Birds Nearby

Getting to Know 45 Common Species of Eastern North America

John Eastman

STACKPOLE BOOKS

Published by
STACKPOLE BOOKS
5067 Ritter Road
Mechanicsburg, PA 17055
www.stackpolebooks.com

Printed in the United States of America

10 9 8 7 6 5 4 3 2 1

First edition
Cover design by Tessa J. Sweigert
Cover images by Michael G. Mill and MVPhoto

Photos courtesy of Shutterstock.com
AHPix, p. 57; BGSmith, p. 26; Biegler, Steve, p. 8; Byland, Steve, pp. 22, 33, 67,
70, 85, 87, 121, 123, 125, 128, 152, 155, 163; Campbell, T. More, p. 63; Chris-
tiaans, Rob, p. 103; claffra, p. 174; DeBoer, Gerald A., p. 93; Erni, p. 83; Fawver,
Melinda, pp. 53, 92; FloridaStock, p. 134; Hebert, Daniel, pp. 6, 178; Hill,
Chris, pp. 88, 158, 161; Hudgins, Lorraine, p. 49; Jessup, Sarah, p. 14; Lemke,
Doug, p. 171; Lukich, Anatoliy, p. 36; MacQueen, Bruce, pp. 28, 165; Marks,
Martha, p. 16; Maton, Ian, p. 51; Middleton, Tom, p. 10; mlorenz, p. 91;
Mulick, Mike, p. 74; Nelson, Jim, p. 140; O'Neal, Sari, p. 25; Oehlenschlager,
Steve, pp. 112, 115; Paul Reeves Photography, pp. 18, 31, 80, 138, 159; Phent,
p. 108; Price, Glenn, p. 111; rck 953, p. 173; Reichner, Tom, pp. 56, 132; Reid,
J. Norman, p. 1; Ron Rowan Photography, p. 145; Steven Russell Smith Pho-
tos, pp. 60, 182; Stubblefield Photography, p. 77; suphanat, p. 148; Swadz-
ba, Marek R., p. 42; Swora, Becky, p. 136; Woodruff, Michael, p. 110

Library of Congress Cataloging-in-Publication Data

Eastman, John (John Andrew)
  Birds nearby : getting to know 45 common species of Eastern North
America / John Eastman. — First edition.
     pages cm
  Includes index.
  ISBN 978-0-8117-1484-6
  1. Birds—East (U.S.) 2. Birds—Canada, Eastern. I. Title.
  QL683.E27E357 2015
  598.0974—dc23
                              2014047348

Contents

American Crow
(*Corvus brachyrhynchos*)

The crow is about twenty inches long and all black. Its gregarious behaviors and loudly distinctive caws, along with other sounds and call notes, also identify it. Both sexes look alike, though adult males are usually an inch or so longer than females. Yearling crows can be distinguished from adults by their frayed, pointed tail feathers, which give the tail a squarish shape, and, close up, by the brownish cast of their plumage; adult crows, whose truncated tail feathers form a more rounded tail, show a purplish cast. In flight, crows plow through the air with distinctive, rowing wingbeats.

Close relatives. Some forty-two *Corvus* species exist worldwide, most residing in the Northern Hemisphere. North American species include the fish crow (*C. ossifragus*) of eastern seacoasts and Florida; the northwestern crow (*C. caurinus*) of British Columbia; and the common and Chihuahuan ravens (*C. corax*, *C. cryptoleucus*). European corvids include the jackdaw (*C. monedula*), rook (*C. frugilegus*), and carrion crow (*C. corone*).

Behaviors. "If a person knows only four birds, one of them will be the crow," wrote early ornithologist Edward Forbush. The more that one observes crows, the more one must agree with Forbush that "each crow is a character." Crows are highly social year-round; even their nesting is an extended family affair. They also display much intelligence and adaptability. A rich anecdotal literature details their cooperative behavior, their ability to distinguish subtle cues and clues, and their apparent strategies for obtaining food. (A friend who feeds crows in his yard believes that they move road-killed animals from road margins into the driving lanes, then perch and wait for passing vehicles to macerate the carcasses.)

Crows can be taught to mimic human words, and in the woods they sometimes imitate barred owl calls. Most of their vocabulary, however, consists of raucous "aw" and "ah" notes, together with a cacophony of bill clacking and moaning, growling, and even musical notes. Once, while sitting alone in the silent woods, I heard several soft, tentative, almost dovelike "cu-koos." Looking around, I saw a single crow eyeing me from a tree across a shallow ravine. These soft notes, I learned, are often uttered as a vocal greeting between crows in unalarmed social contexts.

One index of crow intelligence is what appears to be creative play behavior. Crows are sometimes seen repeatedly sliding down embankments or church domes, perversely yanking the tails of mammals, or provoking chases by other birds. Noisy crow mobbing of hawks and, especially, owls is a common behavior. One noted crow researcher states emphatically that crows think. Yet, as naturalist Bil Gilbert cautions, "Crows, like people, cannot be known generally. All descriptions and judgments about them are necessarily parochial, limited to what some crows, sometimes, in some places have been known to do."

In most of their continent-wide range, American crows are permanent residents. Much winter wandering occurs, however, as the birds seek food, and many northern crows are migratory. A crow's life span may reach about fifteen years; most do not begin breeding until two or more years of age.

Spring. Northern crows have arrived on their breeding range by late winter. By early spring, the birds have settled into basically two groups: small, wandering flocks of non-breeding birds; and family flocks consisting of a previously mated pair and several non-breeding crows, usually one to three yearlings and older offspring, which may remain with the parent birds for up to four years or longer. Such is the complex variability of crow relationships, however, that a breeding-behavior continuum exists, from a single pair nesting alone to a small group endeavor at the nest. Often a family group returns to a previous nesting tree.

The breeding pair spends much time in reciprocal preening and billing. As breeding commences, the male parent becomes more aggressive, driving away some of the hangers-on while allowing selected others to bring in nesting material. From my living room window in April, I often watch crows collecting dead twigs from tree branches and flying off with them. Another sign of incipient nesting is when the pair begins chasing hawks, common ravens, and turkey vultures that happen to fly over the nest site. The unmated helpers seem eager to exercise their own parental impulses by fetching nest materials, feeding the female on the nest, and later feeding the nestlings (male parent permissiveness increases as the season advances). Crows become silent and secretive during the nesting period. Territoriality, like almost everything else in crows, is a group function. The area defended from other family groups may extend to thirty-six acres.

EGGS AND YOUNG: four to six; eggs bluish to olive green, spotted with brown and gray. INCUBATION: by female, which is fed on the nest by male parent and nest helpers; about eighteen days. FEEDING OF YOUNG: by both parents plus nest helpers; insects, small invertebrates and vertebrates, carrion. FLEDGING: four or five weeks.

Summer. Northern crow populations raise only one brood; those in the southern breeding range often raise two. Juveniles, extremely vocal beggars, remain with the family group after fledging. As summer progresses, flocks enlarge as family groups merge and join flocks of unmated crows. Flocks roost together in trees at night and fan out over the countryside to feed in daytime. In midsummer, many observers report crow anting behavior—wallowing in anthills and inserting ants, which release formic acid, into their plumage. Since this is also the period of the annual feather molt, anting behavior may be related to skin irritation as new feathers emerge or to feather parasites.

Fall. Many, though not all, northern crow populations migrate south in September and October. Those from the midwestern Canadian provinces travel farthest—up to two thousand miles—but most eastern migrants move only a few hundred miles south at most.

Winter. Fall and winter are seasons of communal roosting, often in immense flocks. Flocks arrive from miles around in late afternoon, often roosting at sites they have used for generations. They usually fly to roosts along established flight lines, gathering in successively larger staging areas before arrival at the roost. Night roosts may hold from several hundred to millions of birds. In daytime, flocks leave the roosts at staggered intervals and move to feeding grounds that may lie twenty or more miles distant. Most of the larger winter crow roosts occur in midlatitudes between the thirtieth and fortieth parallels. But exceptions, as in all things corvid, abound. Not all crows join the large communal roosts; many remain in or near their summer territories. Crow migrants are usually moving north again in February and March.

Ecology. Crows require open areas for ground feeding and trees for nesting and roosting. Open woodlands, farmland, and forest edges are typical rural habitats. During the past century, however, many crow populations have become urbanized, scavenging from trash bins, loading docks, and shopping malls. Winter roost habitats, as Bil Gilbert points out, are quite similar botanically. Typically they consist of tall, mature trees in a small grove—an island of oaks, ashes, conifers, or others—with thicket understories of locust, box elder, vines, and briers, the whole surrounded by extensive open areas.

Crows seem to prefer nesting in tall conifers when available, usually over thirty feet, often near the top, in a crotch or near the trunk. The paired female builds most of the nest, sometimes after one or two preliminary attempts elsewhere, from materials brought mainly by the helper birds. The bulky nest basket, about two feet across, consists mainly of sticks on the outside, lined with bark fibers, moss, grasses, hair or fur, and leaves. Crows usually build new nests every year; old nests are often adopted by great horned owls.

An adult crow must consume about eleven ounces of food daily to maintain body weight. Both animal and vegetable foods—the latter predominating in winter—are consumed. Road-killed carrion supplies much of the diet in all seasons. We have crows to thank for cleaning up most of the small carcasses left in the wake of our vehicles. This steady food supply probably accounts in large part for the increase of northern crow populations in winter: Up to a half century ago, few crows wintered in northern areas. Animal prey includes a variety of insects plus frogs, salamanders, bird eggs and nestlings, and occasionally mice. The crow's fondness for corn, wheat, and oats has enraged many a farmer, but much of this diet is gleaned from fields after harvest. Crows also consume fruits, including wild cherries, mulberries, grapes, and pokeberries. Acorns are favored foods in fall and winter.

Upon locating a food source, crows often carry and bury the food items, placing them in scattered ground sites and tree crevices. Since many cached items, such as pieces of carrion, are perishable, food caching is usually short-term. Like the blue jay, a crow can carry several acorns, many corn grains, or pieces of other foods in its *antelingual pouch,* the distensible floor of the oral cavity behind the lower bill. Like raptors, crows eject pellets of indigestible materials after feeding.

Carrion competitors include common ravens and turkey vultures, both somewhat better adapted for finding and consuming carcasses than crows. Crows harass and rob these birds at food sites when they can. Because crows are omnivorous feeders, food competition likely is insignificant except, perhaps, for northern crows in winter. Probably crows are their own foremost competitors for nesting habitat. Their abundance may influence the amount of cooperative breeding (that is, with nest helpers) that occurs.

Great horned owls are major predators of American crows. These raptors raid crow nests and roosting sites at night, killing and eating both adults and nestlings. Raccoons are regular nest invaders, consuming eggs and nestlings, and goshawks also threaten. Gray squirrels, daytime intruders, are noisily driven away, and crows attack red-tailed and red-shouldered hawks during the breeding season, although they often tolerate their presence at other times. Their chief predators are humans, and roosting sites become frequent targets of recreational gunners. Federal migratory bird laws have made indiscriminate shooting and poisoning of crows illegal, but shooting is permitted under various state regulations.

Focus. Thoreau rhapsodized about the "delicious sound" of crows in winter, blessing the Lord "for wildness, for crows that will not alight within gunshot!" Capitalizing on the crow's natural wariness of people, scarecrows became stock characters of farm and rural folklore. Many Native American tribes revered the crow as a spiritual being. These peoples probably saw fewer crows than we do, for the birds were far less abundant in the Northeast before agriculture created optimal habitats and abundant food for them. In Michigan, for example, they remained unknown until about 1850, when the landscape was being opened up by logging. Since then, large foraging flocks and piles of droppings beneath roost sites have given crows gigantic pest status in many quarters. Probably the biggest crow massacre occurred in 1940 near Rockford, Illinois, where state officials dynamited some three hundred thousand crows into oblivion.

Yet to view these native birds of legend solely through the biases of farmers and san- itation engineers gives us an incomplete picture of this bird. If crows can indeed think, our inviting habitats and simultaneous crow shoots must seem baffling indeed.

American Goldfinch
(Carduelis tristis)

This five-inch-long "wild canary" can be recognized by its black wings marked with a prominent wing bar. Spring and summer males have bright yellow body plumage and a black forehead patch; females are dull olive-gray. Winter plumage of both sexes is greenish gray with yellowish tinges. Goldfinches bounce in flight, "as if skimming over unseen billows," wrote Thoreau, often uttering an accented "ac-*cip*-i-tee!" as they fly. Also commonly heard is an ascending, querulous "sweee?"

Close relatives. Some thirty *Carduelis* species exist worldwide. The nearest eastern U.S. relatives are the pine siskin (*C. pinus*) and common and hoary redpolls (*C. flammea, C hornemanni*). Lawrence's goldfinch (*C. lawrencei*) and the lesser goldfinch (*C. psaltria*) reside in the western United States. The European goldfinch (*C. carduelis*) is one of several Eurasian relatives, including the greenfinch (*C. chloris*), linnet (*C. cannabina*), chaffinch (*Fringilla coelebs*), and brambling (*F. montifringilla*). The canary (*Serinus canaria*), native of the Canary Islands and a popular cage-bird, is also closely related.

Behaviors. Gregarious in small flocks for most of the year, goldfinches are common year-round visitors at yard feeders. They become especially conspicuous in spring and summer, when the males' bright plumage and warbling, canarylike song convey a sense of exuberance.

Winter goldfinch residents may not be the same goldfinches present in summer, since wandering or south-migrating populations from farther north often supplant the summer residents. Goldfinch diet requires access to plenty of water, and these birds frequently bathe. When perched goldfinches watch other goldfinches bathing, the watchers often flutter wings and tail in imitation movements, as if bathing themselves.

Goldfinch breeding range spans the continent from southern Canada to the southern United States.

Spring. Most winter goldfinches move northward in spring, and north-migrating goldfinches arrive on their breeding areas in April and May. This is one of the few passerine birds that undergo a prenuptial plumage molt, which begins in late winter and extends through spring. Only the body and head feathers are replaced; males transform from blah to brilliant as they gain new yellow body plumage and jet-black crown feathers. Bills of both sexes turn from dull gray to yellow-orange.

Although territory formation and nesting do not occur until several months later, the birds engage in song and courtship behaviors, with males skirmishing and chasing single females. The singing male's flat flight, a high, level, rapidly flapping movement in contrast to the typical looping flight path, is often seen at this time. Previously mated males may disperse to new areas, but females usually return to an earlier nesting vicinity. Pairing soon occurs, but the birds continue to feed together in small flocks. Goldfinches typically remain faithful to one mate for the breeding season but change mates from year to year.

Summer. Goldfinches, among our latest nesters, begin establishing territories in late June or early July. Territories may extend to a quarter acre or more or, in places where the birds nest in loose colonies, to a diameter of only one hundred feet. Males sing from localized perches, chase away other males, and perform high, circular flights over the territory as females build the nests. These circle flights are good indicators of nest locations. As incubation proceeds, defensive behavior wanes and territorial boundaries shrink to the immediate nest area. Parent goldfinches often raise two broods; sometimes females lay the second clutch of eggs in a new nest before the first brood has fledged, in which case the male takes over most of the feeding chores. Nesting often extends into September.

EGGS AND YOUNG: typically five; eggs bluish white, unmarked. INCUBATION: by female, fed by male; about twelve days. FEEDING OF YOUNG: by both sexes; regurgitated seed pulp. FLEDGING: about two weeks.

Fall. As goldfinch families forsake the nest vicinity, they can be recognized by the incessant "chipee chipee" calls of the fledglings as they bounce along in the air, following a parent. Soon the young are independent, and social organization becomes flock oriented; all-juvenile flocks of several hundred often feed and fly together. Late in the fall, goldfinches undergo a complete plumage molt, including wing and tail feathers. The sexes now look much alike, with olive-gray plumage and darker bills, although females

show paler yellowish throats and males more facial yellow and blacker wings.

Goldfinch migration is erratic and age-segregated. Many goldfinches travel long distances south in October and November, often in daytime flocks of several thousand. But others, usually juvenile flocks, may remain in or near the breeding area. Probably food abundance determines the scale and distance of migration in this species as in other so-called irruptive migrators.

Winter. Goldfinch winter range extends from the northern United States to the Gulf Coast and northern Mexico. Often a winter feeding flock advances across a field by leapfrogging, with birds in the rear continually flying to the forefront. Biologist Kenn Kaufman has pointed out the individual variations of goldfinches in winter flocks; on close examination, the amount of facial yellow and subtle differences in other plumage patterns give each bird a distinctive appearance. Yard feeders have probably influenced the winter distribution of goldfinches, causing them to remain in areas they might otherwise vacate.

Ecology. Goldfinches are edge-habitat birds that have benefited from human land clearing and agriculture. They favor open areas with scattered trees and shrubs, overgrown fields, shrub wetlands, and suburban residential areas. Access to water is important, as are thistle-seed food sources; they often nest within one hundred yards or less of the latter.

Favored nest sites include dogwood, shrub willow, and hawthorn thickets. The deeply cupped nest, often attached to several upright branches in a fork, averages four to fourteen feet high. Goldfinches often use milkweed bark strips, giving the nest a yellowish or silvery appearance. For nest lining, they collect cottony materials, mainly thistle and cattail down. Sometimes they raid vacated nests of willow flycatchers, yellow warblers, and Baltimore orioles for nest fibers. The compact cup is so tightly woven that it even holds rainwater, yet is so flexible that it expands as the nestlings grow. In shoreline shrubs, the nests much resemble those of yellow warblers, which also build there, but goldfinch nests typically show droppings on outer edges of the rim, where nestlings have backed up to defecate. The presence of feather sheaths embedded in the nest lining probably indicates a successful nesting, revealing the first growth of juvenile plumage. Goldfinch nests often last through winter and are often recycled by various creatures. White-footed mice may pile them with cattail down, adapting them for their own nests; mice, red squirrels, and chipmunks also use them for seed storage and feeding sites; and next spring's yellow warblers may tear them apart for nesting materials.

The goldfinch's late nesting sequence coincides with its summer seed diet from maturing food plants, especially composites—thistles, dandelions, ragweeds, and sunflowers—plus grasses and many others. Thistle rings, circles of strewn thistledown around the plant, reveal that goldfinches have been there. Birch and alder catkins, elm seeds, flower buds, and berries are also consumed. In spring, goldfinches also devour many cankerworms, tree aphids, and massed aphid eggs; observers report watching goldfinch flocks work tamarack trees from the top down for insect eggs. In fields, goldfinches often alternate between seed feeding on the ground and on the plants.

Two other species—willow flycatchers and yellow warblers—nest in the same shrub habitats as goldfinches, often in close proximity. They usually breed in spring, however, so competition with goldfinches is minimal. Food competition is also insignificant at most times. Winter foraging flocks of up to three hundred goldfinches may associate with pine siskins, common redpolls, and American tree sparrows.

Nest predators include blue jays, common grackles, and weasels. Occasionally goldfinches become entangled in burdock burs and spiderwebs. Many are killed by collisions with automobiles and by salmonellosis, a bacterial infection sometimes transmitted at yard feeders. Brown-headed cowbirds find goldfinches poor prospects for brood parasitism; cowbird nestlings need much more protein than the goldfinch seed diet provides, and they often starve in the nest. Occasionally goldfinches bury cowbird eggs in their nests, reflooring them for their own eggs.

Focus. Watching goldfinches at yard feeders reveals much about their eating habits. Unlike many feeder visitors, they eat in place rather than carry seeds to another perch. They are also most methodical, neatly trimming a sunflower seed of all husk portions and finishing up the edible fragments before taking another seed.

Average goldfinch longevity is probably six years or less; banding records show a maximum of eleven years.

Iowa, New Jersey, and Washington have designated the American goldfinch their state bird.

American Kestrel
(*Falco sparverius*)

The smallest (nine to twelve inches, about killdeer size) and most common North American falcon, the American kestrel, also called sparrow hawk, has distinctive markings. On each side of the head, two black, vertical "sideburns," one of them running through the eye, frame white cheek and chin patches. The top of the head is blue with a rusty cap, usually brighter in males than females. A pair of black spots on the rear of the head, called *ocelli*, or false eyes, may deter possible predators from sneak attack. Males have a rusty back, bluish gray wings, and a rusty-colored tail with a black terminal band; underparts are spotted. Females have rusty wings, back, and tail, all marked with black barring, and brown-streaked underparts. Kestrels voice their alarm calls, rapid, high-pitched "killy killy killy" or "klee klee klee" notes, mainly near the nest.

Close relatives. The genus *Falco* includes, besides the kestrel, five other North American falcons: the Aplomado falcon (*F. femoralis*) of the Southwest, the merlin (*F. columbarius*), the gyrfalcon (*F. rusticolus*), the prairie falcon (*F. mexicanus*), and the peregrine falcon (*F. peregrinus*). Thirty-two other falcons range worldwide. The common kestrel, or windhover (*F. tinnunculus*), of Eurasia is a slightly larger, gray-tailed version of the American kestrel.

Behaviors. Kestrels are easily seen in their open-country habitat as they hover-hunt on rapidly beating wings or perch-hunt from power lines and poles. In flight, the almost two-foot wingspan curves back in sickle shape; a reliable field mark for male kestrels is the line of translucent dots along the rear edge of the wing. Another characteristic is the kestrel's habit of bobbing its tail when perched. The birds are buoyant in flight, gliding more than most falcons, and can also soar on thermal updrafts. Kestrels capture most of their prey on the ground, seizing it in their talons and carrying it to a perch. Primarily solitary birds, kestrels apparently mate for life, but even during the breeding season, mates spend most of their time apart.

American kestrel breeding range spans North and South America from the arctic treeline to Tierra del Fuego. Only the northernmost breeding populations—from the northern Great Plains, northern New England, and northern Great Lakes—migrate.

Spring. Many, if not most, migratory kestrels have already arrived on their northern breeding range by early spring—"after the horned larks and shortly before the bluebirds," one observer noted. Previous breeders are *philopatric,* returning to their previous territories, which vary extensively in size, depending on quality of habitat; 100 acres is probably minimal. Females, arriving some days later than males, often wander in and out of several male territories before settling on the mate's territory, and extrapair copulations with one or more males are common during this period. American kestrels are noted for their frequency of seven-second copulations—up to fifteen times a day over a six-week period, beginning days or weeks before the female's fertile period. Females can store viable sperm up to twelve days in their oviduct tubules before fertilization occurs. But whereas copulations are frequent, actual fertilizations by males other than the bonded mate apparently are not.

In addition to aerial dive displays by males, mate feeding is an important courtship and bonding behavior. A male spends hours afield hunting, transferring prey to his mate at habitual perch sites on the territory. Before egg laying begins, the female stops hunting; her mate supplies all the food until a week or so after the nestlings hatch, a total period of two months or more. Egg laying on the northern range usually begins in April.

EGGS AND YOUNG: usually four or five; eggs white or pinkish, finely dotted with brown. INCUBATION: by both sexes (male about four hours per day, when female vacates to feed and preen in morning and late afternoon); about thirty days. FEEDING OF YOUNG: by female for first few days, from food brought by male, then by both sexes; mainly grasshoppers. FLEDGING: about thirty days.

Summer. Fledglings, which leave the nest from about mid-June to early July, remain perched in the nest vicinity for about two weeks, being fed by the parents and brooded in the nest cavity at night. Over the next few weeks, they learn to hunt for themselves, sometimes merging with other kestrel families or all-juvenile flocks of up to twenty birds. Kestrels nest only once per year in most northern habitats, twice in the southern range.

Juveniles resemble adults but show dark streaking on the breast. During late summer and fall, most juveniles molt into adult plumage. Annual plumage molt of adults begins in midspring and occurs over the entire summer period; females typically molt weeks ahead of males. The molt is usually complete by early September, as the birds begin migrating. Some late-summer migrators, however, are still molting as they travel.

Fall. Peak movements of northern-range kestrels occur in mid-September and early October. Falcon migration relies on fast, direct flight rather than on thermal updrafts that reflect ridge topography, as in most hawks. Kestrels migrate in groups of three or four or in small, loose flocks over a broad interior front and along the seacoasts. Unlike other falcons, they seldom fly far over open water. Many northeastern kestrel migrants augment the resident kestrel populations directly south of the breeding range; many also winter in the southeastern states, especially coastal Florida.

Winter. Resident kestrels in the middle and southern United States may remain year-round in their breeding areas or on winter territories, but many also wander, seeking feeding sites elsewhere. Solitary now, the birds establish and defend individual winter feeding territories of 100 acres or more. In Florida, males tend to forage in edge areas, margins of slash pine woodlots, eucalyptus plantations, cypress swamps, and citrus groves; females seem to favor more open, sparsely vegetated sites. Researchers believe that female kestrels are dominant over males, at least in winter, forming territories in prime feeding habitat and forcing males into more sideline, edge habitats.

Many male kestrels begin moving northward by late February and early March.

Ecology. American kestrels favor open farmland habitats—pastures, hayfields, grasslands, and fields of row crops. Hence they were probably uncommon in the northeastern United States before settlement and land clearing. Marshland, forest openings, clear-cut forest areas, and bogs also host kestrels at times, and median strips of expressways are common foraging sites. Habitats must also contain nest cavities and perch sites, such as power lines and poles, roadside and hedgerow trees. This species has also adapted to urban and suburban areas; kestrels often perch-hunt amid the ample house sparrow populations around skyscrapers and warehouses.

Natural tree cavities, old tree excavations of northern flickers and pileated woodpeckers, vacated holes in cliffs, and crevices in old barns and outbuildings are typical kestrel nest sites. These birds never excavate their own holes. The female selects the site after inspecting a number of cavities located by the male. Many previous breeders probably return to cavities they have previously used. The birds bring in no nesting material; the female lays eggs atop whatever debris already lies on the floor of the cavity. Kestrels perform no nest sanitation and do not carry away nestling fecal sacs. Chicks shoot their feces onto the cavity walls, where they quickly dry. Dermestid beetles (Dermestidae), prevalent in most kestrel nests, scavenge food scraps.

Summer and winter diets vary according to prey availability. The birds capture most of their prey on the ground, though they occasionally forage aloft for aerial insects and capture birds on the wing. Insects—mainly grasshoppers and crickets—are the chief summer foods; in winter, more small mammals, such as voles, and birds up to flicker size are captured. Other food items include lizards, snakes, frogs, upland sandpiper chicks, and bats. In urban habitats, kestrels feed mainly on house sparrows, sometimes raiding ivy-covered walls of buildings where the sparrows nest and roost. Kestrels often cache food items for periods up to seven days, usually in grass clumps or niches in tree limbs. The birds cache dead rodents top side up; the rodents' own protective coloration helps conceal them.

Nest cavities, often scarce in kestrel habitats, are sources of most interspecific competition, mainly from northern flickers, European starlings, and squirrels. Biologist Terry Root has pointed out the inverse relationship kestrels exhibit with northern shrikes; although shrikes are not raptors, they exploit most of the same winter habitat types and prey as kestrels. The chief difference that largely precludes competition between them is the kestrel's preference for warmer areas. "Perhaps these two ecologically similar species are avoiding each other," suggested Root.

Kestrel predators are relatively few. Blue jays sometimes mob them, and larger raptors (mainly sharp-shinned and other accipiter hawks) occasionally capture them.

Focus. Kestrel populations have shown modest trends of increase during the past several decades; recent researchers estimate that more than a million breeding pairs inhabit North America. Probably only about half of the chicks survive to fledge; typical longevity is two to five years, though some have survived in the wild to age eleven. Kestrels are extremely sensitive to cold, rarely remaining in wintering areas where temperatures plunge below 20 degrees F. Tolerant of heat, they even inhabit deserts in the Southwest, obtaining most of their moisture requirement from their diet.

Probably the foremost limitation on kestrel numbers in otherwise adequate habitats is the lack of suitable nesting cavities. Losses of American elm trees from Dutch elm disease have depleted a once-common nest tree for kestrels. Placement of kestrel boxes or roofed nail kegs in open habitats near wet areas has helped restore kestrel populations in many areas. Boxes containing wood chips in the bottom should measure 16 by 12 inches with a 3$^{1}/_{2}$-inch-diameter hole, mounted on 10- to 15-foot cedar poles placed along fence lines or highways and facing into open fields. Since kestrels and eastern bluebirds occupy similar habitats and both use nest boxes (with different-size entrance holes), the helpful house provider should "choose one species or the other," recommended naturalist Emma B. Pitcher; "a hungry kestrel might hassle or even eat a bluebird."

Beginning falconers in America often train themselves by using kestrels before attempting to train larger hawks or falcons.

The name *kestrel* derives from the Old French *cresserelle,* in turn originating from the Latin *crepitare,* "to rattle, creak, or crackle," supposedly suggestive of the bird's call.

American Robin
(Turdus migratorius)

Measuring about ten inches long, this thrush is dark on top with a brick red to orange breast. Males have blacker heads and tails and redder breasts than the grayer females, and juveniles have speckled breasts. The male's "cheeriup, cheerily" is one of the spring's most familiar bird songs.

Close relatives. More than sixty *Turdus* species exist worldwide. Nine European species include the blackbird (*T. merula*), the fieldfare (*T. pilaris*), the song thrush (*T. philomelos*), and the mistle thrush (*T. viscivorus*). The European robin (*Erithacus rubecula*), though a red-breasted thrush, is smaller and does not closely resemble the American robin.

Behaviors. One of the most common residents around human dwellings, the robin is a true yard bird. Its characteristic hop-and-stop gait in the grass, head cocking, and sudden thrust for an earthworm are familiar sights. After years of controversy, researchers have finally established that robins locate earthworms primarily by sight, not by sound. The bird can detect slight movements, undiscernible to our eyes, of a worm in its near-surface burrow. Wet lawns attract robins because saturated soil drives worms to the surface for air.

Robins are gregarious for most of the year. Even during breeding, when pairs aggressively defend their nests, one robin's territory, about one-third of an acre, often overlaps with another's, and feeding and roosting sites are often shared. Night communal roosting, most prevalent in fall and winter, also occurs among male robins during the nesting season; they resume their territories in daytime.

Robin breeding range spans most of the continent from northern Canada and Alaska to the Gulf and southern Mexico. Robins are migrators, though small populations often remain on the breeding range in winter.

Spring. Breeding robins remain faithful to their previous territories, and their arrival in force occurs in late March and early April. In moving northward—as far as Alaska and northern Canada—flocks closely follow the advancing daily temperature mean of 37 degrees F., although harsh early-spring weather can rapidly deplete robin populations. Males precede females by a few days, and territorial formation is marked by hostile chases, attacks, and various courtship rituals—"robin racket," as naturalist John Burroughs called these behaviors. Nesting begins shortly after arrival. Watch for "mustached" robins as they gather dead stems of long grasses, holding them crosswise in the bill, for nesting material. Females, which do most of the nest building, often display a mud line across the breast where they have shaped and pressed against the damp soil rim of the new nest. Sometimes they use the previous year's nest, adding materials to the old nest. Male robins sing most conspicuously just before hatching time. Robin pair bonds, despite territorial fidelity, often last through only one breeding season.

EGGS AND YOUNG: typically four; eggs blue. INCUBATION: by female, which is attended by male; about two weeks. FEEDING OF YOUNG: by both sexes; insects. FLEDGING: about two weeks or slightly longer.

Summer. Usually females have begun incubating a second brood by early summer, often on the same nest. The male is the main feeder of the fledged first brood, some of which follow him about on the ground for two weeks or so. Listen for the loud, screechy "seech-ook!" of fledgling robins calling for parental attention. About the time second broods hatch, first-brood birds are becoming independent. In July and August, the annual feather molt occurs. Now robins begin to gather and roam in large flocks for both feeding and roosting. This diet and behavioral shift is evidenced by the gradual disappearance of pairs from the lawn. Watch for anting behavior—the rubbing of ants, which release formic acid, into the plumage—especially in summer.

Fall. October is the primary month of robin migration southward, often in large flocks. Most flocks travel by day to the milder, generally snowfree climate of the southern states and Gulf Coast. Some robins range as far south as Guatemala.

Winter. Nighttime roosting areas sometimes hold thousands of robins, often mixed with European starlings, common grackles, and brown-headed cowbirds. Observers have noted winter territorial behaviors as robins defend individual fruit trees from other robins. In recent decades, robins seem to be extending their winter range northward.

Ecology. American robins are true habitat generalists, able to occupy almost any land

area that provides enough food. During the breeding season, they favor the artificial parklands so prevalent in shady residential suburbs. Away from town, their frequent haunts include orchards, forest edges, and lake and stream margins. Unless severe weather forces them to move elsewhere, wintering flocks both north and south favor swampy areas for feeding and roosting. The first robins of spring in many areas may actually have been residing in nearby wetlands all winter and are simply beginning to shift habitat.

For nesting, robins usually select a semi-sheltered tree fork, horizontal limb, building ledge, or, often, an eave pipe beneath a roof overhang. Conifers are favored sites in some areas. The nest, which may appear unkempt and not very well camouflaged, is distinctive for its mud construction, with grass binding and lining. One observer reported the use of earthworm castings.

Except for the required protein-rich diet of earthworms when feeding young, robins are mainly frugivores, or fruit eaters, sometimes to the fury of commercial fruit growers. Earthworms are the most conspicuous food we see robins take in spring and form about 15 percent of the total diet, but robins also abundantly reside in areas where earthworms are few or lacking. Ground, snout, and scarab beetles constitute about 40 percent of the diet. Caterpillars also rank high, but other insects, spiders, and snails are also consumed. Wild fruit foods include just about any available, with heavy summer emphasis on rose family plants. Fruits of dogwoods, sumacs, red cedar, and Virginia creeper, as well as wild and domestic cherries, blackberries, and grapes, are all favorites, as are fruits of the cabbage palm in the southern winter range. Robins rarely consume grains or other dry plant seeds.

The robin's adaptability to human environs gives it a competitive edge over many other birds, though wintering robins must compete for food with other frugivores, including northern mockingbirds, cedar waxwings, and European starlings. These same environs, however, expose fledgling robins to that notorious yard predator, the domestic cat. In rural habitats, sharp-shinned hawks occasionally capture robins, and American crows, blue jays, and snakes sometimes raid nests, consuming eggs or nestlings. Robins rapidly eject brown-headed cowbird eggs.

Focus. Their adaptability to human environs has made robins far more abundant today than in presettlement times; many Native Americans and pioneers probably saw them rarely, if at all. During the nineteenth century, robins were widely hunted and consumed for food, especially in the South; Audubon called them "excellent eating." At fruit trees where robins fed, gunners shot them day-long by the bagful. A more insidious killer later appeared in the form of DDT pesticides. Spraying for Dutch elm disease during the 1950s resulted in high concentrations of the poison in earthworm tissues, followed by the death and reproductive failure of many birds. This widely observed lawn avicide formed the basis for Rachel Carson's furiously maligned but scientifically dead-on warning in her classic 1962 book, *Silent Spring*. It took a decade for the United States to ban the use of lethal DDT. U.S. companies, however, still manufacture it and sell it to other nations that continue to use it, including those in which most of our Neotropical birds winter. U.S. robin populations rebounded, and in many areas they are now the most numerous bird species.

The word *robin* is actually a nickname for the French name Robert. Colonists transferred the name of the European robin to the American species.

The robin is the state bird of Connecticut, Michigan, and Wisconsin.

Baltimore Oriole
(*Icterus galbula*)

Flaming orange underparts and black head and wings distinguish the male Baltimore oriole; females are variably yellow-orange beneath and olive-brown above. Both sexes, seven to eight inches long, show two white wing bars. Piping, whistled phrases, voiced by both sexes, are distinctively unrhythmic. A short series of notes on one pitch sounds "like blasts from a tiny trumpet," as one observer wrote, and a loud chatter of alarm notes resembles the rattle notes of brown-headed cowbirds or house wrens.

Close relatives. Of the twenty-six *Icterus* species, eight breed in North America. The orchard oriole (*I. spurius*) is the only other eastern U.S. species. The western U.S. counterpart of the Baltimore is Bullock's oriole (*I. bullockii*). Other western species include Scott's oriole (*I. parisorum*), Audubon's oriole (*I. graduacauda*), the hooded oriole (*I. cucullatus*), and the Altamira oriole (*I. gularis*). The unrelated Old World orioles (tribe Oriolini) belong to the family Corvidae (crows and jays).

Behaviors. Despite the male's gaudy colors, the Baltimore is easier heard than seen. Baltimores spend most of their time in the tree canopy, though they also forage low on occasion. The song pattern of clear, slurred notes is distinctive, revealing this oriole's often common presence where one may have visually missed it. Each oriole voices its own particular pattern of song phrasing and tonal characteristics, enabling individual recognition by careful listening. Males in neighboring territories often countersing back and forth, and one bird may closely imitate the other's song.

Baltimore orioles are migrators, breeding throughout most of the eastern continent from southern Canada almost to the Gulf.

Spring. "To many of us who live in the northern states," wrote orinthologist Winsor M. Tyler, "the Baltimore oriole represents the spirit of spring." Fairly late migrators (late April through May), male Baltimores seldom appear before the trees have leafed out. They precede females by a week or more, usually returning to a previously held territory. First-year males still appear brownish on the head and wings, resembling females, but they acquire full adult plumage in a spring prenuptial molt. Chases, chatter calls, and frequent song from high, conspicuous perches mark the male's establishment of territory, usually two or three acres. When females arrive, one may see courtship displays, especially males bowing in front of females. Females build the nests, usually beginning in late May, though I have watched male Baltimores tugging on loose ends of a clothesline as if trying to collect it. Occasions of extrapair copulation, when a male invades another's territory and copulates with the paired female, are known to occur.

EGGS AND YOUNG: usually four or five; eggs bluish white, brown streaked and blotched, especially at the larger end. INCUBATION: by female; twelve to fourteen days. FEEDING OF YOUNG: by both sexes; regurgitated insects at first, then whole insects. FLEDGING: twelve to fourteen days.

Summer, Fall. Baltimore pairs raise only one brood, but nesting typically extends to late June. Song and nesting cease at the same time. Parents feed the noisy fledglings for two or three weeks, but females sometimes roam away from them, beginning their annual plumage molt a few days before the males stop feeding the young. Males often remain solitary on their territories until completing their molt; orange plumage becomes more vivid as males age. Juvenile males molt into an intermediate femalelike plumage but show a black throat patch, which they will wear until their spring molt. Females and juveniles begin flocking and drifting southward in mid-August, with males following through mid-September.

Winter. Most Baltimore orioles winter in Mexico through Central America to northern South America. Increasing numbers, however, remain in North America, especially along the Gulf and Atlantic coasts north to the Carolinas. On their winter range, the birds remain solitary or associate in small groups. They occasionally sing, and males may also defend feeding territories.

Ecology. Baltimore orioles favor open deciduous woodlands and edges. Orchards, parks, and residential areas with tall shade trees are also frequent habitats. In their winter range, these birds frequent shaded coffee, cacao, and banana plantations, as well as shady thickets and rain-forest canopies.

The Baltimore's suspended, sacklike nest is a durable marvel of tight-woven plant fibers. Usually placed thirty feet high or more at the outermost end of an arched, drooping branch, they are difficult to see when trees are in foliage but easy to spot after leaves drop in the fall. Tall American elms were frequent nesting sites before Dutch elm disease killed so many of these trees. Maples, willows, and apple trees (hosting lower nests) are also common sites, but almost any large tree with arching branches may be selected. Nest building takes the female oriole five to eight days or longer. From a snarl of loose, hanging fibers draped over supporting twigs, she goes to work on the dangling strands. Strips of milkweed, dogbane, or Indian hemp bark often provide the tough suspension fibers, along with pieces of string, grapevine bark, and grasses. She feverishly pushes and pulls in shuttlelike movements, randomly weaving from all sides, to create a flexible, suspended pouch, open at the top. She lines the chamber with hair, fine grasses, and plant down. Occasionally a female repairs and reuses a nest of the previous spring, but usually she builds a new one each year. House finches may sometimes adopt vacated oriole nests.

Caterpillars form the bulk of oriole diet year-round. This bird is one of the foremost consumers of hairy and spiny larvae, including tent, gypsy, webworm, and tussock moth caterpillars. Orioles forage in the dense webs of eastern tent caterpillars, which few other birds do. Irruptions of these destructive foliage eaters may attract orioles, temporarily increasing their local populations. Orioles also consume many other insects, plus spiders and snails. Buds, flower nectar, fruits, and some seeds are frequent food items, as are garden peas, mulberries, shadbush berries, and blackberries. These birds relish orange slices at yard feeders and also visit hummingbird feeders. Some researchers believe that yard feeding accounts for the in-creasing winter presence of orioles in the United States. Winter range foods include caterpillars, beetles, winged termites, and cecropia fruits.

Competition between Baltimore and Bullock's orioles is difficult to judge. Both are currently expanding their ranges at each other's expense in certain areas. Plumage and adaptive variations—such as the Baltimore's tendency to suspend its nest from thinner branches, possibly a defense against more numerous squirrel predators in the East—distinguish the two species.

Baltimore predators include screech-owls, American crows, and red and gray squirrels. Baltimores seldom tolerate brown-headed cowbird parasitism, rapidly ejecting cowbird eggs from their nests.

Focus. The word *oriole* stems from the Latin *aureus*, meaning "golden," first applied to the unrelated Eurasian golden oriole (*Oriolus oriolus*), which resembles a large goldfinch. New World orioles, though more orange than yellow, were named after their supposed resemblance to this bird. Thoreau called orioles "golden robins." Pioneering naturalist Mark Catesby named the Baltimore for its fancied resemblance to the black and orange livery of Maryland colonist George Calvert, Baron Baltimore. But modern ornithologists have vacillated to a more than ordinary degree over this bird's rightful name. In 1973, data seemed to indicate that Baltimore and Bullock's orioles were actually a single species, so taxonomists officially lumped them together as two subspecies of the northern oriole, a new designation. This was because landscape alteration in the western United States had brought the two into contact, and they hybridized. But the hybrid population, it was discovered, soon melted away, and Baltimore and Bullock's maintained their separate identities in the border zones—"an excellent example of evolution in action," as one observer noted. Selective pressures, obviously, were operating against hybridization in this case.

The initial lumping into a single species had seemed gratuitous at best to many birders—and was roundly cursed by baseball fans of the Baltimore Orioles. Twenty years later, armed with new data, scholarly opinion was swinging back. By 1995, Baltimore and Bullock's orioles were again officially classified as two separate species, and northern orioles, so briefly among us, were suddenly defunct. Maryland dwellers, who never considered renaming their state bird in the first place, thus remain on track.

Black-capped Chickadee
(Parus atricapillus)

This five-inch-long parid is marked by a black cap, throat, and bib; buffy flanks; and a white belly. Commonly heard sounds are a clear, whistled "fee-bee," the first note a full tone above the second, and a buzzy "chick-a-dee-dee-dee" or variations thereof. Sexes look alike.

Close relatives. Of the six North American chickadees, two besides the black-capped reside in the East: the Carolina chickadee (*P. carolinensis*) of the southern states, and the boreal chickadee (*P. hudsonicus*), which inhabits northern coniferous forests across the continent. Western species include the Mexican chickadee (*P. sclateri*), the mountain chickadee (*P. gambeli*), and the chestnut-backed chickadee (*P. rufescens*). The genus *Parus* also includes titmice. England's twelve *Parus* species are called tits.

Behaviors. Most people see black-capped chickadees at winter yard feeders. Typically a chickadee rushes in, snatches a seed, and flies to nearby cover, where it vigorously attacks the seed by holding it down with a foot and hammering it to pieces.

Chickadees operate in small territorial flocks of about ten birds for most of the year. Their social relations are rigidly stratified, with a dominant pair forming the nucleus of the group. This system of status and precedence may easily be seen at the yard feeder, where a low-ranking chickadee invariably gives way to a higher-ranking bird. Males are dominant over females in most flocks, but older females rank over younger females and occasionally over young males as well. Relative size of the bird and seniority in the flock are other rank-determining factors. Apparently a chickadee can spot the flock ranking of another chickadee from some distance away, so some degree of individual recognition is involved. Various vocal signals in a feeding flock maintain contact among birds and warn of possible predators.

Their well-known curiosity makes chickadees easy to attract by pishing or by playing owl tapes. Watch them watch you while they "pretend" to be exploring a twig, "as if they were minding their own business all the while," observed Thoreau. Researchers believe that this *displacement behavior,* common in many bird species, provides an outlet for surplus energy generated by curiosity—interest in an observer, for example. Chickadees also quickly respond to distress calls of other birds, and they frequently mob predators with incessant "dee-dee-dee" calls.

Black-capped chickadees mate for life. They inhabit the northern two-thirds of the United States plus much of Canada. In most of their range, they remain on year-round flock territories, but portions of northernmost chickadee populations migrate.

Spring. Most chickadee pairing has already occurred by late winter and early spring. Winter flocks are now breaking up as high-ranking pairs become territorially aggressive, driving away lower-ranking birds. The latter disperse to nearby areas, usually within the flock range, some to establish breeding territories of their own. The size of

chickadee territories often fluctuates depending on local abundance of breeding chickadees, habitat quality, relative social rankings, and time progression of the breeding cycle. A pair that begins defending a ten-acre territory, for example, often decreases its territory size as nesting progresses—until, at fledging time, the territory disappears altogether. No courtship behaviors have been identified in this species. Instances of both *polyandry* (one female, two males) and *polygyny* (one male, two females) sometimes occur.

Black-capped chickadees utter at least fifteen kinds of notes or note patterns. Most often heard in spring are the whistled "fee-bee" notes, given mostly by males when establishing breeding territories. Softer "fee-bee" calls from either sex usually indicate incubation or brood-rearing stages of nesting. Gargle notes, a kind of musical sputter, often occur during territorial skirmishes. A common behavior when threatened by an intruding finger or pencil in the nest cavity is a startling hiss and swaying motion followed by a sudden lunge at the intruder. This so-called snake display has been cited as an example of *Batesian mimicry,* in which a prey species mimics the appearance or behaviors of a predator. To see a chickadee mimic a snake can be a bit unnerving even to a human observer.

EGGS AND YOUNG: about seven; eggs white, dotted with reddish-brown spots. INCUBATION: by female, which is fed by male; about twelve days. FEEDING OF YOUNG: by both sexes; insects. FLEDGING: about sixteen days.

Summer. Most pairs of chickadees nest only once a year. After nestlings fledge, family groups move off their territories and wander about, rarely challenged by still-territorial pairs. Loudly begging juveniles remain dependent on food brought by parent birds for up to a month, then suddenly disperse in random directions, often to areas several miles away. Chickadee mobbing of such predators as owls reaches a peak in summer; perhaps, one researcher suggests, this is how the juveniles (as well as other birds such as warblers, which often join late-summer chickadee feeding flocks) learn to recognize predators. The annual feather molt begins in July or early August, lasting into fall. Molting chickadees become secretive and sedentary during this period.

Fall. In late summer and fall, a major shift in chickadee social organization occurs. Dispersing juveniles join flocks consisting of local breeding pairs. A typical flock numbers six to ten birds. Pair formation of singles occurs in the flocks, which persist over winter. Most chickadee flocks begin with equal sex ratios, though mortality factors eventually tip them either way. A hierarchy of pairs rather than of individuals dominates the flock. If both members of a pair survive until spring, they will then mate. The flock range, occupying twenty or more acres, usually encompasses the former breeding territory of the dominant pair in the flock. Flocks often vigorously defend their ranges from other chickadee flocks.

Southward migrations of black-capped chickadees appear irregular, both in frequency and in numbers. Most chickadee migrants are young birds. In some years, hardly any southward movement occurs; in irruption years, thousands of chickadees travel. Irruption years in the Northeast seem to correlate strongly with seasons of low conifer seed production.

Winter. Food resources grow leaner as food needs become greater in winter, the only real crunch time for most chickadees. Many of them do not survive this season. Young birds appear most vulnerable to predation and starvation. Up to 25 percent of a post-fledgling population may die before their first winter; more than 70 percent do not survive their first year. "To the chickadee," wrote Aldo Leopold, "winter wind is the boundary of the habitable world." During cold winter nights, black-capped chickadees roost singly, often in dense conifers or tree cavities. "One of the most amazing adaptations they possess," one researcher noted, is *regulated hypothermia*, the ability to decrease body temperature at night by about half—from about 108 degrees F. to about 50 degrees—thus preserving energy. Hummingbirds, swifts, and whip-poor-wills also become hypothermic at night.

Chickadee researcher Susan M. Smith found that two sorts of chickadees populate winter flocks: *regulars,* consisting of pairs, and *floaters,* unpaired birds that freely range between three or four flocks. Floaters are always subordinate birds except when a high-ranking pair member dies, in which case a floater fills the empty slot, thus leaving intact the pairings of the other regulars. Although complex shiftings and variations occur, floaters essentially provide the key to flock stability. Floaters that find no missing pair slots to fill remain unpaired but always available flock switchers. Young chickadees usually enter the flock system as floaters or low-ranked regulars. The "chick-a-dee-dee-dee" call, commonly heard in winter, serves to hold the flock together and coordinate movements.

Mixed-species flocks are another characteristic grouping in winter. Individual downy woodpeckers, tufted titmice, brown creepers, nuthatches, or kinglets may join chickadee foraging flocks for short or long periods, moving along with them as they feed and responding to chickadee alarm calls. In such transient groups, larger species such as tufted titmice usually outrank chickadees, which in turn are dominant over kinglets. Food availability apparently determines to what extent mixed flocking occurs; the multiple eyes of a mixed flock may increase the birds' foraging efficiency.

As flocks begin to break up in late winter, the "fee-bee" territorial call becomes increasingly frequent.

Ecology. Black-capped chickadees reside mainly in forest and edge habitats. They inhabit almost any sort of woodland or thicket, plus swamps and urban residential areas. The main habitat requirements are for nesting sites and plenty of bark and shrub microhabitats that contain an abundance of insect food.

Black-capped chickadees excavate their own nests, usually a new one each year, in stumps and dead tree stubs. Their bills are not adapted for powerful wood excavation like those of woodpeckers, so they must select sites that are soft-rotted and far advanced in decay. They usually excavate in the side of a trunk about four to eight feet high, sometimes higher. Dead birches, their tough, intact bark holding in the rotted wood tissue, are favored sites. Alders, aspens, cherries, and willows are also commonly used. Both sexes excavate the nest hole, carrying away the wood chips and dropping them; a litter of wood chips on the ground away from a tree base often indicates that there is a chickadee nest cavity nearby. Sometimes the pair excavates two or more cavities before settling on one.

Females collect most of the nesting materials. Mosses often form the base of the cavity; on this bed the female builds a cup lined with soft plant fibers, fern down, cottony seed fluff, insect cocoons, rabbit fur or other hairs, and feathers. Occasionally, instead of excavating, chickadees use natural cavities, old woodpecker holes, or nest boxes.

Although animal matter constitutes about 70 percent of the total diet, seasonal diets vary considerably. In early spring, chickadees show a fondness for maple sap icicles, formed on broken branches as the sap begins running. But spring and summer foods consist mainly of moth and butterfly caterpillars and spiders, both gleaned from vegetation. Irruptive hairy caterpillars, such as gypsy and eastern tent moths, which remain untouched by many birds, are frequently consumed in their smaller growth stages by chickadees. Experiments

The Carolina chickadee is hard to distinguish from the black-capped chickadee—there are slight differences in appearance, and their songs vary, as well. The biggest difference is range. Black-capped chickadees live in the Northeast and New England; Carolinas live in the South and Southeast. The ranges overlap in only a few areas.

have demonstrated that black-capped chickadees use a range of insect leaf-damage clues when foraging, and that they can associate these clues in various foliage types with the presence of palatable caterpillars.

Seeds and fruits supplement the insect fare in late summer and fall. Ragweed, goldenrod, staghorn sumac, and tulip tree seeds are common food items, as are blueberries, blackberries, and wild cherries. Chickadees cache seeds and other food items mainly in the fall. Common caching sites include bark crevices, leaf and birch bark curls, needle clusters, knotholes, and branch undersides. About half of the winter diet consists of

seeds. Waxy berries such as those of poison-ivy and bayberry are favorites, as are birch, pine, and hemlock seeds. The birds also glean spider and insect eggs and cocoons from bark crevices.

Research indicates that chickadees survive winter in about the same flock abundance whether or not yard feeders are provided. Only during periods of extremely cold or harsh weather, when the birds' energy needs are greater than usual, may yard feeders make the difference between survival and starvation. Although yard feeding may be expanding the winter ranges of some seed-eating birds, the weight of evidence suggests that, on the whole, yard feeding is more important to people than to birds. Indeed, an argument exists for *not* feeding chickadees in winter: A chickadee well provided with sunflower seeds may seek and consume fewer hibernating insects and insect eggs than it normally would; thus, in the spring, the unthinned populations of foliage-eating insects may produce a larger-than-normal abundance of plant pests.

In any hierarchical flock, food competition bears hardest on the subordinate members, which must give priority access to the dominants. Studies of winter chickadee flocks confirm that the survival rate of dominants exceeds that of low-ranking birds in the same flock. Food competition seems offset to some extent, however, by the advantage each bird derives from the multiple eyes and ears of the mixed or unmixed flock in detecting food and potential predators. The chickadee's omnivorous diet also works to its advantage.

Nest site competition is often from other chickadees, as territorial contests evict subordinate pairs and floaters from prime habitats. Most of these evacuees must settle for inferior habitats, and many do not breed at all. Tufted titmice, whose range expansion has brought them into increasing contact with black-capped chickadees, may contend for nest sites. House wrens often invade chickadee nests on or near wren territories, puncturing eggs, killing nestlings, and removing nesting material.

Frequent chickadee predators include sharp-shinned hawks, American kestrels, eastern screech-owls, and, in the far north, northern shrikes. Raccoons, squirrels, and snakes sometimes raid nests. Domestic cats are the foremost predators around yard feeders. Brood parasitism on chickadees by brown-headed cowbirds is negligible, probably because of the small entrance holes of chickadee nest cavities.

Focus. Chickadees are favorites of people who like to watch their antics and feed them in winter, and few other passerine species have received more attention from field researchers. Hundreds of scholarly papers have inspected and analyzed almost every aspect of chickadee existence, and more appear each year. Yet new questions about their territorial and flock behaviors, their reproduction, and their group dynamics continue to arise. We are far from knowing everything about these feisty little parids.

For example, recent research suggests that chickadee food caching and retrieval in the fall is an amazing complex of behavior and anatomy. The birds apparently regenerate new cells in the hippocampus, a brain area associated with spatial memory. Although this process occurs year-round, its peak occurs in October, when about 2 percent of the neurons are replaced daily. This peak coincides with the chickadee's main period of seed caching, when short-term memory of deposit sites becomes vital. The memory cells later die when the information they contain is no longer needed. Such cell economy ensures that the brain remains at a consistently small size, important in an airborne creature.

Black-capped chickadees have been known to survive more than twelve years, but average longevity is about two and one-half years.

Blue Jay
(*Cyanocitta cristata*)

Its foot-long size; blue crest, back, and tail; black "necklace"; gregarious behaviors; and harsh "jay" calls easily identify this common corvid. Actually, it produces a whole repertoire of sounds, including imitations of other birds. Sexes look alike, but summer jays in worn plumage sometimes appear more gray than blue.

Close relatives. Steller's jay (*C. stelleri*) is the blue jay's western counterpart, often hybridizing with it where their ranges meet. The gray jay (*Perisoreus canadensis*) of northern forests is the only other northeastern jay. Three scrub-jay species (*Aphelocoma*) inhabit

Florida and the western states. About forty jay species exist worldwide.

Behaviors. Flocking in blue jays is common at most times of the year. A troop of blue jays invariably announces its presence, but when blue jays pair during the breeding season, these birds seem to change personality and become silent, even secretive. Blue jays are noisiest when they spot a hawk, owl, prowling cat, squirrel, or snake, often mobbing the creature and excitedly advertising its presence (listening for blue jay caucuses is a good way of locating perched raptors). When not nesting, blue jays vocalize numerous sounds. Besides the familiar raucous alarm or attention calls, the squeaky gate call—"queedle queedle"—and a rattle that sounds like stones clicking together are commonly heard. Blue jays also imitate to perfection the "kee-yer" calls of red-shouldered hawks and, less commonly, the calls of red-tailed and broad-winged hawks. Amid all this jay cacophony, count yourself favored if you hear a much more infrequent sound—the soft, sweet, musical soliloquy of a solitary blue jay perched in dense foliage. In contrast to most birds, vocal behaviors of blue jays apparently have little to do with territorial defense or attracting mates; instead, they are most often flock related, serving as messages of contact, stimulation, and alarm. At food sources, a blue jay often gobbles as fast as it can, storing nuts and seeds in its expandable throat, later disgorging them for caching or feeding. When actually feeding, it grasps the seed or nut between its feet, pounding with unerring aim until the shell cracks open.

Northern blue jay populations migrate in large daytime flocks to and from the upper Great Lakes and Canada. The birds are year-round residents, however, throughout most of the eastern states.

Spring. Northern breeding populations move northward in April and May, often in noisy flocks of thousands. Nowhere have I seen so many blue jays massed as at White-fish Point Bird Observatory on Lake Superior, a prominent migratory channel. Here the passage of some fifty thousand blue jays has been recorded in one spring.

Blue jay courtship, as so many of their behaviors, occurs in the flock context. Small groups of three to ten males (probably yearling birds) attach to one female, bobbing and uttering bell-like "toolool" and rattle calls.

Gradually the males drop out, perhaps intimidated by displays of other males, until only a male-female pair is left. Older jays that have previously bred apparently pair earlier without joining courtship flocks. After pairing, the male often feeds the female, transferring food from bill to bill. Blue jays strongly defend their nests from intruders but seem oblivious to other jays in the vicinity except those in the same stage of the breeding cycle. Away from the nest, territorial boundaries seem ill defined in this species, though the birds usually remain within a given home range (also of indeterminate size) throughout the breeding season. Two or three pairs per hundred acres is probably an average figure. Nesting jays fall silent until the nestlings fledge but often rob and consume the contents of other species' nests at this time. Most jays probably remain monogamous only for a single breeding season.

EGGS AND YOUNG: four or five; eggs olive or buff, brown spotted. INCUBATION: by female; about seventeen days. FEEDING OF YOUNG: by both sexes; insects, other invertebrates, carrion. FLEDGING: about twenty days.

Summer. Blue jays raise only one brood in their northern range, two in the southern. Family groups remain together for one to two months, the parents continuing to feed clamorous juveniles even when full-grown. The annual feather molt occurs in late July and August, and observers sometimes report bald blue jays when head feathers molt.

Fall. With fresh plumage, the birds appear their most immaculate blue. Family groups join in late summer and fall to form larger foraging flocks, which disperse into smaller flocks as the weather chills. Farthest north populations in Canada withdraw south in September and October, and the juveniles of northern U.S. populations also move south. None of these migrants, however, depart the continental United States.

Winter. Blue jays remain throughout winter in most of their central and southern range. Farther north—in Michigan, for example—winter jays may be either local year-round residents or wintering migrants. Winter flocks average four to six birds, which feed and roam together, though solitary jays are not uncommon. Larger flocks begin to form in late winter as courtship activities commence.

Ecology. Mature, deciduous, mixed, and pine forests are the blue jay's foremost breeding habitats. Jays also reside in open woods and savannas, small woodlots, orchards, conifer plantations, and suburban areas. This bird's adaptable use of so many habitat types accounts in large part for its abundance.

Both sexes gather nesting materials, males breaking twigs directly off trees, and several preliminary nest platforms may be started and abandoned. This mock nest building is apparently also a courtship behavior. The actual breeding nest, built mainly by the female, nears completion when mating occurs. Blue jay nests are bulky masses of sticks, bark strips, mosses, string, paper, and occasionally mud, holding a cup lined with fine rootlets. Nests are usually well camouflaged, placed ten to twenty feet high in a crotch or outer branch. The birds often build in pines and red cedars, as well as in other trees, woodland shrubs, and even garden vines and trellises.

Although it consumes many sorts of plant and animal foods, this omnivorous bird is mainly vegetarian; acorns, beechnuts, fruits, and seeds are its staples. But in spring, as it seeks protein foods, it frequently becomes a bird predator, devouring eggs or nestlings in any nest it can find; these are important food items for many, if not most, blue jays. Insect food includes ants, caterpillars, grasshoppers, and beetles. Frogs, mice, and carrion are also occasionally consumed. Fall foods, besides nuts, include corn and blackberries. Jays occasionally raid ripening fruit crops in berry and tree orchards. They have also been observed eating sand and paint flakes from buildings, presumably for digestive and mineral needs.

Blue jay food habits are ecologically important in at least two ways. In spring, the birds are major consumers of hairy caterpillars, which include gypsy and tent moths, two of the most common irruptive pests of northeastern forests, and which most insect-eating birds won't touch. In the fall, blue jays cache many acorns and other nuts, collectively called mast, in the ground for later retrieval, sometimes transporting them a mile or more. I have even found acorns, beechnuts, and corn cached in cattail seed heads, probably also placed by blue jays. Many observers have reported watching streams of nut-laden blue jays disperse from woodlots during peak nut seasons. Forest clearings and fallow meadows are their favorite cache sites. The stored food items become important winter sources of nourishment. Since blue jays never retrieve all the nuts they bury, however, new oaks and beeches sprout. Blue jays thus become important agents of forest regeneration, especially on burnt and cut-over lands.

Competing mast feeders and cachers include many birds and mammals. Woodpeckers and squirrels are probably the blue jay's foremost nut competitors. This bird's

aggressiveness probably gives it advantage over some food collectors. Also, because it feeds more omnivorously than some of its competitors, jays enjoy more food options, thereby offsetting competitive pressures. Nut production in any given year may be poor or bountiful, and a poor mast year increases competition for the crop that exists. For northern blue jays, the abundance or scarcity of mast in the autumn may determine the extent of their southward migration.

Accipiter hawks are probably the blue jay's foremost predators, especially in northern areas during jay migrations. I have watched sharp-shinned hawks attack mist-netted jays captured for banding, sometimes also entangling themselves in the nets. These hawks often accompany jay flocks like wolf predators, capturing unwary or weakened birds. Peregrine falcons also capture blue jays, and American crows raid their nests. Blue jays are rare victims of brown-headed cowbird nest parasitism.

Focus. The blue jay longevity record is sixteen years, though few reach anywhere near that age. Estimated annual adult survival rate is 55 percent.

Predation by jays where dense populations exist may affect the abundance of small, non-cavity-nesting birds, such as vireos, warblers, and sparrows. Biologist Stephen Fretwell's analysis of breeding bird census records for one area concluded that "every blue jay costs a woodland seven pairs of small, open-nesting birds, but appears to add two pairs of hole nesters," such as woodpeckers, nuthatches, chickadees, or titmice, presumably because of reduced food competition. One of the negative effects of forest fragmentation is that it gives blue jays and other predators easier access to the nests of smaller woodland birds.

Yet, in contrast to its influence as a predator, the blue jay's ecological importance as a forest regenerator—thus creating new habitats for many more species—can hardly be overestimated. Pioneering botanist William Bartram recognized almost two centuries ago that "these birds are capable, in a few years' time, to replant all the cleared land." Biogeographers believe that the rapid northward spread of oaks—almost four hundred yards per year—following the retreat of Pleistocene glaciers was primarily due to blue jay acorn dispersal. The association of blue jays and oaks, in fact, appears rather tight. Another study concluded that "the distribution of oaks in nature may mirror the collective behavioral decisions made by the community of jays as they select, disperse, cache, and retrieve nuts." Blue jays far surpass nut-burying squirrels as oak planters. Probably natural selection has "opted" for relatively small acorn size in most oaks, thus favoring dispersion by jays. As naturalist Vaughan Edmonds writes, "If the oaks had had an age-old contract with the squirrels, acorns might be as large as pecans or walnuts."

If you hold a blue jay feather directly between your eyes and the sun, its blue color disappears. That's because, unlike the pigment-produced coloration of most plumage, blue in birds is a structural color, resulting from physics instead of chemistry. Minute air pockets, or *vacuoles*, that cannot absorb the blue part of the spectrum cause light reflected from any angle on the feather to scatter blue wavelengths. Light transmitted through the feather, on the other hand, is not reflected, and the feather appears dark.

Brown Thrasher
(*Toxostoma rufum*)

The brown thrasher's long, red-brown tail makes up about half of its twelve-inch length. Our largest and shiest mimid also has red-brown back and wings, heavy brown breast striping, and yellow eyes. It voices its loud, musical song in paired phrases, and often utters the smack call, which sounds like a loud kiss, when it is alarmed. Sexes look alike.

Close relatives. Six other *Toxostoma* species reside in the western United States. Most, like the sage thrasher (*Oreoscoptes montanus*), are desert birds. Some ten other species reside mainly in the West Indies.

Behaviors. Thrushlike in plumage and wrenlike in behaviors, brown thrashers are slimmer than thrushes and much larger than wrens. The thrasher's conspicuous behaviors, long tail, and twice-repeated song pattern make it easy to identify. This bird spends most of its time on or near the ground except when singing—often from a high, conspicuous perch—and migrating. Mainly a ground forager, it bill-sweeps dead leaves and other debris as it feeds. Its breeding range spans the continent, corresponding closely with that of its relative, the gray catbird. Also like the catbird, it occasionally includes mimicry of other birds—northern flickers, tufted titmice, wood thrushes, and northern cardinals, among others—in its song phrases. Unlike the catbird, however, it tends to shun human proximity. Brown thrashers are migrators, but a few often linger on the breeding range over winter.

Spring. Brown thrashers usually arrive on their northern breeding range in April, males preceding females. Territories may cover two to ten acres, depending on the habitat and thrasher abundance. The male's loud treetop song gives way to softer versions on lower perches as pairing begins. Few courtship behaviors have been observed. In May, both sexes collect nesting materials, but females do the actual building. Males, unless unmated, seldom sing conspicuously after nesting begins.

EGGS AND YOUNG: four or five; eggs bluish white, thickly dotted with brown. INCUBATION: by both sexes, sometimes singing on the nest; about two weeks. FEEDING OF YOUNG: by both sexes; mainly insects. FLEDGING: about ten days.

Summer. Despite bold thrasher defense of their nests, predation apparently causes many nesting failures in this species. Because of first-nest failure or double brooding, many, if not most, brown thrashers renest in early summer. Males continue feeding the fledged first brood while females begin the second nesting. Many thrashers apparently do not pair for life and may even switch mates between nestings. By late summer, when the annual feather molt occurs, young thrashers are on their own, and the birds become silent and secretive.

Fall, Winter. Southward migration occurs mainly in September. Most brown thrashers winter south of the Ohio River to the Gulf states. These birds are site faithful to both summer and winter territories. In parts of Texas, they share their winter range with long-billed and curve-billed thrashers (*T. longirostre, T. curvirostre*).

Ecology. Brown thrashers favor thickets—the denser and thornier the better. Dry forest edges and brushy undergrowth are common breeding habitats, as are conifer plantations.

Nests vary in height. In New England, thrashers often nest on the ground; elsewhere, they usually build less than seven feet high in such shrubs as hawthorns and viburnums, often placing late-season nests higher than earlier ones. The bulky nests are typically four-layered: large foundation sticks; dead leaves and grapevine bark; grass stems and dirt-encrusted rootlets; and a clean rootlet lining.

During the breeding season, thrashers feed chiefly on beetles, as well as ants, caterpillars, crickets, and other insects. Spiders, earthworms, and frogs are also consumed. At other seasons, blackberries, wild cherries, common elderberries, dogwood fruits, blueberries, corn, and acorns rank high in the diet.

Gray catbirds and northern cardinals compete with brown thrashers for breeding habitat. Somewhat less opportunistic than these species in diet and habitat use, thrashers may sometimes be driven out of areas where one or both are numerous. In their western winter range, brown thrashers occupy dense riverbottom thickets; the other two thrasher species with which they may share their winter range favor chaparral scrub.

Predators are generally the same as for gray catbirds. Brown-headed cowbird parasitism occurs, but usually at low levels. Thrashers may eject cowbird eggs. Research suggests that cowbirds may mistakenly eject their own eggs from thrasher nests, on the basis of size; thrashers are the largest passerines victimized by cowbirds, and unlike eggs in most host nests, thrasher eggs are larger than those of cowbirds.

Focus. While the related northern mockingbird has a large song repertoire, the thrasher's is larger—indeed, with an estimated three thousand or more song types, the largest of any North American bird's. The names *thrasher* and *thrush* derive from the same Anglo-Saxon root. Brown thrush is a colloquial label for this thrasher.

Unlike catbirds and most other edge species, brown thrashers appear to be declining in most of their breeding range. Causes remain unclear. Individual thrashers have been known to survive almost thirteen years, but most probably live less than half that long.

The brown thrasher is Georgia's state bird.

Brown-headed Cowbird
(Molothrus ater)

This seven-inch-long black-bird has a thick, sparrowlike bill. Males are black with clove brown heads; females are a uniform gray-brown with no distinctive markings. The male's song, a liquid, squeaky "glug-lug-glee," sounds as if he is swallowing his own notes. A long, squeaky whistle is also common. Females often utter a series of chattering notes similar to those of house wrens or eastern meadowlarks.

Close relatives. Of the five other cowbird species, only the shiny cowbird (*M. bonariensis*) of the Southeast and the bronzed cowbird (*M. aeneus*), a southwestern desert dweller, reside in North America. The rest are South American species, only one of which, the bay-winged cowbird (*M. badius*), is not a brood parasite and raises its own young.

Behaviors. Note the cowbird's habit of uptilting its tail when (like most blackbirds) it walks. Cowbirds are highly gregarious for most of the year, associating in large flocks with other blackbirds and European starlings.

All brown-headed cowbirds are step-children, having been raised in nests of other species—"the ultimate form of day care," in the words of one researcher. Cowbird nestlings often coexist with host nestlings, but often too they supplant them by more rapid hatching, growth, and aggressive begging behavior, resulting in starvation or crowding out of the host nestlings.

Cowbird numbers relate directly to habitat. Originally a Great Plains species that associated with bison herds, giving them the vernacular name buffalo bird, cowbirds have extended their range eastward since agriculture cleared ample new habitats for them. As a result, several eastern passerine species, especially certain warblers, are today seriously threatened by cowbird brood parasitism. Some birds, including blue jays, American robins, gray catbirds, brown thrashers, and Baltimore orioles, have learned to recognize cowbird eggs and eject them from their nests. Other species abandon parasitized nests. One theory even attributes the evolution of blue egg color, as in robins, catbirds, and chipping sparrows, to defense against cowbird parasitism, enabling the blue-egg hosts to discriminate the cowbird egg from their own and eject it from the nest. But most eastern passerines have not yet evolved defensive behaviors and thus, on occasion, may raise more cowbird young than their own.

The cowbird female is an opportunistic egg layer in open nests, but rarely in cavity nests. She shows little discrimination in nest choice and will often deposit eggs in nests of inappropriate species whose type of nestling food will not sustain young cowbirds. Nest accessibility and timing of host presence at the nest are the key factors in choosing where to deposit her eggs. Of some two hundred twenty host species recorded, about one hundred forty-four are successfully parasitized and fledge cowbird young.

Cowbirds expend a huge amount of energy to reproduce themselves. Although only about 3 percent of cowbird eggs laid result in adult cowbirds, this percentage produces enough cowbirds to threaten the survival of several host species that are already threatened or endangered, such as Kirtland's and prothonotary warblers. This is because, as one researcher writes, "each pair of cowbirds replaces itself with an average of 1.2 pairs—which will double a cowbird population in eight years." Population numbers of the most common victims, however, seem little affected by cowbird parasitism, though as cowbird numbers increase, this could change. Red-eyed vireos, song and chipping sparrows, American redstarts, and yellow warblers, though most frequently and successfully parasitized, show stable or increasing abundance in most areas. Cowbird parasitism ordinarily affects host bird populations only when other factors—often human-induced habitat changes—lead to cowbird overabundance. We have strongly invited cowbirds to succeed—and they have.

Several other North American bird species, including cuckoos, pheasants, and a few ducks, occasionally dump eggs in nests of their own or other species; such occurrences are fairly common among several passerine species as well. But the cowbird is our only *obligate* brood parasite—it *must* parasitize nests for its own survival. Worldwide, obligate brood parasites include the European cuckoo (*Cuculus canorus*), the honeyguides (*Indicator*), and several weavers (Passeridae). Thus brood parasitism is not an anomalous or abnormal biological situation, but a complex, highly evolved reproductive strategy.

Brown-headed cowbirds breed throughout North America, except for peninsular Florida, from mid-Canada into Mexico. Northern populations migrate, but the birds occupy a large, year-round midcontinental range from New England and the Great Lakes southward.

Spring. Northern cowbird populations usually arrive on their breeding range in early spring, often mid-March. Males usually appear before females. Studies reveal that of all blackbirds, yearling cowbirds are least likely to return to their birth sites in spring. Until egg laying begins in late April, I often observe the birds in trios of two highly attentive males to one female, the males perching and singing wherever she perches and following wherever she flies. Also conspicuous is the male topple-over display as he fluffs, arches, spreads wings and tail, tips forward as if about to fall, and creaks out a song.

More than for most species, cowbird courtship and territorial behaviors are keyed to their habitats. In eastern North America, females are the territorial sex, defending areas of ten to fifty acres from other female cowbirds. Territories often overlap, however, which may be why some host nests receive multiple cowbird eggs. Cowbirds are generally monogamous and sometimes retain the same partners over successive years. Courting males may wander in and out of several female territories until a female pairs with one; the chosen male then follows and guards his mate from invading males but does not defend her territory. At certain times of day, territorial boundaries lapse, and all cowbirds in an area may gather to forage gregariously in prime feeding spots. Midwestern farmlands, where host species and their nests are scattered over much wider distances, present a different picture. There males tend to group in small, loose flocks and remain in areas of twenty to one hundred acres. The females establish no territories, wander widely in search of host nests, and mate promiscuously with dominant males of a flock wherever they can.

Having mated, a female cowbird searches out a host nest by three main methods: by perching in silent observation, by walking on the ground while watching for birds in the vicinity, and by raising a ruckus—noisily rummaging on the ground and in tree foliage as if trying to flush out hidden potential hosts. She usually selects a nest in which at least one host egg is already present. If she finds more than one, she often removes one of the host eggs the day before laying one of her own. She never lays more than one egg at a time in a given nest, though another cowbird female may repeat her performance in the same nest. This operation is performed quickly, usually in seconds, often just before dawn when the host bird leaves its nest to feed.

EGGS AND YOUNG: Female cowbirds often lay an egg a day for five or six consecutive days, quit for a few days, then begin again (some sources say a female lays an average of forty eggs per breeding season, others say up to forty); eggs grayish white, brown dotted, especially at the larger end. INCUBATION: by host species; ten to twelve days (about the same period as that of the smallest passerines), the egg often hatching the day before the host's eggs hatch, thus gaining the cowbird nestling a head start. FEEDING OF YOUNG: by host species, though there have been rare observations of female cowbirds feeding nestling cowbirds in host nests; food consists of whatever the foster parents feed their own young, in most cases insects; cowbird nestlings may starve without a high-protein diet. FLEDGING: ten or eleven days.

Summer. Female cowbirds continue laying at progressively less frequent intervals until about mid-July. Thus, as the season advances, many later- or repeat-nesting species escape cowbird parasitism. Cowbird nestlings, often growing much larger than their foster parents, receive the most attention and thus most of the food brought to the nest. The foster parents also continue to feed fledgling cowbirds from two weeks to a month. Marked behavioral differences between host and parasite species sometimes become apparent during this period. Researcher Harry W. Hann, describing the behavior of cowbird fledglings from ovenbird nests, noted that their tendency to fly up to a perch was "quite disconcerting to the foster parents, which like to keep the young on the ground." Soon the juveniles disperse to nearby areas.

Do cowbirds have the avian equivalent of an identity crisis? Having supposedly become imprinted on a host species, how does a young cowbird achieve cowbirdhood? And does having a particular species as foster parents result in an adult cowbird's favoritism toward that species as a future host? Researchers continue to grapple with these and other puzzles posed by this intriguing bird. As the season advances, young cowbirds, resembling female adults, seek out their own kind, joining also with other blackbirds in foraging and roosting flocks.

Adult cowbirds undergo their annual plumage molt in late summer and early fall.

Fall. After the breeding season, cowbirds might almost be said to lose their social identity as a species. They blend into a larger entity, the blackbird flock, mixing with other blackbirds as if these were their true siblings. Huge mixed flocks of red-winged and rusty blackbirds, common grackles, and cowbirds—which may constitute only 1 to 3 percent of the flock—move southward from their northern ranges mainly in October. Flying by day, they forage in fields and spend nights in transient roosts, often marshes or conifer groves. Northeastern cowbirds may travel five hundred miles or more to their wintering areas.

Winter. Researchers long believed that young male cowbirds learned and developed their species song from older males during winter, when the birds are associated in roosts. Recent work, however, suggests that they learn their song by female feedback—that is, the wing-stroke reactions by a female to a song she "likes" may "teach" a male his song even if he has never heard another male cowbird. Most cowbirds winter from New England, the southern Great Lakes and Great Plains, and California to the Gulf and into Central America.

Ecology. Cowbirds were originally native to the short-grass plains, which they still inhabit and where they associate with grazing cattle, horses, and bison. They began expanding their populations both east and west concurrently with land clearing and cultivation. Their feeding association with grazing mammals was seen to be unnecessary to their survival and reproductive success. It took them more than a century, however, to span the continent. Optimal cowbird habitats in the East include open forest and edge mosaics amid plenty of open land for ground foraging. Residential areas and farm country with woodlots, hedgerows, roadside vegetation—almost any landscape with a tree-shrub-field mix—serve cowbird needs. Because of these habitat preferences, most cowbird hosts are edge-dwelling species. Yet this is changing. Forest fragmentation has increased the vulnerability of many interior woodland birds to cowbird parasitism. Since cowbirds often penetrate woodlands several hundred feet—and occasionally much farther—from their edges in seeking out host nests, virtually every nest in a fragmented stand may become accessible to these parasites.

Cowbirds construct no nests of their own, though ancestral cowbirds probably did so. How and why the parasitic nesting habit evolved in these birds remains a subject of endless theory and speculation. Likely it had something to do with the birds' transient lifestyle as they followed the bison herds.

Primarily insect eaters during the summer, cowbirds consume many leafhoppers, beetles, and caterpillars, but almost half their insect food consists of grasshoppers. From the farmer's point of view, the cowbird's consumption of destructive insects makes it a beneficial bird. Spiders, snails, and eggs from host nests are also eaten. Early observers, watching cowbirds perch on the backs of cattle, believed that they benefited grazers by feeding on the animals' skin parasites. Perhaps they do to some extent, but probably the association is mainly *commensal*—that is, cowbirds capture insect food stirred up by the grazers, which neither benefit nor suffer. About 75 percent of the cowbird's annual diet consists of weed and grass seeds; ragweeds, knotweeds, foxtail grasses, and crab-

grasses rank high, as do corn, oats, and wheat. Since cowbirds feed mainly on the ground, most of their grain consumption is harvest waste.

Probably the cowbird's foremost competitor is itself, especially in host nests where two or more large cowbird nestlings must contend with each other for food. They also compete against high statistical odds: If the host bird does not eject, bury, or abandon the cowbird egg, and if, once hatched, the cowbird nestling receives enough protein food and does not fall victim to a nest predator, its chances for survival to adulthood are good. But only a small percentage of cowbirds make it that far.

Though many host species show hostility to adult cowbirds in or near their territories, few succeed in driving the silent female stalkers completely away. Cowbird eggs and nestlings are vulnerable to any host nest predator, and flock roosts may be raided by owls. Hawks and falcons also capture cowbirds.

Focus. Thoreau sometimes called this bird the "cow troopial" (troupials are related to South American orioles); cow bunting and cow blackbird were other common names. Audubon and other early naturalists misidentified the juvenile cowbird, naming it a separate species, the "ambiguous sparrow."

Brown-headed cowbirds have been known to live for almost sixteen years; average longevity is probably half that or less. Researchers estimate that twenty to forty million cowbirds currently inhabit North America.

In areas managed for certain host populations threatened by cowbirds, trapping and killing the parasites has provided at least temporary relief for the victimized. Yet these birds, posing as many problems as they do for bird conservation and research, offer a wealth of interest. And their gamble on the successfulness of deceit reminds us of the endlessly variable survival strategies evolved for living on Earth—that nature's "agendas" far transcend the values of human community. For that reason alone should cowbirds intrigue us.

Canada Goose
(Branta canadensis)

The most abundant, widespread, and familiar goose in North America as well as the world, the Canada goose is readily identified by its white "chinstrap," its black head and neck contrasting with paler breast and brownish wings, and its resonant, honking calls. Sizes range from the almost swan-size giant Canada goose *(B. c. maxima)* to the mallard-size cackling goose *(B. c. minima)*. The giant race, one of the most common, often shows other markings: a white neck ring, a white forehead spot, and a distinctive "hawk's-head" pattern (facing rear) as part of the cheek-patch profile.

Waterfowl biologists have classified eleven distinct subspecies of Canada geese in North America, based on sizes, plumages, breeding range locales, migration routes, and wintering locales. (Some biologists believe there are many more, possibly up to forty.) Most of the medium to large subspecies migrate and reside east of the hundredth parallel of longitude; the smaller, darker races dominate west of that line. The six eastern populations, with their dominant races or subspecies, are as follows, from east to west: north Atlantic (Atlantic race), mid-Atlantic (interior race), Tennessee Valley (interior and giant races),

Mississippi Valley (interior race), eastern prairie (interior race), and tallgrass prairie (Hutchins's, lesser race). The giant race is common in all areas. Each race breeds apart, and they seldom hybridize; in a practical sense, they are distinct species. Two or more races often mix together during migrations, however, and on the winter range. Size and plumage differences between giant and interior races of Canada geese (which commonly occur together) are obvious in the field. Male Canadas are slightly larger than females. The male's two-syllable honk, "ke-ronk," is lower toned than the female's "kink kink."

Close relatives. Five *Branta* species range worldwide. In North America, the only other resident *Branta* is the brent goose (*B. bernicla*), often called brant. The barnacle goose (*B. leucopsis*) is a native of Greenland and arctic Europe. Another European species, the red-breasted goose (*B. ruficollis*), is the smallest goose of all. The endangered nene or Hawaiian goose (*B. sandvicensis*) is restricted to Hawaii.

Behaviors. The Canada goose is the bird most people think of as *the* wild goose or honker. Its high, migratory V formations and nasal, quavering chant from the sky herald the arrivals of spring and winter. Thoreau called Canada geese "grenadiers of the air . . . coming to unlock the fetters of northern rivers." Yet this creature that so conspicuously travels the continent twice a year, even occasionally competing with the airlines for high-traffic lanes, nests in utter stealth. A goose spotting you from a pond thicket can freeze still as a rock, its head outstretched with not a feather ruffled by breeze, not a pond ripple set forth by slightest movement.

Canada geese have a large repertoire of display postures, a body language fairly easy to interpret once you learn its details. Many of these movements are easily seen in any flock year-round, and most of them involve motions of the head and neck. Threat or aggressive displays include folded-neck and extended-neck postures with head lowered and pointed at the opponent; vertical head pumping, often preceding a direct attack; and vigorous swinging of the outstretched neck, rotating the head. Geese convey other messages during courtship (see Spring). A flock of geese on water often signals its imminent takeoff by suddenly erupting into loud honking, head pumping, and facing into the wind. Landing seems trickier for them; they stretch their feet forward and their necks downward before splashing down, an awkward-appearing performance. Landing in strong wind, a goose may "whiffle" on its descent, turning on its side (or sometimes flipping completely over), stalling its airlift, and plummeting five or ten feet before righting itself. These giddy acrobatics seem more characteristic of younger geese than older adults, which seem more inclined to sober landings.

Like most waterfowl, Canada geese mate for life. Should one partner die, the other usually bonds to a new mate within a year or less. Most large flocks consist of subflocks made up of individual family units. These smaller groupings are easily observed in any large flock on water. In the goose social hierarchy, large families dominate smaller ones. Families in turn dominate pairs, which dominate single geese. Males dominate family units.

Canada geese, native to North America, range from the high Arctic to the southern United States and northern Mexico. They have also been introduced into Europe and New Zealand.

Spring. "For the farmer, the rancher, the city dweller, and the Cree Indian," wrote biologist Frank Bellrose, "the northward flight of Canada geese symbolizes spring." Likewise, to Aldo Leopold, "one swallow does not make a summer, but one skein of geese, clearing the murk of a March thaw, is the spring." Observers have noted differential migrations in some areas, with two peak movements: March-April and May-June. Except for far-northern populations, however, most Canada geese have arrived on their breeding ranges by earliest spring. They usually return as family units to the previous year's nesting site, but yearling geese soon separate into flocks by themselves and depart their first home, often traveling up to several hundred miles (usually northward) from the natal area. Some yearlings may form lifelong pair bonds now, but their first nesting seldom occurs until their second or third year.

Within most of their breeding range, as snow and ice begin to retreat, Canada geese are among the first birds of the year to nest (great horned owls, crossbills, and a few others precede them). The female leads her mate on a search, often inspecting old nest sites, perhaps choosing one she has previously used or scraping a new hollow nearby. Now the pair, especially the male, becomes aggressively territorial, defending an area that may vary from a quarter acre to many acres in size, depending upon density of population and height of surrounding vegetation. Throughout the incubation period, males may readily attack any intruder, including other geese and humans. Following a successful challenge to an intruder, the pair typically performs a mutual action called the greeting or triumph ceremony. This consists of head shaking, neck stretching, male snoring notes, and strident honking in perfectly timed duet. Head and neck dipping precedes copulation. The female builds the nest, beginning with a slight scrape, then reaches from it to pluck adjacent vegetation. Gradually she forms a base and rim around herself, adding down from her breast after egg laying begins. The male stands guard near the nest as incubation begins. He accompanies his mate when she leaves the nest, usually twice daily (early morning and afternoon) for short periods of feeding and bathing.

After hatching, nest territorial bounds immediately dissolve, and the family moves about together in mobile territory, often in single file on water. Sources differ on whether the male or female usually leads or trails the family procession.

EGGS AND YOUNG: typically five or six; eggs creamy white, becoming nest stained. INCUBATION: by female; about four weeks. FLEDGING: about two months, sometimes less.

Summer. After hatching, goslings leave the nest with parents in a day or less, but brooding continues for the first few days. An oft-noted occurrence is the *creche* or gang brood, a mixed brood of ten to twenty goslings swimming and feeding under the care of a single pair of adults—a kind of day-care system also seen in flamingos, ostriches, penguins, and a few other species. Creching occurs mainly in densely occupied nesting areas, where many goslings hatch at once. Their imprinting on a single female parent may be incomplete or delayed for two or three weeks. Some studies suggest that such brood interchange results from a literal mix-up of abundant progeny. Other studies indicate that younger, inexperienced females may sometimes lose their goslings to the care of older adults, resulting in formation of large extended families.

Yearling and other nonbreeding adult geese begin their annual feather molt some ten days after parent adults, usually in June. The birds remain flightless for four to six weeks. Family groups become secretive, moving to more secluded areas during this period. During this flightless period, the Inuit and other natives hunt Canada geese for food. By late summer, molting is completed, goslings are fledged, and family groups often join large multifamily flocks on open land and water areas.

Fall. Canada goose populations vary extensively in timing of fall migration. Many populations depart their breeding areas in early fall or before; others (such as the giant Canada goose), wrote Frank C. Bellrose, "are notorious for their late fall departures." Peak travel occurs in September and October, but thousands of geese *stage,* or gather, at large wildlife refuges in the northern tier of states. They often associate with snow goose or brant migrants on these areas. If open water is available and food is plentiful, many remain over winter in these areas or until harsh weather sends them farther south. Most eastern populations, however, winter inland from southern Illinois to Kentucky. Incoming migrants join resident year-round geese, swelling numbers to hundreds of thousands.

Flying both day and night, Canada geese travel in flocks that may number from 30 or less to 100 or more birds. Observer opinions differ on the gender and constancy of the lead bird in a flying flock. In a migrating flock, thinks Frank C. Bellrose, the leader "is probably the gander of the largest family." In a life-time of observing geese, he never witnessed the point goose in a migratory flock changing positions, as has been reported. Most flocks travel about 40 miles per hour at an altitude around 2,000 feet, though occasionally much higher flocks are spotted by pilots. As they fly, they voice their constant contact calls— "goose music," as Aldo Leopold called it. Their voices precede their wedge formations, often drifting down from the night sky as you lie snug abed.

Winter. As on their breeding ranges, flocks *home* to particular wintering areas, resulting in highly localized populations, often of mixed races, that return year after year. Family groups remain together in subflocks and in large flocks on the winter range. Early morning and evening hours are preferred feeding times, but flocks may stay on feeding grounds all day if not disturbed. At night, they usually roost in open water. Winter storms or cold snaps may send resident flocks southward on minimigrations for brief periods, but the birds often bounce back when weather abates. Winter is barely half over when flocks in many locales begin restless behaviors. From their southernmost range, they may depart northward as early as mid-January. More northern wintering flocks begin moving about mid-February or early March. These early migrants often travel in 50- to 100-mile leaps, generally keeping apace with the 35-degree F. isotherm, where melting snow and ice expose food and patches of open water. Later migrants tend to move longer distances at once, thus making up in some measure for the time lapse.

Ecology. A variety of wetland habitats may host Canada geese. In the breeding range, a pair usually requires at least five acres of open water plus access, near or far, to upland fields or open land for grazing. Primary requirements on the winter range are grazing habitats for feeding and open water for drinking and resting sites. Canada geese, as we know, are exceedingly adaptable to human environs and readily become semi-domesticated. Suburban parks, lawns, and golf courses provide ample grazing habitats.

Canada geese probably show greater diversity in nest sites than any other waterfowl. The site is usually located within fifty yards of water (often much closer), contains some amount of cover (usually emergent aquatic vegetation), and is on high enough ground to give the nesting goose a clear overview of the surroundings. Typically the birds nest atop muskrat and beaver lodges, bulrush mats, and marsh hummocks, and on dikes, ditch banks, and small islands. (In certain prairie and delta marshes, the presence of muskrat lodges may be chief attractants.) Occasionally the geese inhabit above-ground structures such as abandoned heron, hawk, and osprey nests, human-made tree platforms, or elevated washtubs. Nest materials consist of sticks, cattails, reeds, and grasses, all gathered from the immediate vicinity.

Canada geese are almost wholly vegetarian grazers. Their natural food consists mainly of shoots and seeds of grasses, legumes, and such aquatic vegetation as spike-rushes and bulrushes. They cannot digest cellulose well, however, and must consume large amounts of vegetation to satisfy their energy needs. The passage of food from gullet to excretion averages about two hours. (One researcher conducted a heroic quest for science: "I know from personal experience," wrote M. A. Ogilvie in his book *Wild Geese*, "that a fresh goose dropping from a bird feeding on grass has little or no taste, except perhaps that of chewed grass.") But Canada goose food habits, especially during migrations and winter, have changed extensively since presettlement times. Such changes reflect the countrywide expansion of agriculture; these changes also account in large part for the phenomenal increase of goose populations and shifts in their winter distribution over the past several decades. Wintering Canada geese show marked preference for farm-grown grains (especially corn) and grain shoots (such as winter wheat). Stubble fields with their waste grain are also favored feeding sites. Aldo Leopold pointed out the "prairie-bias" of feeding Canada geese, noting the "conspicuous fact that the corn stubbles selected by geese for feeding are usually those occupying former prairies. No man knows whether this bias for prairie corn reflects some superior nutritional value or some ancestral tradition" or merely "the simpler fact that prairie cornfields tend to be large." Today much of the forage grains and greens that migrant and wintering Canada geese consume is provided expressly for them in state and federal wildlife refuges. As a consequence, many formerly transient flocks have become permanent winter residents in these areas. The birds (mainly goslings) also consume small amounts of invertebrates.

Competition with other waterfowl is negligible in most areas. Canada geese seem highly tolerant of other species such as ducks and herons, often nesting in proximity to them. Canada geese do not regularly associate with other waterfowl. On upland feeding sites, however, other goose species plus grazing ducks such as mallards often mingle freely with them. The recent increase of mute swan populations in the eastern United States offers potentially competitive situations; conflicts often occur between these species in areas where they are both breeding.

Predators, which consume mainly eggs and goslings, include jaegers, gulls, common ravens, American crows, magpies, foxes, coyotes, minks, and (in some areas) dogs. Goslings, even when very young, are able to dive, thus avoiding the beaks or talons of predatory birds. Attacks by blackflies (Simuliidae) and snapping turtles sometimes kill goslings.

Focus. Trends of rapid increase in Canada goose populations over the past several decades continue. The spectacular comeback of this once-depleted species, especially in middle and eastern North America, is an oft-cited victory of wildlife conservation efforts. Overhunted to extirpation in many areas, most breeding Canada geese had vanished from the north-central states by 1900. Severe drought during the 1930s reduced many migratory populations as well. Since then, the growth of federal and state refuge systems has helped build eastern Canada goose populations to numbers that probably far exceed their presettlement abundance. Especially notable is the recovery of the giant Canada goose, the largest race, once believed to have become extinct by 1920. In 1962, however, a surviving population was identified in Minnesota, and subsequent management efforts have produced a success story that for waterfowl biologists "may well have become one of their greatest nightmares," as ornithologist James Granlund remarks. Today, as a consequence, two large populations of Canada geese reside in eastern North America: the wild migrants and the more or less permanent residential population of the suburbs, introduced since World War II. The latter population has become the larger by far.

The present overpopulation of Canada geese in open suburban areas—parks, airports, golf courses—has given the bird an increasingly negative image. From a bird of near-legendary status venerated by Aldo Leopold and other conservation pioneers when Canada geese were far fewer in number, its subsequent transformation into a "trash bird" of urban areas is a case of familiarity breeding contempt. Honkers defecate about once every three minutes—almost a pound per day per goose—wherever they graze, and lawns full of goose manure lose their appeal for human sunbathing and picnicking. Control of nuisance geese by removal, extended hunting seasons, and planting of distasteful grasses such as tall fescue has had little widespread success. The birds also trouble farmers at times, especially by ravaging soybean crops in some areas; most grain feeding, however, occurs during the postharvest season, and mainly on wildlife refuges planted for the purpose.

"Wawa," the Ojibwa word for the Canada goose, is perpetuated in the town name of Wawa, Ontario, where a large statue of the goose welcomes visitors. Fennville, Michigan, located near a large goose refuge, hosts an annual goose festival for hunters (motto: "Get your goose in Fennville"). Long a staple source of meat for Native Americans, Canada geese also provided flight feathers for arrow fletching and goosedown for bedding. Goose grease became a popular medicinal and cooking ingredient. And Canada goose migrations, which sky watchers invariably declare as happening earlier or later than usual, still provide an endless seasonal topic and bellwether.

Captive Canada geese may survive for several decades, but most wild geese probably live only five or six years. Annual mortality rates of fledged geese average less than 30 percent. Canadian naturalist Jack Miner, who established an Ontario migration refuge for Canada geese as early as 1904, was an early proponent of their conservation. Miner spread much information and folk wisdom (along with some notable misinformation) about the species in his many books. Most ornithologists discredit the widely reported "piggyback phenomenon"—tales of hummingbirds or sparrows hitching rides on Canada geese during migration. Such behavior involves too many anomalies to be true.

Cedar Waxwing
(Bombycilla cedrorum)

Waxwing family (Bombycillidae). Sleekly brown and crested, cedar waxwings are seven to eight inches long. They have a yellowish belly, yellow band at the tail tip, and waxy red tips on the wing secondaries. Their wheezy, high-pitched notes are distinctive. Sexes look much alike, but juveniles show brown streaking.

Close relatives. The Bohemian waxwing (*B. garrulus*), a larger version of its cousin, is a northwestern species that also resides in Eurasia. The only other species is the Japanese waxwing (*B. japonica*) of Asia.

Behaviors. Debonair, dapper, and elegant are adjectives frequently used to describe the color-dabbed cedar waxwing. Waxwings are gregarious and nonchalant, even almost sluggish. They sometimes resemble starlings in flight, with an undulating pattern of quick wingflaps and soars. They also make brief sallies from perches, capturing aerial insects much as flycatchers do. In flocks, their thin, sibilant notes sound almost incessantly as they feed, fly, and perch.

Breeding and winter ranges span the continent, but seasonal movements are irregular. In many northern areas, waxwings are nomadic rather than migratory, but substantial north-south migrations also occur.

Spring. Waxwings move to their breeding sites from early to late spring. Some observers suggest that spring migrations occur in double waves—one in March, and one in May or June. Traveling in large flocks, waxwings pair during migration, but they may not return to the previous year's breeding sites. They often delay territory formation and actual nesting until summer—thus, unlike many birds, females select mates on the basis of individual attraction rather than quality of territory. In the meantime, the birds split into smaller flocks of six or more. A common courtship display is the side-hop: A pair sidles alongside each other, hopping close, then away, passing a berry or cherry back and forth for up to fifteen minutes before one of the birds eats it.

Summer. Breeding territories (up to an acre in size) and nest sites are largely determined by the proximity of fruiting trees or shrubs. Territorial food sources are not defended, however, and the birds continue to feed communally. A prominent territorial feature is the male's sentinel perch, from which he watches as nesting proceeds. Nesting usually begins in mid-June, often continuing into late summer, especially when the birds raise two broods. Subtle differences in waxwing call notes are good indicators of the precise phase of nesting. Often several pairs may nest semicolonially, with nests as close as twenty-five feet. Nesting overlap is common, with nestlings fledging in the first nest while egg laying begins in a second. Pairs probably remain monogamous for the entire season. After the young achieve total independence—about twenty-five days—they join other juveniles to feed in small flocks. Mixed juvenile-adult flocks occur in late summer.

Various theories explain the delayed breeding dates of the waxwings—the latest passerine nesters, except for American goldfinches. One theory suggests that their late timing is a recently evolved response to brood parasitism of brown-headed cowbirds, which breed earlier. More likely, perhaps, is the theory that waxwing breeding coincides with seasonal fruit ripening, since berries and tree fruits constitute the main diet of nestlings.

EGGS AND YOUNG: four or five; eggs gray, brown spotted. INCUBATION: by female, which is fed by male; about twelve days. FEEDING OF YOUNG: by both sexes; insects for first two days, regurgitated berries thereafter. FLEDGING: about fifteen days.

Fall. The annual feather molt occurs in late summer and early fall. Most waxwings do not gain their red secondary tips until their second-year molt, though exceptions do occur. Many, if not most, waxwings migrate south in September and October, some moving as far as Panama.

Winter. Most eastern waxwing populations winter on the coastal plain from South Carolina to Texas. Little interchange of western and eastern populations occurs; birds west of the Rockies probably form the bulk of Central American migrants. Roaming flocks, however, remain in the northern breeding range, appearing locally wherever there are food sources. Their occurrence and abundance fluctuate from year to year.

Ecology. Cedar waxwings favor edge habitats—open woodlands, thickets, hedgerows, orchards, and suburban yards—almost anyplace that offers fruiting trees or shrubs. In winter, they often frequent swamps. They avoid densely forested areas.

Nests vary in placement, height, materials used, and even general form. Some are large, loose, and bulky, others relatively neat and compact. I have found them on red pine branches built against the trunk about eight feet high, but often they build much higher on horizontal limbs, away from the trunk or in an upright fork. They use twigs in the nest foundation, as well as grasses, weed stems, and string or twine if available. They line the nest with fine grasses, pine needles, plant down, and sometimes wool. Waxwings often raid nests of other birds for nesting materials.

This is one of our most *frugivorous*, or fruit-eating, birds, with an annual diet consisting of some 70 percent fruits. Highly favored are the berrylike cones of eastern red cedar (commonly called juniper), wild cherries, and flowering dogwood fruits. Blackberries, hackberries, chokeberries, mulberries, grapes, and hawthorn and viburnum fruits also rank high, but waxwings are essentially fruit opportunists, taking whatever nature offers in abundance. Apple blossom petals are especially relished in spring. Waxwings perched on a wire often pass a cherry, petal, or caterpillar one to the other, a similar behavior to their courtship display. The birds are often gluttonous; after gorging on overripe, fermented berries, they may droop like sodden couch potatoes or become comically tipsy. On their southern winter range, waxwings consume mistletoe, privet, and persimmon fruits in abundance. North-wintering flocks seek out wetland shrubs that hold their fruits for long duration. Insect consumption is also important; waxwings are

efficient predators of foliage-eating geometrid moth caterpillars (cankerworms) and also consume many leaf beetles.

Food competitors include other frugivores, such as American robins, northern mockingbirds, and European starlings. Occasionally waxwings also compete with berry and orchard farmers. Predators are relatively few, although accipiter hawks probably capture some waxwings. Waxwings vary in response to brown-headed cowbird parasitism; most waxwings eject cowbird eggs, especially during early incubation stages, but some 8 percent of waxwing nests raise one or more cowbirds.

Focus. Cedarbird, cankerbird, and cherry bird are common nicknames. The dropletlike red dabs on the tips of adult secondaries are pigmented extensions of the feather shafts. Astaxanthin, the red carotenoid pigment found mainly in red fruits, originates in the diet. Research confirms that these color markings are age related and probably confer some breeding and status advantage. Since the 1960s, a color variation in the tail band—orange instead of yellow-has been observed in many northeastern juvenile waxwings. This variation seems to have coincided with the introduction from Japan of an ornamental fruit-bearing shrub, Morrow's honeysuckle (*Lonicera morrowii.*) The fruits contain the carotenoid pigment rhodoxanthin, which remains unsynthesized in the waxwing's orange tail band. The second-year molt brings normal yellow-banded tail feathers; whether this is from age-related changes in fruit diet or digestive efficiency remains unknown.

Cedar waxwings were once hunted for food; Audubon described them as "tender and juicy." Their wide habitat and food tolerances have made cedar waxwings common to abundant throughout most of their range.

Chipping Sparrow
(Spizella passerina)

This five-inch-long sparrow can be recognized by its unstreaked pale gray breast, bright reddish brown cap, white line over the eye, and black line through it. Its song is a rattling trill on one pitch. Sexes look alike.

Close relatives. Other northeastern *Spizella* species include the American tree sparrow (*S. arborea*), field sparrow (*S. pusilla*), and clay-colored sparrow (*S. pallida*). Brewer's sparrow (*S. breweri*) and the black-chinned sparrow (*S. atrogularis*) are western U.S. species. These six species form the entire genus.

Behaviors. Before the unrelated house sparrow's invasion of North America, the "chippy" was widely regarded as the most domestic of all the sparrows. It remains one of the most common summer residents of suburban yards, always voicing its monotonic trill, which varies in tempo and pitch among individual males but remains consistent for each. Some males emit a relatively slow succession of "chips" or almost cricketlike trills; others sing faster and sound drier and more staccato. Though mainly ground foragers, chipping sparrows always sing from elevated perches and occasionally at night.

Chipping sparrows breed across the continent from the tree line in Canada south to Nicaragua. Northern populations migrate.

Spring. A molt of head and throat feathers in early spring gives chipping sparrows their breeding plumage of reddish crown and white brow line. Males arrive on their breeding range in April a week or so before females; in my yard, their arrival coincides with daffodil flowering). Singing establishes the territory, ranging from half an acre to more than an acre in size. Few courtship displays greet the arrival of females, but copulation on the ground or a perch is frequent and conspicuous, often in the morning. Females, often interrupted by these couplings, collect materials and build the nest, usually in early May.

EGGS AND YOUNG: usually four; eggs pale blue, brown spotted at the larger end. INCUBATION: by female, which is fed by male; about twelve days. FEEDING OF YOUNG: by both sexes; insects. FLEDGING: seven to ten days.

Summer. Chipping sparrows usually raise two broods, sometimes three, and nesting may extend into mid-August. Most pairs probably remain monogamous for the entire season, though polygyny, in which the male mates with an outside female, sometimes occurs as incubation begins; usually few extra females are available, however. Renewed singing by males and nest building by females herald the beginning of each new breeding cycle. Older nestlings may fledge a few days early if the nest is disturbed. Last year, as I observed an early-August nest, one of four nestlings fledged directly into my face,

scrambling all over me before dropping to the ground—a case of instinctual offense as best defense or of utter confusion? Well pummeled in any case, I retreated.

One researcher estimated that about 60 percent of chipping sparrow nests prove successful—that is, fledge birds—a relatively high proportion among passerines. Parents continue to feed the fledglings for several weeks even as renesting commences. Family flocks desert their territories in August and wander widely, often combining with other family groups, as well as with song and field sparrows. In late summer, the birds molt, acquiring a duller plumage of brown-streaked crowns and tan eye stripes. They rarely sing after August.

Fall. Chipping sparrows travel southward through September and October, usually in nighttime flocks of about thirty, resting and feeding during the day.

Winter. A few chipping sparrows may remain on the northern breeding range through winter, and some travel as far south as Central America, but most settle inland in the Gulf states. Typically the birds forage in flocks of twenty-five to fifty, sometimes mixing with field sparrows and dark-eyed juncos.

Ecology. Optimal habitat for this upland edge resident is a mixture of shrubs, small conifers, and open ground—exactly the landscape of many suburban lawns. Chipping sparrows also favor pine groves and plantations, orchards, and shrubby, overgrown fields. Before humans provided these kinds of habitat, the birds, much less abundant then, probably inhabited dry pine and oak savannas (often the result of fires), plus a variety of mixed open-edge sites.

Chipping sparrows usually nest three to ten feet high, often on an outer horizontal branch of a pine, red cedar, spruce, or hawthorn. The small, compact cup formed of dead grasses, weed stalks, and rootlets is lined with fine grasses and hairs. "In our rural past," wrote ecologist Richard Brewer, "[this bird] was known for lining the nest with horsehair and, even today, the birds usually find some type of hair for the lining." This led to the birds' former name of hair-birds. Often they remove and reuse the hair lining from the previous nest when rebuilding.

Chipping sparrows forage on or near the ground, as well as in low shrubs and trees. Like most seed-eating birds, they feed mainly on insects during the breeding season, when nestlings require a high-protein diet. The June diet may consist of some 90 percent insects, with large proportions of grasshoppers, caterpillars (including destructive gypsy moth larvae), and beetles. After the nestlings fledge, the seeds of many grasses and weeds become the staples, including those of oats, chickweeds, pigweed, ragweeds, and crab, foxtail, timothy, and panic grasses. Chipping sparrows apparently obtain most of their water from their diet and may survive without drinking for up to three weeks, a useful adaptation for their dry-habitat preference.

Competition appears negligible. In earlier decades, chipping sparrows may have declined in some areas because of seed competition with house sparrows; the decline of house sparrows plus the widespread growth of suburban habitats since World War II have apparently offset this effect, however. Blue jays, snakes, and domestic cats are probably the foremost chipping sparrow predators. Brown-headed cowbirds often parasitize their nests, especially those containing first broods; since subsequent sparrow nestings extend beyond the period of cowbird breeding, however, long-term negative effects on chipping sparrows appear minimal.

Focus. Chipping sparrow song bears close similarity to that of several other passerine birds, notably the pine warbler, worm-eating warbler, dark-eyed junco, and swamp sparrow, each of which has deceived me at times. The differences are subtle and, because of the chippy's individual variations in speed and pitch, not invariably distinctive. Differences in typical breeding habitats help narrow voice identification where summer ranges of two or more of these species coincide. Together with American robins and house finches, chipping sparrows have probably become our most common native birds in suburbia.

Common Grackle
(*Quiscalus quiscula*)

Our largest northeastern blackbird, at a foot long, is marked by a "striking yellow eye amidst a sea of iridescence," as one observer described. Its long, broad-tipped tail and stout, sharp-pointed bill are also distinctive. Males have shiny iridescent purple, blue, or green heads and deep bronze or iridescent coloration on the back; females, smaller than males, show less iridescence and browner plumage. The song is a discordant creak—"like a great rusty spring," wrote Thoreau—accomplished with effortful fluffing and hunching; loud, croaking "cack" notes are also common.

Close relatives. The seven *Quiscalus* species all reside in the Western Hemisphere. Only the common grackle, one of three North American grackles, breeds in the Northeast. The boat-tailed grackle (*Q. major*) mainly inhabits southeastern coastal marshes, the lower Mississippi valley, and the arid Southwest; great-tailed grackles (*Q. mexicanus*) also reside in the Southwest.

Behaviors. The grackle seldom hops, but walks. A long-tailed bird strutting in stately gait across your lawn, or uttering harsh, unmusical squeaks that sound as if its syrinx, or "song box," needs oiling, is this familiar blackbird. Unlike their red-winged blackbird relatives, which undulate in flight, grackles fly evenly with steady wingbeats. Males often crease their tails lengthwise, forming a keel, when in flight or on the ground.

Grackles are frequent predators on nests of smaller birds, consuming eggs and nestlings, often decapitating their victims. They habitually dump the white fecal sacs of their own nestlings in water, often birdbaths. Some grackles also dunk food items in water before swallowing them. Another common grackle habit is anting—picking up ants, which release formic acid, and rubbing them into their plumage. Grackles anoint themselves with other aromatic items as well, presumably as antiparasitic insecticides; mothballs, marigold flowers, and walnut hulls are favorites. Gregarious at all seasons, grackles frequently mix and roost in large flocks with other blackbirds and European starlings after the breeding season.

Common grackles breed throughout most of eastern North America east of the Rockies and south of the arctic tundra. Northern and central continental populations migrate.

Spring. Grackles usually occupy their breeding range by early to mid-March. Adult birds likely return to previous nesting sites or areas, though pairings with prior mates are probably infrequent. Song is hardly territorial in this species; flocks of up to twenty birds may chorus in a tree, creating a cacophony of rasping "scoo-de-leek" notes. Grackle song is a strenuous, full-body exertion that finally produces an anticlimactic noise. Both sexes sing, often alternatively when paired. Small groups of interchangeable males often follow single females about, gradually decreasing in number as pairing occurs.

Both sexes carry long grasses to the chosen nest site, an activity that may continue for several weeks before the female begins building in earnest by late April or early May. Even then she may abandon one site and rebuild in another. Nesting is often loosely colonial, with a few or many pairs residing within a tree grove; a pair's defended territory usually consists of only a few yards' distance surrounding the nest site. Grackle night roosts become smallest in size at this season, when only unmated birds and paired males—leaving their incubating partners on the nest—inhabit them. During incubation, many male grackles opportunistically mate with females other than their original mates.

EGGS AND YOUNG: typically five; eggs greenish white with brown spots and blotches. INCUBATION: by female; about twelve days. FEEDING OF YOUNG: by both sexes if male remains after incubation, by female if not; insects, other invertebrates, eggs and nestlings of other birds. FLEDGING: about twelve days.

Summer. Most females raise only one brood. Parent grackles—or just the female in some cases—feed their young for only a few days after they leave the nest. You can often see one or more large fledglings begging, following, and being fed by adult foragers on the ground at this time. Soon the fledglings achieve independence and form large flocks that feed and roost together. Adult grackles also consolidate into flocks that roost communally at night in shade trees, usually in habitual sites throughout the year. Flocks wander and feed at widely separate locations during daytime, then fly to the roost before dusk. A seemingly endless line of grackles passing overhead in the evening is always roost-bound. As summer advances, roosts grow in size. Grackles gradually molt into new plumage in August and September; juveniles lose their dark brown color and acquire full adult plumage. A fork-tailed grackle flying overhead indicates a beginning tail molt, when the long central rectrices drop first.

Fall. Roosts become largest in late summer and fall, with thousands (sometimes millions) of grackles plus red-winged blackbirds, brown-headed cowbirds, European starlings, and American robins. Most grackle migration occurs by day; northern populations have largely vacated their breeding range by early November.

Winter. Grackles winter on this continent, most in the southern United States from Texas eastward. Year-round resident populations may remain as far north as the lower Great Lakes and southern New England; single birds or small flocks sometimes winter even farther north. The amount of snow cover may be a crucial factor governing their northern distribution in winter. Grackle existence remains entirely flock oriented through this season. Huge roosts of up to ten million birds may assemble, mainly south of latitude 38 degrees and east of longitude 100 degrees. Individual grackles shift among roost sites, displaying no constant fidelity to a given site. Migrants begin moving northward in late winter; in southern Michigan, vanguard grackle arrivals often coincide with those of red-winged blackbirds in late February.

Ecology. Common grackles fare well in a variety of open-woods and edge habitats. Originally they probably inhabited wetland areas almost exclusively, and many still nest and feed in marsh, swamp, and shoreline areas, sometimes wading into shallow water.

Today they also frequent residential areas, parks, orchards, plantations, and hedgerows. Flocks often feed in fields and along roadsides. Roosting habitats are generally the same as for European starlings.

Grackles frequently nest in colonies of twenty to thirty pairs, often in dense groves of conifers. Blue and Norway spruces, white pine, and red cedars are common sites; marsh vegetation, low shrubs, orchard trees, climbing vines, and tree and building cavities are also used at times. The birds favor sites near water, but many nest far from water as well. Nests are often placed near the tops of trees, up to sixty feet high or more but usually much lower, two to twelve feet being typical. The bulky nest consists of coarse grasses and weed stalks, often reinforced with a middle layer of mud and lined with finer grasses and plant fibers. A pair of grackles—though not necessarily the same pair—has nested in a white cedar tree in my yard for many years, probably in the same annually repaired nest located three feet from the top.

Grackles forage in trees, on the ground, and at all points between. Local nuisance flocks of grackles have aroused the enmity of farmers for their food habits. Flocks especially relish corn in the preripened milk stage, sometimes stripping husks to devour just a few kernels. Sprouting wheat is another favorite. Almost half of the grackle's annual diet consists of grain, much of it gleaned from farmyards and fields. Ragweed and smartweed seeds also rank high, as do blackberries and mulberries. Favored fall items include corn and acorns. In contrast to most blackbirds, grackles' *abductor,* or jaw-closing, muscles are stronger than their *depressor,* or jaw-opening, muscles, and they are not strong gapers. A prominent lengthwise ridge in the upper mandible of the bill enables them to crack acorns with ease. During the breeding season, animal matter dominates the diet. Bees, beetles, grasshoppers, and crickets are favored items, as are cutworms, noctuid moth caterpillars that ravage grain sprouts, perhaps accounting for some grackle damage in pulling up shoots. Grackles also forage extensively on lawn grubs, especially those of the destructive Japanese beetle. In addition to a variety of insects, these omnivores consume many spiders, earthworms, snails, and crayfish. They are adept at catching emerald shiner minnows in shallow water. They are foremost predators on American robin eggs and nestlings and aggressively rob foraging robins of their earthworm prey. At other seasons, however, robins and grackles often roost together.

Often the more adaptable the species in terms of nest sites and food, the less competition it faces from other species; this generally holds true for grackles, as their abundance attests. Occasions may arise when a limited food resource, such as acorns or small fruits, which are consumed by many bird and mammal species, leads to brief episodic competition. A marsh-nesting grackle encounters competition from different sources—red-winged blackbirds, for example—than a yard grackle competing with robins for earthworms. Grackle size and aggressiveness make them winners in most conflict situations.

Grackle predators include owls, accipiter hawks, and falcons, which attack mainly at roosts. Nests are sometimes raided by bullsnakes, American crows, blue jays, and squirrels. Brown-headed cowbird parasitism is rare in this species, perhaps because of its semi-colonial nesting habits.

Focus. The name of this bird derives from the Latin *graculus,* which was used to refer to several blackbirds, including cormorants (*Phalacrocorax*) and the jackdaw (*Corvus monedula*), a Eurasian crow whose calls the word *grackle* supposedly echoes. Crow blackbird, as Thoreau called the common grackle, remains a frequent vernacular name. Until several decades ago, this bird was classified as two species: the bronzed grackle, inhabiting New England and westward, and the purple grackle, of Atlantic and Gulf coastal distribution. These are now classified as subspecies that show minor differences in plumage coloration. At least one leg-banded grackle survived to age twenty-two, but average longevity is certainly far less.

Iridescence, so plainly seen in grackles, some waterfowl and gamebirds, hummingbirds, starlings, and a few others, is a pattern of structural colors, as is blue.

Iridescent colors are as much the work of our own eyes as of feather structure and light, for these colors vary as our angle of vision to the feather changes. Twisted, highly modified feather *barbules*—tiny branches that normally interlock and hold the feather *vane,* or web, together—cast differential reflections of light, and our eyesight does the rest. Iridescent feather barbules, unlike most barbules, do not interlock; hence these feathers are relatively weak.

Immense communal roosts of grackles and other blackbirds sometimes annoy human residents, especially in urban areas. Aggressive efforts to wipe out the largest roosts have somewhat reduced grackle populations since the 1970s, but grackles remain abundant on their seasonal ranges.

Dark-eyed Junco
(Junco hyemalis)

This sparrow-size bird is dark hooded down to its breast, with a whitish belly, pinkish bill, and white outer tail feathers, its most conspicuous feature as it flushes from the ground. Males have blacker heads than the grayer females. The junco's trilling song resembles that of the chipping sparrow, and junco flocks often utter twittering notes as they fly up. They also voice musical, finchlike "tew tew tew" notes.

Close relatives. Not so long ago, ornithologists recognized ten separate *Junco* species. All were North and Central American residents, and each varied somewhat in plumage. In 1983, these were demoted to races or subspecies of just two species: the dark-eyed junco and yellow-eyed junco (*J. phaeonotus*). Five distinct races, often hybridizing where their ranges overlap, are now lumped as the dark-eyed junco. The most widely distributed race, formerly known as the slate-colored junco species, is the typical junco of eastern North America. The other races are the Oregon, white-winged, gray-headed, and Guadeloupe juncos.

Behaviors. Most of us see dark-eyed juncos only in winter, when their twittering flocks populate the hedgerows and the ground beneath yard feeders; they only occasionally venture as high as the feeder itself.

This ground-loving habit characterizes juncos throughout most of the year. A distinctive junco feeding characteristic is its double-scratching in leaf litter or snow; it jumps forward and back with both feet, a quick hop-step observable wherever the birds are foraging. Like most flocking birds, juncos show rigid dominance hierarchies, an evolutionary adaptation that apparently maintains social stability.

Junco breeding range spans the continent from Canada's tree line south to the upper Great Lakes, New England, and the Appalachians to Georgia. Juncos are migrants.

Spring. Males precede females on the breeding range by a week or more in April and early May. Adult males probably return to their previous territories; a junco territory may span two or three acres or, in prime nesting habitats, may be much smaller. Males often sing from the tallest trees in their territories; this is the only time of year when juncos spend much time high off the ground. As in many songbirds, male singing contrasts with initially hostile behavior when a female actually arrives; he chases, but she lingers. Male song decreases, and soon the birds are reciprocally displaying with drooping wings, fanned tails, and a nodding head dance. Females build the nests, mainly in June.

EGGS AND YOUNG: typically four; eggs bluish white, brown speckled, especially at the larger end. INCUBATION: by female; about twelve days. FEEDING OF YOUNG: by both sexes; regurgitated insects at first, then soft-bodied insects. FLEDGING: nine to thirteen days.

Summer. Many junco pairs raise two broods, nesting into early July. The female builds a new nest for the second brood soon after the first brood fledges, and the male feeds the first-brood fledglings. One or both parents feed the brown, streaked young for up to a month before the latter disperse. From mid-August into September, adult juncos undergo their complete annual molt.

Fall. Juncos move southward in flocks through September into early November, with the largest numbers traveling in October. This species demonstrates a movement pattern called differential migration, also seen in several other passerine species. Adult females migrate farther south than young females. Young males remain farthest north, and adult males may winter with, or slightly south of, young males. Thus most juncos in a flock often consist of same-sex, same-age birds (though mixed flocks do occur). Such sex and age segregation probably relates to the birds' rigid dominance hierarchies.

Winter. Dark-eyed juncos winter from southern Canada to the Gulf states and northern Mexico. They narrowly overlap their breeding range in the upper Great Lakes, New England, and Appalachia. Adult juncos usually return to their previous wintering areas. At night the flock, generally fifteen to thirty birds, roosts in a habitual place, usually a densely foliaged conifer. Winter flocks are fixed but flexible units, each with a foraging range of ten to twelve acres that seldom overlaps into another flock's range. A junco flock may subdivide and reform at irregular times through the day, but all birds of a flock remain in the flock range, associating with American tree sparrows, black-capped chickadees, white-throated sparrows, and other weed- and ground-feeding species. Each junco in the flock knows its place in the pecking order; in mixed flocks, males tend to dominate females, and adults dominate juveniles. By March, males are beginning to sing, and some flocks are moving northward.

Ecology. Dark-eyed juncos breed in the drier coniferous and mixed forest regions of North America. They seldom inhabit dense forests, however, favoring brushy edges and natural openings. During migrations and winter, they frequent hedgerows, brush piles, thickets, and weedy fields.

Juncos typically nest at the edge of forest clearings, along woodland roads or power lines, rarely in deeply shaded sites. Nests are built on the ground, occasionally in low vegetation, often in slight depressions against a vertical bank or in upturned tree roots overhung by sod or plants. I have also found them sheltered amid grass clumps or small shrubs on hillside slopes. Occasionally juncos build in such untypical sites as trellises, open cans on the ground, and semiopen cavities in stumps or walls. The nest of dried grasses lined with pine needles, bark strips, rootlets, and sometimes hair much resembles the nests of its ground sparrow relatives.

Juncos are mainly ground-feeding seed eaters, but they consume about 50 percent animal matter—mainly caterpillars, beetles, ants, and spiders—during the breeding season. Even in winter, they feed avidly on winter gnats and springtails ("snow fleas"). Most of their diet, however, consists of weed and grass seeds. Ragweeds plus foxtail, crab, panic, timothy, and drop-seed grasses rank high, as do smartweeds and pigweed.

Competition with other species is probably negligible. Potential users of similar bank or tree-root nesting sites might include yellow-bellied flycatchers, winter wrens, and waterthrushes. Competition between sexes for food may provide impetus to differential migration.

Accipiter hawks and northern shrikes occasionally capture juncos. In some areas, garter snakes are the foremost nest predators. Others include red squirrels, chipmunks, weasels, skunks, and raccoons. Brown-headed cowbird parasitism appears infrequent.

Focus. Flocking in birds has been described as a mixture of "gregariousness and intolerance, a compromise of costs and benefits"—as is evolution itself. So it is with juncos. Many people know juncos as snowbirds, since in most areas of the United States their arrival forecasts winter. Wrote Thoreau, "You see them come drifting over a rising ground just like the snowflakes before the northeast wind." Another writer described junco coloration as "a sort of meteorological microcosm of a snowy winter day (leaden sky above, snow below)."

The name junco, from the Latin *juncus*, meaning "rush," resulted from the bird's supposed marshland habitat, a misnomer sanctified by time and conservatism. Audubon, who often recycled his artistic models by eating them, reported junco flesh as "extremely delicate and juicy." The junco's maximum recorded life span is ten years, a longevity that most never approach.

Downy and Hairy Woodpeckers
(Picoides pubescens and P. villosus)

These two common black-and-white woodpeckers are similar in plumage but differ in size; downies, our smallest woodpeckers, are about six inches long, hairies about nine inches. Both display small regional variations in plumage pattern. The only North American woodpeckers with white backs, they have white-spotted black wings, black tails edged with white, and black-and-white heads. Males have a small red patch on the back of the head. Bill size is the best field mark: Hairies have disproportionately longer, stouter bills. Both species utter a sharp, emphatic "peek!" note. Downies also utter a descending "whinny" of notes; the hairy's loud rattle resembles that of a belted kingfisher.

Close relatives. Three-toed woodpeckers (*P. tridactylus*) and black-backed woodpeckers (*P. arcticus*) are boreal forest species. Southwestern species include the ladder-backed woodpecker (*P. scalaris*), Nuttall's woodpecker (*P. nuttallii*), and Strickland's woodpecker (*P. stricklandi*). White-headed woodpeckers (*P. albolarvatus*) occupy western montane forests. The red-cockaded woodpecker (*P. borealis*), an endangered species, inhabits southeastern pinelands.

Behaviors. Like most woodpeckers, downies and hairies are most typically seen on tree trunks as they forage or drum. A downy climbs a tree in jerky, fidgety movements; hairies hitch their way up in short leaps. Downies rarely excavate far into wood for food; hairies pound deeply. Watch for sexual differences in feeding behaviors. Downies *partition* the feeding site, with males foraging in the upper parts of a tree, females in the middle canopy. With hairies, the difference lies in feeding method: Males tend to excavate deep into the wood for insects; the more opportunistic females glean the trunk surface. These behavioral differences, suggests one researcher, enable the woodpeckers "to exploit the resources of a particular piece of woodland more effectively." Some seasonal variation in feeding sites also occurs. When foraging for nestlings, downies often start at the base of a tree, work rapidly upward, then drop to another tree base; hairies often forage on the ground. Downies are present year-round, though summer birds are not necessarily the same ones present in winter. Some seasonal shifts and southward movements occur, probably depending on local food supply, but neither bird is a true migrant. Both species range across North America.

Spring. Territories and pair bonds of these monogamous species are usually already formed by early spring. Signs of breeding activity include courtship rituals: drumming by both sexes on separate drumming posts and bill waving. Frequent triangle encounters occur when a third bird of either sex intrudes on a pair, resulting in much chasing and aggressive displaying. In April, nest cavity excavation averages sixteen days for downies, twenty for hairies. Female downies and male hairies select the sites. As with all woodpeckers, nestlings are loud, incessant beepers

until about two weeks old, so nest holes are fairly easy to locate.

EGGS AND YOUNG: four or five; eggs white. INCUBATION: by both sexes; twelve to fifteen days. FEEDING OF YOUNG: by both sexes; insects. FLEDGING: about three weeks for downies, four for hairies.

Summer. After fledging, the young are fed outside the nest, remaining in the vicinity for several weeks before dispersing. Parent birds usually raise only one brood. The adult birds undergo their annual molt from midsummer to early fall, hairies earlier than downies. The downies' new white plumage shows a yellowish tint that soon wears off. Some juveniles of both sexes display red crown patches, lost when they acquire their first adult plumage in late summer. "Juvenile woodpeckers usually have a geeky air," noted one observer, "a slight clumsiness that sets them apart."

Fall. Food supply probably determines the extent of seasonal movements in these birds. In downies, females tend to travel more often than males; in hairies, the first-year birds seem to move more frequently. Hairies seem generally more sedentary than downies, but except for northernmost populations, the majority of both species remains on the breeding ranges through winter. Pairs are now split, each bird excavating one or more roosting cavities for itself. Though instances of food caching occur, downies and hairies store far fewer items than red-headed and red-bellied woodpeckers.

Winter. One or two downies often mingle with mixed feeding flocks of black-capped chickadees, tufted titmice, white-breasted nuthatches, brown creepers, and kinglets. Such interspecies mingling, suggests one researcher, enables downies to rely on the flock for vigilance, thus increasing their foraging efficiency.

Hairy woodpeckers commence territorial activities—mainly drumming—in December and January; downies begin a bit later. Over a period of weeks, previously mated pairs resume courtship displays and reestablish the home range—anywhere from five to thirty-five acres—and later, within this area, the territory in a radius of forty to one hundred feet from the selected nest site. As in most woodpecker pairs, home ranges and territories tend to remain the same year after year. The birds actively defend their territories from other woodpeckers, but home ranges, which contain favorite drumming posts, often overlap with those of other pairs.

Ecology. Although the woodland habitats of these species often overlap, each has its preferences. Hairies favor mature woodlands and extensive forest areas, but downies more often frequent woodland edges, openings, and residential areas.

Mature aspen trees infected with *Phellinus* heartrot fungus are the choice nest cavity sites for both species; hairies favor live aspens, and downies prefer dead stubs or branches, often excavating near their tops or beneath an exposed limb. Typically the cavity entrance of the hairy is larger in diameter, by about an inch, than that of the downy and is somewhat elongated, whereas that of the downy is perfectly circular. Both species excavate new cavities each year; downies often return to the same tree, but hairies usually select a different one. Dutch elm disease, which has ravaged American elm trees throughout their range, has benefited both woodpeckers by providing dead standing trees and ample insect food within them.

Primarily insect eaters, downies and hairies often feed in upper dead branches, but downies focus on gleaning spiders, aphids, scale insects, ants, and caterpillars from bark crevices. Hairies seek wood-boring grubs and other larvae; tapping on the wood apparently tells them where to excavate. Downy tongues are relatively short, but the hairy's tongue is long and barb tipped. As the season advances, both birds also consume wild fruits; they relish poison-ivy berries, sometimes caching them in bark crevices. Both also feed at sapsucker drill holes; sometimes they drill for sap and cambium themselves, creating wider, larger holes than sapsuckers. Downies are foremost fall and winter predators of the fruit fly larvae (*Eurosta soladiginis,* called goldenrod gall flies) that create the familiar ball-shaped galls on goldenrod stems. Groves of white birch trees are also favored feeding sites of downies in winter. They often seek defective trees infested with a dormant scale insect (*Xylocculus betulae*) that, in summer, feeds on sap just beneath the outer bark. Downies peck around the bark containing the insect, then open the hinged fragment to expose the insect. Inspect birch trunks for these tiny trapdoors, sure signs of downy feeding.

Tree cavities are always at a premium for hole-nesting birds and denning mammals, many of which cannot excavate cavities themselves. The size of the entrance hole often determines which competitors may occupy it. Downy competitors include nuthatches, house sparrows, flying squirrels, and deer mice. Hairies contend mainly with European starlings, especially if the nest tree borders an open area; the starlings almost always win such contests. Flying and red squirrels also vie for new cavities but are usually driven off. Yellow-bellied sapsuckers sometimes compete with hairies for a nest tree, as do red-headed woodpeckers. The somewhat differing habitat preferences of downies and hairies tend to reduce nest site competition between them.

Food competition among woodpecker species appears minimal. The species focus their foraging activities in separate *niches,* using different parts of the habitat, or they use different feeding techniques.

Some of the competitors for tree cavities may, at times, become woodpecker predators. Probably the foremost predator is the European starling, which may destroy woodpecker eggs or young by poking its head into a cavity, even if the entrance hole is too small to admit its body. Raccoons can chew and claw into cavities excavated in dead, weak wood, and gray squirrels sometimes enlarge entrance holes by gnawing to gain entrance. The worst habitat enemies of all woodpecker species are salvage-harvesting foresters and landowners who like to clean out the dead standing trees from their woodlots, thus depriving the birds of nest sites and food.

Focus. Note the back-of-the head patterns of black, white, and—in males—red. "I have never found two with the same pattern," re-

ports one eminent woodpecker researcher. These head variations, almost as individual as fingerprints, enable an observer to identify one bird from another, an invaluable aid to research.

Hairy woodpeckers, usually younger ones, often peck habitually on human-made structures—house walls, roofs, eaves, window frames, utility poles, even trash cans and boats. The louder the resonance, the better the object or material serves as a territorial drumming post. Such drumming can be highly destructive, and once the birds become habituated to such a site, they are not easily driven away. One researcher believes that this behavior begins as a displacement activity, an outlet for energy aroused by crowding or other stress situations. As the habit continues, the pecking may turn to serious food searching and excavation, and the damage multiplies.

Downy and hairy woodpeckers were stupidly misnamed, and the errors remain condoned by a wink of science. Downies have no more underlying down feathers than many other birds, and hairies have no hair. Both birds were saddled with these inappropriate names by a few early observers of questionable visual acuity who stated that both species looked somewhat hairy. Ornithologists, for some reason, often prefer to maintain long-accepted misnomers than to correct them.

Eastern Bluebird
(Sialia sialis)

Thrush family (Muscicapidae), order Passeriformes. Recognize the eastern bluebird by its sky blue upper parts and robin red breast and belly. Females are somewhat duller in color than males. When perched, bluebirds appear somewhat hunched, about seven inches long. The musical "chur-a-lee" song, sometimes described as a pure contralto and voiced by both sexes, carries far; other sounds include a "chir-wi" flight call, soft gurgling notes, and an alarm chatter.

Close relatives. The only other *Sialia* species are the western and mountain bluebirds *(S. mexicana, S. currucoides),* which inhabit western North America. Some 450 thrush species exist worldwide. North American family members include the *Catharus* thrushes (the veery and gray-cheeked, Swainson's, hermit, and wood thrushes) and the American robin (*Turdus migratorius*). (See page 14.)

Behaviors. Bluebirds often perch on wires, fences, or low branches, periodically sailing to the ground and capturing an insect. More infrequently they catch insects on the wing or glean them in the treetops. Casual bird observers cherish the bluebird not only for its colorful plumage, gentle mien, and chortling song but also for a domestic lifestyle that seems to coincide neatly with human family values. Actually, bluebirds exhibit an often confusing array of domestic arrangements, the more startling as research brings them to light. Little evidence exists, for example, that bluebird monogamy lasts beyond a single season, and findings now indicate that in many cases, it endures hardly that long. Matings fairly commonly occur outside the primary pair bond. From 9 to 25 percent of bluebird nestlings, blood type studies reveal, show biological parentage from an adult other than the incubating female or her mate. Such cases of multiple parentage in a brood can only result from less than total mate fidelity by either parent or from egg dumping in the nest by another female. Both of these reproductive strategies are known to occur in bluebirds. "Divorce" among bluebirds can occur after an unsuccessful first nesting, usually a result of harsh weather or nest predation. The birds rapidly abandon sites of nest failure, even though such sites may be otherwise optimal. In such cases, the pair sometimes stays together and renests elsewhere; often, however, the pair may split and travel some miles away, the male to establish a new territory, the female to find another mate. Thus nest-site fidelity (*philopatry*), so common in most species, seems to depend in bluebirds mainly on the degree of nesting success at that site.

The eastern bluebird, wearing "the sky on his back," in Thoreau's phrase, exhibits a characteristic hunched, neckless posture that can be observed even when the bird is too distant for its colors to be visible.

Bluebirds are also among those species that use nest "helpers"—usually one or more juveniles from the previous seasonal brood or an unmated adult bluebird that lingers at the nest and helps feed the current nestlings.

Such systems of *cooperative breeding,* seen to a much greater degree in such species as common ravens, American crows, and scrub jays, may develop when certain environmental pressures (in this case, the number of available cavities for nesting) limit opportunities for younger birds to breed and tend to force birds into group parentage systems. Nest helpers also gain experience for their own future parental roles.

Eastern bluebird breeding range extends eastward from the Great Plains to the Atlantic and from southern Canada to the Caribbean and parts of Mexico and Central America. The birds migrate to and from about the northern half of this range (above latitude 40 degrees N).

Spring. Eastern bluebirds reside year-round in their southern range, and nesting commences there in February and March. Each 10 degrees of latitude farther north translates to about 3 weeks later in time for the onset of breeding activity. In the northern range, eastern bluebirds begin arriving in March, with migration peaking in early to middle April. Sometimes the male moves several days ahead of the female; other times the pair arrives together. Spring snowstorms may descend upon migrating bluebirds with devastating results.

Some studies indicate that a relatively small percentage of first-year bluebirds return to their natal sites to breed. Males establish territories of two to twenty-five acres, depending on habitat resources and bluebird population density. Territory centers on a nest cavity in a tree or nest box, and territory size usually shrinks as the season advances. Episodic chasing and grappling with other bluebirds occur as the birds defend their sites. The fullest intensity of male song, sometimes voiced up to twenty times per minute, occurs before a female arrives on the territory. When she appears, his song rate slows to five to ten times per minute. He moves from perch to perch, often flying in lopsided or fluttery fashion, and lifts and quivers one or both wings while perched. Another stylized courtship maneuver is landing at the cavity entrance, perching there, and rocking head and shoulders in and out of the hole. When a female joins him and enters the hole, the birds may be said to be paired. Courtship feeding, in which the male brings food to the female, is another common behavior. Aggressive encounters reach a peak during nest building and egg laying, the period when nest cavities are most vulnerable to takeover by other bluebirds or house sparrows. Female bluebirds fight fiercely against female interlopers.

Yet bluebirds rarely battle intruders of the opposite sex, and this—together with a population of unmated adults termed *floaters*—sets the stage for extrapair matings while the nominal mate is absent. Apparently, to judge from DNA analyses, a paired male frequently mates with a single floater, which then invades the nest of the paired female and lays an egg. "Because bluebird nest sites are in short supply," suggested researcher Patricia A. Gowaty, "perhaps the only way some females can successfully reproduce is to be opportunistic—to lay their fertile eggs in nests holding some other bluebird mother's eggs." Another theory suggests that male nonaggression toward a female territorial intruder may pay off with survival benefits in the long run: If he opportunistically mates with her, he increases the evolutionary advantages of producing extra offspring.

First-brood nestlings in the North usually fledge in May. The pair typically remains to-gether for a second nesting, beginning in late May, if the first nesting was successful. A pair may begin renesting in the same or another nest site as soon as three or four days after the first brood fledges.

EGGS AND YOUNG: typically four or five; eggs glossy, pale blue or white. INCUBATION: by female, which is occasionally fed at the nest by male; about two weeks; hatching synchronous; altricial young. FEEDING OF YOUNG: by both sexes and (especially in second broods) by occasional nest helpers; caterpillars, beetles, grasshoppers, sometimes berries. FLEDGING: sixteen to twenty days; most fledge within a period of two hours.

Summer. Many eastern bluebirds raise 2 broods throughout most of their northern range (often three in the South), but many also raise only a single brood. Second-brood nestlings usually fledge in late June. First nestings, in which 75 to 95 percent of the nestlings typically survive to fledge, usually prove more successful than later ones, which may fledge only 55 percent or so of nestlings. The male continues to feed first-brood fledglings for three or four weeks, sometimes more, while the female incubates the second brood. Territorial defensive-ness rapidly declines after hatching, becoming almost nonexistent as nestlings and fledglings are fed. Birds still raising young in July and August are probably renesting after a previous nesting failure.

Juvenile plumage resembles the female bluebird's except that the breast is brown spotted until the molt of body plumage in late summer, when juveniles acquire adult coloration. The annual molt of adult birds also occurs in late summer. The final family

group of the season often remains together, feeding and wandering until migration. During this period, they often return to the nest site. "Parents and offspring from one or several broods gather," wrote naturalist Connie Toops, "investigating the cavity inside and out. Sometimes one or more of the birds will carry a few pieces of grass or pine needles into the box, as though reinforcing the idea that this is a place to nest."

Fall, Winter. Many, if not all, eastern bluebirds that reside north of latitude 40 degrees N migrate south, traveling from late September through early November in small or medium-size flocks in daytime. Those few that occasionally remain in the northern range over winter tend to be experienced adult birds. Eastern bluebirds on the winter range usually remain in loose flocks of five to ten or more birds, sometimes associating with other fruit eaters, including American robins, cedar waxwings, and purple finches. During cold nights, several may roost together in nest boxes or other shelters, sometimes huddling in warmth-sharing clusters. By March, many northern-range bluebirds are moving northward, while overwintering and southern-range bluebirds are establishing territories.

Eastern bluebird winter range spans the southeastern and south-central United States, with individual birds moving into Mexico, Central America, and the West Indies.

Ecology. Eastern bluebirds favor neither forest nor completely open field habitats but something in between—a semiopen or savanna mixture of small trees or shrubs, such as open oak or pine woodlands, old fields, pastures, orchards, even golf courses and suburban lawns. "Relatively poor, sandy soils apparently contribute to favorable habitat conditions," wrote one researcher. Vital to bluebird habitat are elevated perches for visual food finding—fence posts, wires, low or sparse ground vegetation, scattered trees or shrubs—and, for nesting, cavities in trees, fence posts, or nest boxes. In fall and winter, because of the birds' diet change from insects to tree and shrub fruits, they often occupy somewhat more wooded or marshy habitats. Before European settlement in North America, eastern bluebirds probably frequented forest edges and openings created by fire, storms, and beaver floodings.

What would cavity-nesting wildlife do without woodpeckers? As cavity nesters, eastern bluebirds do not excavate holes themselves but adopt cavities created mainly by woodpeckers. Often these holes have been long vacated by woodpeckers, some species of which excavate new holes every year (see page 63), but since many birds and some mammals vie for nest cavities, the work of woodpeckers is always prime real estate for wildlife. Today, however, after precipitous decline and partial restoration of bluebird abundance, most eastern bluebirds probably nest in human-built nest boxes, the placement and maintenance of which have become a major environmental activity for naturalists. The nest within the cavity, built solely by the female, consists mainly of dried grasses and weed stalks, lined with finer grasses or unlined. Building may not begin for a week or more after the cavity is claimed; actual construction usually takes four or five days. Throughout incubation and brooding, the female engages in a behavior called the *tremble-thrust,* in which she pokes her bill into the nesting material and shakes it, perhaps

dislodging parasites and organic debris toward the base of the nest. Nests average about $2^{1}/_{2}$ inches inside diameter and about 2 inches deep. When bluebirds take over a vacated nest box or one currently used by another bird, such as a tree swallow, they do not clean out the contents but bury the previous nest along with any eggs or nestlings it may contain with fresh materials.

Choice foods include ground beetles, grasshoppers, crickets, caterpillars, spiders, and snails. In summer and fall, eastern bluebirds add many fruits to their diet, mainly berries. The winter diet is almost exclusively frugivorous—fruits of dogwoods, eastern red cedar, bayberry, Virginia-creeper, and sumac, plus wild grapes and multiflora rose hips are widely consumed. Ecologist Richard Brewer reports observing bluebirds capturing insect naiads from shallow streams in winter.

Competition, as in most cavity nesters, largely consists of contention for suitable nest sites. Probably the most frequent contest for bluebirds occurs with tree swallows; each species is known to invade nest sites of the other on occasion. The swallows are most aggressive in late April and early May when searching for nest sites and when many bluebirds are already incubating. Bluebirds, on the other hand, tend to and early June before beginning their second broods. When such invasions successfully occur, each species simply builds a nest atop that of the other. Yet each seems widely tolerant of the other when both are nesting. In recent years, a popular—though still controversial—method of providing housing for both species while discouraging invasive takeovers is the pairing of nest boxes; each box is placed 15 to 25 feet from the other, with 250 to 300 feet separating each pair of boxes. Such pairing has several advantages: With increased tree swallow populations, pairing allows some boxes to remain available for bluebirds, since tree swallow territorialism prevents other tree swallow pairs from nesting nearby; bluebird pairs likewise will not nest in both of the closely adjacent boxes but can easily defend their single nest box from a tree swallow pair; and tree swallow neighbors closely adjacent to a bluebird pair help defend both boxes from other competitive invaders such as house wrens and house sparrows. Most bluebird nest boxes cannot be sparrow proofed. Placement of the boxes at least 200 yards from buildings, however, reduces house sparrow competition. European starlings also compete for nest cavities; bluebird nest boxes with 1½-inch entrance holes successfully prevent their invasion. White-footed and deer mouse and squirrel usage of nest boxes generally occurs in winter and thus rarely competes with bluebird nesting. Bluebirds and tree swallows do not compete for food to any large extent, since tree swallows feed aerially and bluebirds feed mainly from the ground. Eastern and mountain bluebirds, where they overlap ranges in the Great Plains, rarely hybridize. The rapid transition from eastern to western and mountain bluebird range occurs within only 2 degrees of longitude (100th to 102nd meridian).

Sumac fruits remain on this shrub or small tree over winter, providing a reliable, if not preferred, food for bluebirds and other frugivores.

Bluebird predators include all the aforementioned competitors at times, especially house wrens and house sparrows. Other occasional bird predators include American kestrels; Cooper's, sharp-shinned, and red-tailed hawks; and shrikes. Bull and rat snakes,

raccoons, opossums, and domestic cats raid unprotected nest boxes at times. Brown-headed cowbird parasitism is rarely a problem in bluebird nest boxes since the entrance holes are too small to admit them. Blowfly larvae infest many, if not most, bluebird nests, especially during second nestings; the larvae parasitize nestlings at night but seldom weaken them so much as to cause death unless the infestation is very severe. In Ontario, a 1994 study indicated that blowfly infestation followed by house wren and house sparrow predation were the main causes of bluebird nesting failure there, but other studies seem to show that blowfly parasitism does not affect fledging success. Paper wasps and ants occasionally invade nest boxes, the latter when a broken egg or dead nestling attracts them.

Focus. Ever since English naturalist Mark Catesby first identified "the blew bird" in America in 1731, this species has been a popular "birder's bird." The bluebird, waxed researcher Lawrence Zeleny, "is American idealism personified—a flying piece of sky, a living poem, a crystal note, an emblem of nature's moral conscience." Early colonists called it "blue robin" for its resemblance to the European robin. Naturalist John Burroughs claimed that bluebird arrival in New York and New England signaled the rise of sap in sugar maple; and bluebird song, according to one folktale, inspires the full bloom of apple trees. The "bluebird of happiness" and bluebirds flying "somewhere over the rainbow" suggest the symbolic load this bird carries in addition to "the sky on its back," as Thoreau wrote. Missouri and New York have named it their state bird, as Idaho and Nevada have claimed the mountain bluebird. Hardly another bird is so uncritically adored by casual observers, yet it is astonishing how many people have never seen one. Indeed, most of an entire generation of Americans missed out on bluebirds, for during the decades of their precipitous decline (1950s–70s), the birds became rare throughout much of their range. Today, thanks to hard work by people unwilling to let the species perish, it seems well advanced on the comeback trail.

Bluebird nest boxes, often established along "bluebird trails," have probably helped restore populations of this charismatic bird in many areas.

The number of bluebird societies that exist throughout the United States also attests to the popularity of this bird. During the nineteenth century, bluebirds were probably about as numerous as robins today. A combination of starling competition, scarcity of cavity nesting habitats, blanket pesticide applications, and several harsh winters were primarily blamed for the decline. Publicity campaigns led by the North American Bluebird Society brought awareness of the bluebird's plight and inspired direct action to help recover bluebird populations. To that end, bluebird nesting programs, which employed a variety of nest box designs, and bluebird trails, with several to many nest boxes placed and spaced in good bluebird habitats and regularly monitored by volunteers, headed the recovery efforts. A Transcontinental Bluebird Trail project, launched by the North American Bluebird Society in 1999, aims to place nest box networks across the continent. "Strategic placement of nest boxes," wrote researcher Ben Pinkowski, "remains the principal conservation measure for bluebirds." These projects plus fortuitously kinder weather and reductions in pesticide use have paid off, restoring bluebird populations in many areas to levels of stable abundance. From 1966, when breeding bird surveys began, to 1996, the latest figures, eastern bluebird populations increased 103 percent. Northern bluebird populations always will, however, be subject to periodic crashes—probably about once every 10 to 15 years—because of harsh weather, which results in widespread insect decreases and consequent bluebird starvation.

As in all blue-plumaged birds, the bluebird's blue—unlike the colors produced by pigments in most bird plumages—is an optical illusion governed by the physics of scattered light waves from reflective cells in the feathers. Thus the intensity of light shining on a bluebird (or blue jay or indigo bunting, among others) largely determines how blue it looks. Worn or molting plumage can also affect the blue appearance.

Eastern bluebirds sometimes survive for six or seven years, but the typical adult bluebird averages about two years old. After the bird's first year, during which mortality is highest, its chances for survival increase.

The North American Bluebird Society continues to provide information and aid to persons who want to establish and maintain bluebird trails and nest boxes.

Eastern Screech-Owl
(Otus asio)

This small (seven- to ten-inch-long) woodland owl shows conspicuous ear tufts resembling erect horns over its yellow eyes. Sexes look alike except that females are somewhat larger. Plumage coloration occurs in one of two phases, or *morphs*: reddish brown or gray, permanent for each bird. Gray morphs are most numerous in this owl's northern range, red morphs more common in its southern range, but both morphs readily interbreed. Two commonly heard calls are a tremulous, descending whinny and a whistling trill or bounce call. (The screech is seldom heard). Males usually voice lower-toned call notes.

Close relatives. Similar species include the western screech-owl (*O. kennicottii*), whiskered screech-owl (*O. trichopsis*), and flammulated owl (*O. flammeolus*), all residing in the western United States; and the scops-owl (*O. scops*), a Eurasian resident.

Behavior. These are probably the most common owls of eastern North America, more abundant than most of us realize. One most often detects them by hearing their calls during the evening and night. In the daytime they roost in tree cavities or huddle on branches close to the trunk, resembling bark-colored stubs of the branch itself. They become active after sunset, often hunting prey and feeding throughout the night. On launching from a perch, they drop, then fly straight and low to the ground, rising abruptly to another perch. This low-flying habit results in many collisions with vehicles along highways. Nonmigratory and sedentary, a pair often resides in the same area year-round if food sources remain sufficient. Feeding areas typically cover about fifteen to one hundred acres. Screech-owls are monogamous and apparently mate for life.

Spring. Screech-owls are cavity nesters. The cavity vicinity—a tree, nest box, or wall crevice—is the only territory they defend, though aggressive encounters with other screech-owls occasionally occur outside the territory. A pair often reuses the same cavity, or finds another in the same vicinity, each year. In late winter and early spring, both sexes begin to voice the monotonic trill call, signal that a cavity home exists. Courtship activities include male bowing, blinking, and bringing food to the perched female, and the pair may reciprocally preen and duet. After the owlets hatch, both parents become busy hunters, making many back-and-forth trips each night, bringing prey from a usual distance of several hundred feet or less. When fledging occurs, parental attention centers on the first owlet to leave the cavity, still unable to fly. Its ignored siblings soon scramble to leave too, and feeding is resumed outside the cavity, where the owlets often huddle together on a branch. This is the stage when parent owls, especially the female, become vigorously defensive, attacking any intruders, including humans, with needle-sharp talons. As they gain strength and flight feathers, the owlets begin following the parents as they hunt, gradually learning to feed themselves. Screech-owls raise only one brood per year.

EGGS AND YOUNG: four or five; eggs white, round. INCUBATION: by female, which is fed by male; about one month. FEEDING OF YOUNG: by both sexes; large insects, small mammal prey. FLEDGING: about three weeks.

Summer, Fall. Owlets continue to be fed by the parents at intervals, but by late summer they begin to disperse in all directions. They usually settle in home ranges less than a mile from their original nest cavity. Territorial disputes often occur, and the screech-owl's whinny call is most often heard at these seasons. The annual feather molt, beginning in July or August, continues into late fall. Until leaves drop, a screech-owl pair usually roosts on branches or in vine tangles outside the nest cavity.

Winter. Pairs now roost during the day in tree cavities. Winter mortality, from predation, starvation, or flying into cars or windows, takes a heavy toll, especially of the juvenile owls. As food becomes scarcer, screech-owls often range widely to seek prey. Studies indicate that gray morphs may be better adapted than the red for withstanding extreme cold. By late winter, courtship activities become increasingly apparent as pairs prepare to mate.

Ecology. In rural areas, screech-owls favor open woodland and deciduous woodlots, often near water. They tend to avoid dense or dry forest habitats. Screech-owls have also adapted to the plant mosaic of older suburban areas that contain large trees or groves. Parks, cemeteries, and residential areas often provide more plentiful food than rural woodland and have become frequent nesting habitats. Screech-owls tend to avoid conifer groves for both nesting and roosting.

Screech-owls do not excavate their own tree cavities. They use natural hollows or holes previously excavated by northern flickers and other woodpeckers. They bring no nesting materials, but prey remnants and owl pellets often accumulate to form a deep litter. A screech-owl peering from its cavity makes the cavity hole disappear, as the owl's plumage blends with the pattern of tree bark.

A curious owl-snake association occurs in the south-central and southwestern United States, where screech-owls capture Texas blind snakes as live prey. These wormlike snakes often escape from the owls inside the nest cavity and thrive there, feeding on nest debris and probably on larval insect parasites. Owlets in these nests seem to grow faster and survive in greater numbers than those in nests without the resident snakes.

Screech-owls are exclusively carnivorous, capturing any prey they can seize and carry with bill or talons. During warmer seasons, their diet mainly consists of large insects, including moths, June beetles, katydids, cicadas, and crickets, many captured from around lights at night. They also raid songbird nests for adult and nestling birds; wade in the shallows for frogs, crayfish, and minnows; and consume earthworms on wet pavements. Mammal prey includes many mice and shrews. Much of their fall and winter diet consists of small birds such as sparrows and juncos, as well as rock pigeons and mourning doves. Screech-owls often decapitate their vertebrate prey when they capture it.

Woodpeckers, European starlings, and squirrels are probably the screech-owl's main competitors for cavity sites. Since a screech-owl pair sometimes roosts apart in separate cavities, a high screech-owl population may increase territorial conflicts among the owls.

Screech-owls often become the prey of other nocturnal predators. Great horned owls capture many. Raccoons, opossums, and squirrels rob the nest cavities of eggs and owlets. Day-roosting owls outside their cavities are often discovered and mobbed by American crows, blue jays, and smaller birds, driving them to flight and thus exposing them to daytime raptors, mainly hawks.

Focus. The average adult screech-owl lives two or three years, some much longer. Screech-owl abundance, though probably much greater today than in presettlement North America, is declining. Urbanization, loss of hedgerows and fields conducive to mice, and the forester's compulsion to "clean up" woodlots by eliminating dead trees have tended to drive out screech-owls. Where tree cavities are sparse, a nest box placed in the right habitat may attract a pair.

Birders have made increasing use of taped screech-owl calls in the field, not only for owling at night but also for year-round daytime censusing of songbirds, since the calls excite mobbing behavior in many species. These tapes should generally not be used during the breeding season, as the calls may evoke unnecessary disruption and territorial disturbances.

Eastern Towhee
(*Pipilo erythrophthalmus*)

This seven- or eight-inch-long bird can be identified by its long tail and distinctive pattern of robin-red sides, white belly, dark upper parts, white tail corners, and red irises. Male heads and upper parts are black; those of females are dark brown. The contrasting solid-color patterns of towhee plumage provide effective camouflage in the light-and-shadow mosaic of its habitats. The towhee's song is likewise distinctive: a loud, three-part phrase—"drink-your teee"—the last syllable higher and trilled. The two-note call, "too-WHEE," is also commonly heard.

Close relatives. The four other North American towhees—spotted towhee (*P. maculatus*), green-tailed towhee (*P. chlorurus*), brown towhee (*P. fuscus*), and Abert's towhee (*P. aberti*)—reside in the western United States. Two others are Mexican residents.

Behaviors. The towhee spends most of its time on or near the ground. It often reveals its presence, when not singing, by its vigorous rummaging in the leaf litter, where it double-scratches in a manner similar to juncos. Towhees display much tail action, pumping, spreading, and flicking their white-splashed rectrices as they move about, accenting the fact that this is our longest-tailed northeastern finch. A lover of bathing, it often flutters in dew-heavy foliage, thoroughly drenching itself, then fluffs and preens on a perch.

Eastern towhees range east of the Great Plains, breeding from southern Canada to the southeastern states. The northern population migrates.

Spring. In the northeastern range of this species, peak migration occurs in late March and early April. Males precede females, remaining in small flocks for a few days before establishing territories of half an acre to two acres in size, probably on or near previously held territories. They sing from low perches or on the ground. When the females arrive, there is much chasing, usually in triads of two males and a female, before pairing occurs on the territory. A common courtship display by both sexes while perched is a brief spread of wings and tail, exhibiting the birds' white markings. The female builds the nest, often accompanied by male song from an overhead perch as she collects materials. About mid-May, both song and territory diminish somewhat as nesting begins. Unmated males continue to sing, however.

EGGS AND YOUNG: three to five; eggs grayish, brown spotted, especially at the larger end. INCUBATION: by female; about twelve days. FEEDING OF YOUNG: by both sexes; mainly insects, some fruits. FLEDGING: about ten days.

Summer. Fledglings begin flying a week or so after leaving the nest. They continue to be fed for about a month on the territory. Towhee parents remain monogamous for the entire breeding season, often raising two broods in the original territory. A week or more after the first brood fledges, the female begins building anew, and this nesting may extend into July or August. The independent young often form small flocks with other juvenile towhees and wander widely, usually ignored by the still-territorial adults. Juveniles are heavily brown streaked until their first molt in midsummer, and the males possess brown wing primaries until their second-year molt. Song largely ceases by August, when the adult towhees also acquire new plumage.

Fall. Migration from the northern range proceeds leisurely in September and October, mainly at night with daytime rest stops. Most towhees travel to the southern United States, many leapfrogging past year-round residents of the central states. Females travel the farthest south, an example of differential migration.

Winter. Most towhee migrants join year-round resident towhees, whose range extends from south of the Great Lakes and New England to the Gulf. Flocks of fifteen to twenty-five birds forage over areas of twenty to thirty acres, often mixing with northern cardinals, various sparrows, and dark-eyed juncos. Small numbers of male towhees spend the winter on the northern breeding range, and males also outnumber females on the northern winter range.

Ecology. Towhees are not as tolerant of humans as American robins are and rarely reside in suburban yards or farmland. Yet their favored habitats result mainly from human activities. Dense, shrubby edges and deciduous and mixed open woodlands with heavy leaf litter characterize both summer and winter habitats.

A female scratches a depression in the litter, building the nest rim flush with the ground surface. She lines the bulky cup of leaves, grasses, twigs, and bark strips (especially grapevine bark) with fine grasses, pine needles, and sometimes hair. Nests usually lie sheltered beneath a grass tuft, low shrub, or brush tangle. Occasionally, especially for later nestings, towhees build a foot or two high in a dense, low shrub.

Towhees consume almost any sort of invertebrate they can find in the leaf litter, chiefly beetles, plus caterpillars, ants, spiders, and snails. Towhees are foremost predators of late-stage gypsy moth caterpillars and the adult moths. The diet turns mainly vegetarian in summer and fall, and they consume many kinds of fruits and seeds. Seeds of ragweeds, smartweeds, sedges, and foxtail grasses are favored, as are corn, blueberries, and blackberries. The birds also eat acorns in fall and winter.

Although towhees inhabit the same upland thicket sites as cuckoos, brown thrashers, and white-throated sparrows, among other edge dwellers, competition for nest sites and food appears minimal, except for north-wintering towhees.

Ground nests are always vulnerable to foraging predators, including pilot black snakes and mammals such as weasels, skunks, and raccoons. Probably the towhee's foremost nemesis, however, is the brown-headed cowbird, which often deposits eggs in towhee nests. The towhee's tolerance for forest fragmentation places it on a collision course with cowbirds, which favor patchy forest tracts and edges. If not for the fact that many towhees nest into summer, when most cowbirds have ceased breeding, probably fewer towhees would exist.

Focus. The name towhee is one of many transliterations of this bird's call notes. Vernacular names include chewink, red-eyed towhee, and ground robin. Banding data show a longevity record of ten years; four to six years, one researcher judged, "is not an uncommonly long life span for this species."

As edge habitats are transitional, towhee abundance varies locally over time. A dramatic trend of decrease in New England—some 8 to 10 percent per year since 1966—has been attributed mainly to forest regeneration.

European Starling
(*Sturnus vulgaris*)

A short-tailed, seven- or eight-inch-long black bird is probably this species. Sexes look alike, except that females have a yellow iris ring in the eye, but the dark plumage patterns vary seasonally. With practice, one can instantly identify starlings aloft by their triangular shape; short, pointed wings; and swift, direct flight. Starlings voice numerous sounds; common songs and notes include a squealing "tseeer," a breathy "hooee," clear whistles, chuckles, gargles, and rattles.

Close relatives. More than one hundred starling species range throughout Africa and Eurasia. Two European species are the spot-less and rose-coloured starlings (*S. unicolor, S. roseus*). The crested mynah (*Acridotheres cristatellus*) and hill mynah (*Gracula religiosa*), introduced to western Canada and Florida, respectively, are Asian imports whose North American populations have remained localized.

Behaviors. Like blackbirds, starlings are gregarious, have black plumage, feed mainly on the ground, and walk instead of hop. Starlings often associate with blackbirds in mixed flocks but are not closely related to them. Starling body shape is stubbier; its flight is steady and direct, unlike the hill-and-dale flight of blackbirds; and its vocal capacity is far greater. Starlings are also more abundant, probably numbering upwards of two hundred million in North America alone. Flocks in flight often maneuver as a single unit, raising some intriguing questions about how they communicate. A foraging flock moves steadily across a field by leapfrogging, as birds in the rear fly over the vanguard, and by spreading out in radial circles and arcs.

Starlings forage by probing bill length into the soil. Their jaw muscles work the bill in a reverse fashion called *gaping*. As the bird inserts its closed bill into the sod, the bill snaps open, prying apart grass roots and often exposing hidden and winter-dormant grubs. At the same time, the eyes move forward, giving the bird a narrow range of binocular vision as it probes. Some researchers attribute much of the starling's winter survival success to gaping.

This is a sociable bird at all seasons. Though it displays territorial behaviors when nesting, a pair, unless incubating eggs or brooding young, typically joins other starlings at night to roost at fixed sites, usually tree groves or ivy-covered buildings, where they noisily screech and babble. Though not as frequent or convincing a mimic as the mockingbird (a statement with which some ornithologists disagree), a starling may voice brief snatches of other bird song—some sixty species imitations have been listed—plus sounds of dogs, cats, and machinery. Males sing during the breeding season, but both sexes do so at other seasons and when roosting.

Starling migration is peculiar; some migrate and some don't. Current breeding range extends across the continent from southern Canada into Mexico and throughout temperate regions around the globe.

Spring. By early spring, starlings exhibit their glossy blue-black plumage, a result of feather tip erosion. Also by this time, the male starling has usually established his territory, the area immediately surrounding a potential nesting cavity in a tree or building. Often he preempts cavities excavated by other birds, frequently evicting the occupants. When another starling flies overhead, perchance a female, he waves his wings in a circular motion and utters squeal calls. An attracted female views his suggestive behaviors of repeated entry and exit of the prospective nest hole. When the two begin to fly and forage together, pairing has occurred. The male soon begins bringing materials into the nest cavity, but the female cleans out his contributions and collects fresh materials.

Starlings use a number of breeding strategies. Sometimes, where several cavities occur close together, they breed colonially. Bachelor nest helpers may feed nestlings and guard the nest tree. Males, which tend to outnumber females, occasionally exhibit polygyny, breeding with more than one female. Females may dump eggs in other starling nests, and a solitary, intact egg found on the ground is often a starling's—presumably the bird was unable to get back to the nest in time.

Night roosts in spring are mainly occupied by unmated and yearling males, later by paired males during female incubation. Females join the roosts after nestlings no longer need brooding for warmth.

EGGS AND YOUNG: four to six; eggs bluish or greenish white. INCUBATION: by both sexes (female at night); about twelve days. FEEDING OF YOUNG: by both sexes; caterpillars and other insects. FLEDGING: about three weeks.

Summer. Starlings often raise two broods, beginning the second in midsummer. A male may renest with his previous mate or shift to another while continuing to feed first-brood fledglings. These soon join with other young starlings to form all-juvenile flocks that forage the countryside, often in huge numbers. This age segregation occurs only in summer. In August, after breeding, starlings undergo their annual molt, replacing their worn iridescence with light-tipped feathers that give the birds a duller, speckled appearance. Starlings are one of the few American birds in which juveniles replace all their plumage, including flight and tail feathers, at this time. The yellow bills of adults also change to grayish. A common behavior in summer is anting—the rubbing of ants, which release formic acid, into the plumage. This is often done in company with American robins. This period also marks the formation of the largest starling assemblages, when birds of all ages gather, sometimes by the thousands, to roost each night in the communal site. Often they share these roosts with common grackles, brown-headed cowbirds, and American robins. They also join grackles, cowbirds, and red-winged blackbirds in large daytime feeding flocks.

Fall. For those starlings that migrate, seasonal timing (late September through November) and directional movements closely follow the migrational patterns of starlings in Europe, their native continent. West of the Appalachians, the directional pattern is northeast to southwest in fall, and the reverse in spring. Movements of young and non-breeding birds seem more random and nomadic.

For the nonmigrators, concurrent with flocking behaviors comes a renewal of nest cavity territoriality by single birds, both males and females. Most of these birds are probably previous breeders.

Winter. This most stressful season results in much starling mortality. Studies indicate that about half of all the starlings alive in January, and 60 percent of first-year starlings, will die during the coming year; one-third of that mortality occurs in February and March. Yet huge numbers survive the winter because of their omnivorous diet and their feeding and behavioral adaptations. During the coldest weather, rooftop starlings often group around chimneys or near hot-air vents. Observers in Europe have noted starlings smoke bathing on chimneys—a behavior that some suggest may serve similar functions to anting.

Starling flocks decline in size and the birds split off in pairs beginning in February. In midwinter, perhaps because of energy deficits, nest site defense diminishes, but it increases again in late winter. By now, feather tips of the starling's speckled plumage are wearing off to reveal the bird's iridescent breeding plumage, and the bills are turning yellow, brighter in males. Migrants are winging north in February and March. Upon arrival, older birds usually choose nest sites located within a half mile of the previous year's nest cavity.

Ecology. The starling's abundance owes much to its success in exploiting a variety of human environs. Equally at home in urban, suburban, farm, and edge habitats, it needs tree cavities or building crevices for nesting, lawns and open meadows for foraging, and tree groves or urban structures for communal roosting. About the only places starlings do not thrive are extensive woodlands and marshes.

Starlings cannot enter cavity entrance holes one and one-half inches or less in

diameter. Almost any cavity with a hole larger than this, even if already occupied, may be claimed for a nest site. The birds load the cavity with coarse plant materials plus feathers, pieces of cloth, and other items, lining the nest cup with fine grasses and feathers. Throughout incubation, starlings also bring in sprigs of green plants that may repel mite and insect parasites, often aromatic mints such as wild bergamot, spearmint, and catnip, as well as parsleys. Starling nestlings produce excessively wet fecal matter; fecal sacs are removed by parent birds only until the nestlings begin to develop feathers, when nest sanitation ceases. The nest quickly becomes a sodden, swarming, "pest-ridden compost," as one observer noted.

Though birding protocol seems to demand that we revile these nonnative birds wherever they appear, their omnivorous food habits often prove highly beneficial to humans. Starlings feed on root parasites in lawns and short-grass fields, primarily the larvae of ground beetles, snout beetles, and scarab beetles, including the infamous Japanese beetle (*Popillia japonica*), plus ants and earthworms. They also devour many irruptive hairy caterpillars, including gypsy and tent moths. Age segregation in feeding habitats occurs in summer; juveniles, apparently less able to find soil invertebrates, forage largely on seeds and fruits in weedy fields, whereas adult flocks seek insect larvae in short-grass areas. But in later summer, as roosts approach maximal size, a diet shift occurs in many adult starlings, and wild cherries, berries, and many other fruits are now sought.

The chief source of the starling's vast unpopularity among birders is its aggressive takeover of nest cavities, thus depriving our native cavity nesters of available sites. Woodpecker cavities rank high as favored nest sites, but starlings also compete with American kestrels, great crested flycatchers, tree swallows, purple martins, house wrens, and eastern bluebirds for cavities. In spring, because of their early-timed first brood, starlings often occupy many unspoken-for cavities. Later, as they seek new cavities for second broods after royally fouling their own nests, they often attack other cavity occupants. Few native birds can withstand a determined starling onslaught. Starlings also compete with themselves, not only for nest sites but also by brood parasitism, often laying an egg or two in each other's nests. Food competition becomes significant mainly in fall and winter, when the diet turns largely to fruits. Starling flocks may vie with American robins, cedar waxwings, and other frugivores for survival nourishment during these seasons.

Though vulnerable to predation by accipiter hawks in daytime and roost-raiding owls at night, plus domestic cats, raccoons, and a few other nest robbers, starling populations are hardly dented by predators. Human efforts to break up the enormous starling roosts that sometimes invade and foul urban areas—using all sorts of explosives, noisemakers, and ingenious technological scarecrows—have shown only partial success at best. The average adult starling lives for about a year and a half, although the maximum life span is about twenty years.

Focus. It was no lack of sweet intentions that brought European starlings to America. Blame William Shakespeare, the inspiration if not the boneheaded instigator. New York businessman-dilettante Eugene Scheifflin decided to show his love of country by acclimating to America all sixty-odd bird species mentioned by Shakespeare (Bible birds having already been unsuccessfully done). The enterprise required persistent efforts to achieve, for several previous tries had not worked. In 1890, Scheifflin released sixty starlings at Central Park in New York City, and the following year, forty more. From these hundred starlings arose the multiple progeny we see about us. Starlings reached the Midwest by the 1920s, the West Coast by the early 1940s. Scheifflin's act led directly to the establishment of federal laws restricting introductions of other wild exotics.

Despite the anathemas hurled at them by American bird lovers (for starlings remain a "respectable" species in Europe), starlings are here to stay. And they have taught us much. Working with starlings in wind tunnels, researchers discovered possible functions of the *furcula*, or wishbone, in many birds. This U-shaped bone, with each of its free ends attached to a shoulder, bends and recoils with great flexibility, pulling apart each time the wings press down. Its movements may help push airflow between the lungs and air sacs of the bones, ultimately aiding the bird's respiration, heat control, and buoyancy in flight.

Ecologists rightly voice concern about starling abundance and what it may signify regarding trends toward less diversity and more uniformity of species in our increasingly urbanized environments. Yet again, without applauding Eugene Scheifflin, one may find much to admire about starlings. Watching their behaviors, hearing their mimicry, noting their complex social interactions and plumage changes—all offer a condensed ornithology course in your backyard.

Gray Catbird
(Dumetella carolinensis)

This nine-inch-long mimid can be identified by its gray-black plumage, black head cap, rusty undertail coverts, or *crissum,* tail-flicking habit, and catlike mewing notes. Sexes look alike. Partially albino catbirds are sometimes seen, usually showing white patches or banding.

Close relatives. The black catbird (*Melanoptila glabrirostris*), a resident of Mexico and Central America, is the only other catbird.

Behaviors. Its curiosity and conspicuous sounds and behaviors make this smallest, most common North American mimid easily observable in its habitats. Catbird breeding range spans almost the entire continental United States. Although not so frequent or accomplished a mimic as some of its family relatives, the catbird has been known to imitate songs and calls of at least thirty-five bird species, plus occasional tree frogs and wagon wheels; its familiar mewing note, however, is not mimicry. Ornithologist James Granlund has observed that the birds seem to increase their song repertoires with age. The catbird also sings a sweet song of its own, consisting of jumbled musical phrases always interspersed with a few harsh squealing notes. Catbirds feed both on the ground, where they often forage by bill-sweeping, and in shrub and tree foliage. Most catbirds migrate.

Spring. Traveling at night, many of them directly over the Gulf of Mexico, catbirds arrive on their breeding range in late April and early May. Male catbirds precede females by a week or more and immediately establish territories by loud singing and chasing of other catbirds. Territories average one to three acres in size, usually in a previous nesting area. Males pursue females on their territories; they strut and fluff, erecting their tails to exhibit their only real color marking, the rusty crissum. Females construct the nests, and males cease singing when incubation begins. A pair never leaves its initial territory, even to feed, until nesting is completed. As nesting progresses, however, the vigorously defended area shrinks in size to the nest vicinity. Some catbirds remain paired over several breeding seasons.

EGGS AND YOUNG: usually four; eggs blue-green. INCUBATION: by female, which is fed by male; male also guards the nest; about twelve days. FEEDING OF YOUNG: by both sexes; insects and spiders, berries in late nestling stages. FLEDGING: ten or eleven days.

Summer. While first-brood fledglings remain in the nest vicinity, fed mainly by the male parent for about two weeks, the male also resumes singing, and a shift in territorial size and shape occurs. The female begins building a second nest in early summer, usually in the vicinity of the first. In a few areas, catbirds may even raise third broods. Then the birds congregate in heavier lowland cover. The annual feather molt occurs in August.

Fall. Listen now for the catbird's whisper song, a soft soliloquy version of the spring song, uttered anytime but most frequently in autumn. Most catbirds move south in September and October, but small populations remain on parts of the breeding range during most winters.

Winter. Catbird winter range includes the southern coastal states, the Caribbean islands, and Central America to Panama. Often they feed in flocks, but they remain mostly silent.

Ecology. On their breeding range, catbirds favor wetland edge habitats, especially dense thickets bordering swamps, ponds, and other lowland areas. Willow-dogwood shrublands are favored sites, but almost any thicket habitat, including hedgerows and yard shrubbery, may host a resident pair. On their winter range, catbirds forage in dense rain-forest habitats, banana plantations, and thickets.

The crucial element for catbird nesting is foliage density. Tartarian honeysuckle, hawthorns, and grape tangles are commonly used sites in drier thickets. Usually the bulky, ragged-looking nest, seldom placed higher than ten feet, occupies the densest, innermost heart of the thicket. Leaves in the foundation plus twigs, weed stalks, grapevine bark, and often pieces of paper or cellophane form the nest's outer construction; its deep cup is lined with dark rootlets. The otherwise similar nests of northern cardinals show few if any leaves in the foundation and a lining of fine grasses. Vacated catbird nests are frequently recycled by other creatures. White-footed mice pile additional materials on them for their own nests, and red squirrels and American robins also sometimes build on catbird nest foundations. Chipmunks, mice, and squirrels use the nests as storage and feeding platforms.

The catbird's diet is roughly half animal, half vegetable. Ants, beetles, caterpillars, grasshoppers, and spiders constitute much of its spring and summer food; its seasonal consumption of blackberries, cherries, elder-berries, and grapes, among other fruits, makes the catbird one of our foremost fruit eaters, or frugivores. Occasionally it raids cultivated fruit crops but usually causes few losses. Economically, the catbird's consumption of irruptive cankerworms, armyworms, cicadas, and sawfly larvae more than compensates for its orchard forays.

Its foremost nest-site competitors are northern cardinals and brown thrashers, both upland thicket dwellers. Where numerous enough, catbirds are usually territorially dominant over both species, but either may usurp catbird nests on occasion. In areas of habitat overlap, red-winged blackbirds may also conflict with catbirds. Catbirds may compete with other frugivores at certain times and places for food, but except for north-wintering catbirds, food competition is probably negligible.

Nest predators include red squirrels, chipmunks, raccoons, domestic cats, American crows, house wrens, and several snakes: blue racers and black rat, fox, garter, and milk snakes. Catbirds share with thrushes two parasites of the nasal passages, both rhinonyssine mites. I will never forget reaching overhead one day to feel into a catbird nest and experiencing the peculiar sensation of a wave moving down my arm from the empty nest—an almost invisible swarm of mites. Brown-headed cowbirds do not effectively parasitize catbird broods; catbirds quickly pierce and eject cowbird eggs.

Focus. The catbird's song, or perhaps its harsh mewing notes, seemed like mourning sounds to the Chippewa, who named it "the bird that cries with grief." The only other mewing bird of the Northeast is the yellow-bellied sapsucker.

Records of seven-year-old catbirds exist, but the average life span is probably two or three years. Catbirds have amply benefited from the creation of edge habitats and fruit culture, and it is likely that their current numbers vastly surpass their presettlement populations. Their trend of increase continues in many areas.

Great Horned Owl
(Bubo virginianus)

This brown woodland owl can be recognized by its large size (eighteen to twenty-five inches), erect ear tufts, yellow eyes, white throat bib, and horizontal barring on breast and belly. Sexes look alike except that females are larger. Identify this owl on the wing by its four-foot wingspread, large head, and neckless appearance. When flying, a great horned owl typically glides from its roost, courses low, then abruptly rises at a steep angle to land on its perch. More often heard than seen despite their large size, these are true "hoot owls," voicing several mellow "hoo" notes in rhythmic succession. The male usually utters four or five notes, the female six to eight. Much controversy exists over whether male or female notes are lower pitched; there are owl experts who firmly opine each way. Often a pair duets back and forth. The notes, though resonant, sound curiously muffled, resembling a low-pitched foghorn that nevertheless carries over great distances. Other sounds—hisses, bill snapping, and a medley of barks, squeals, grunts, and shrieks—are occasioned by territorial or aggressive encounters.

Close relatives. The eagle owl (*B. bubo*) of Europe is even larger than the great horned. In North America, only the great gray owl (*Strix nebulosa*) of boreal forests and sometimes the snowy owl (*Nyctea scandiaca*) are larger.

Behavior. A great horned owl specializes in surprise, not pursuit. Like most owls, it is a nocturnal still-hunter; it waits for sight or sound of prey on the ground, then drops in a swift, silent dive. It slams its prey feetfirst, its fisted talons locking into the victim's body. It carries prey, however, in its bill. Except for larger prey, which it tears apart, most of its captures are swallowed whole, head end first after it has been decapitated. If prey is abundant, the owl sometimes eats only the skull contents, leaving the rest of the carcass. Bird prey is often plucked. Great horned owls periodically regurgitate undigested fur, feathers, and bones in pellets two to four inches long. Pellets form in the stomach about eight hours after feeding and are usually ejected before the owl launches forth at night, about one per day. "Each pellet is a mystery," wrote zoologist Bernd Heinrich, "and behind it is the drama of a predator lurking in the night."

Great horned owls often shift their roost locations. An exception may be feeding roosts—particular stumps, branches, or old nests where they regularly bring their prey, often littering the ground beneath with prey remnants. Some researchers believe that this owl's night vision is only slightly better than that of humans and that it does most of its hunting in late evening and predawn hours and on moonlit nights.

Its distribution spans both North and South America. Great horned owls are non-migratory throughout most of their range, often residing in the same vicinity year-round.

Spring. In many localities, great horned owls are completing incubation by mid-March. Human intrusion at this stage may result in viciously aggressive attacks by the parent owls, whose talons can inflict serious damage. The male often brings huge quantities of prey items to the nest, sometimes overloading it. Owlet fledglings often tumble to the ground, then clamber up leaning trees to perch and await feeding. Parent owls continue to feed owlets in the nest vicinity for three or more months. Such long dependency on the parents, rare in birds, accounts for the winter breeding of this species. Parent owls are mostly nonvocal during nesting.

EGGS AND YOUNG: two or three; eggs dull white. INCUBATION: mainly by female, also male at intervals; about one month. FEEDING OF YOUNG: by both sexes; small mammals, birds. FLEDGING: six to eight weeks.

Summer. Many great horned owls abandon their territories and squalling owlets in summer and wander for several weeks. Pairs may remain together or drift apart. For juveniles, this is a prolonged learning period; they make clumsy mock attacks on various objects and just about anything moving. During hot weather, these essentially cold-climate birds, covered to their toes in thick plumage, suffer obvious discomfort. They become mostly inactive, drooping their wings, like other birds, and pumping their throat muscles to aid breathing because they cannot expand the chest cavity. The annual molt begins in midsummer, lasting until late fall.

Juveniles of the previous year now gain their first complete adult plumage.

Fall. Juvenile owls disperse at this season, seldom more than twenty miles or so, where they begin to establish their own territories. Adult owls return from wandering to their breeding territories. Males, especially, begin to hoot in evening and predawn hours, and an old or future nest may also be selected and defended at this time. Size of the home range depends on food resources; two or three square miles is probably a typical size, within which the owls occupy nesting and roosting territories that may shift at intervals before nesting begins.

Winter. Courtship activity, beginning about January, consists of much hooting, bowing, fluffing, bill snapping and rubbing, and ritual feeding. Incubation has begun by mid-February in many areas. Snowfall often covers the female as she sits on the nest.

These owls typically begin breeding in their second year; older mated pairs often breed only every other year or two. Prey abundance may determine whether a pair nests in any given year. In this owl's northern range, a cyclic drop in snowshoe hare populations, occurring about once per decade, brings winter influxes of owls south into the northern United States, sometimes in large numbers.

Ecology. Home ranges of great horned owls are typified by a mixture of large woodlots, either deciduous or coniferous, with adjacent fields and smaller tree groves. Often this owl will roost in a distinctive tree of a grove or woodlot—the tallest or shortest pine, for example, or a lone hemlock or white pine in a stand of other trees. Winter roosting sites are often evergreens with high grapevine tangles or dense foliage.

Great horned owls are prime nest recyclers and do not build nests of their own. They often select the previous nest of a red-tailed hawk. They also use old nests of great blue herons, bald eagles, ospreys, American crows, and common ravens, as well as leaf nests of fox squirrels, which they flatten and scoop out. Occasionally these owls nest atop a tall, dead tree stub or inside a tree cavity. Their nests often have a skunky odor, as do the birds themselves.

Much has been made of great horned owl association with the red-tailed hawk, the latter a daytime raptor nesting in the same upland woods habitats favored by this owl. Each species is sometimes closely tolerated by the other, and the presence of one may indicate *possible* residence by the other. Yet the mutual occurrence of these predators as day-night counterparts is, in my experience, hardly consistent enough to call it an equation. Since red-tailed hawks tend to reuse their own previous nests, a hawk pair building a nest from scratch may indicate that the earlier-nesting owls have taken over the hawk pair's previous, and often nearby, nest.

Exclusively meat eaters, great horned owls are opportunistic hunters. Rabbits are the preferred staple, but frequent mammal prey also includes flying squirrels and other rodents, domestic cats, opossums, and skunks. Porcupines are also occasional—if dangerous—prey. Bird prey, often captured on nests or roosts, includes ducks, geese, grouse, pheasants, American crows, a variety of songbirds, and occasionally poultry. Screech-owls are sometimes captured as they hunt. Great horned owls also capture snakes, amphibians, and insects.

Since most of its prey consists of nocturnal creatures, this owl's chief food competi-

tors are other night hunters, including other owl species, foxes, coyotes, raccoons, skunks, and opossums. Its early breeding gives it a competitive edge over the later-breeding hawks and American crows, whose previous nests it often adopts.

Aside from human gunners and occasional large hawks that attack roosting owls, the great horned owl has few predators, although American crows are known to kill owlets in the nest if the parent owls are absent. The great horned owl attracts numerous bird mobbers and harassers, however. American crows and blue jays express noisy antipathy to all raptors. Songbirds, too, hearing the excitement, often join this raucous ganging, which never approaches the owl *too* closely. The owl, lethargic in daytime, usual-ly ignores the yelling until its tormentors tire and drift away. (One of the best ways to locate roosting raptors is to listen for these loud mob actions).

Focus. Young owls suffer the highest annual mortality of the great horned population; about half of them succumb, mainly from starvation. Many, when they disperse, fail to find prey-rich habitats. Great horned owls may live thirteen or fourteen years, seldom longer.

Great horned owls can sometimes be attracted by other owl calls and by distress squeaks, simulated by rapidly kissing the back of the hand. Look for roosting great horned owls in the middle part of a tree's crown, especially close to the trunk.

Herring Gull
(*Larus argentatus*)

easuring about two feet long, adult herring gulls have white heads, underparts, and tails; a pearl gray mantle (back and wings) with black wing tips; and pinkish legs and feet. The heavy, yellow bill shows a red spot near the tip of the lower mandible. Immature herring gulls—that is, birds four years old and under—exhibit varying degrees of darker plumage. This bird's "hiyah hiyah," "ow ow ow," and "klee-ah klee-ah" cries, along with other squealing and wailing notes, are familiar sounds of beach and port.

Close relatives. All other *Larus* species are closely related.

Behaviors. Visibly larger than the ring-billed gull, the herring gull is the gregarious, widely distributed "seagull" (a generic vernacular term—no gull species of that name exists). This bird's complex behavioral traits, especially during the breeding season, were notably observed and reported by Dutch biologist Niko Tinbergen in his classic *The Herring Gull's World* (1953), a book that helped establish the scientific study of animal behavior *(ethology)*. Tinbergen observed entire repertoires of ritualized motions, postures, calls, and other interactions of this gull, providing one of the most richly detailed biographies of any bird species.

In flight, herring gulls make ample use of air currents and updrafts of their windy environment, often soaring effortlessly, slightly adjusting the bend or plane of wings and tail as they glide. Few birds are so intimately united with the wind as these and other gulls; they exhibit a visible poetry of motion. If you have ever been on a ship forging into a headwind and watched the accompanying gulls, you have seen their ability to keep pace with the ship by expert use of updrafts from the vessel.

Their social interactions in the flock are not so poetic. Except between a breeding pair, they exhibit no cooperative behaviors, often pirate food from one another, and their noisy squabbles, especially when feeding, are incessant. They readily attack (or occasionally adopt) stray chicks in the breeding colony and also consume eggs from unguarded nests of their own and other species. Roosting flocks on a sandbar or wharf, however, appear sedate as they bask in the sun. On the water, herring gulls swim and float buoyantly, feeding mainly from the surface. Occasionally, spotting small fishes, they plummet ternlike from the air in a splashing dive, but this is not a common behavior. Their buoyancy prevents them from diving deeper than a few feet.

One familiar feeding strategy of herring gulls is to carry a mollusk (usually a clam) aloft, then drop it. If the shell breaks on the ground (or ice), the bird lands and consumes the inner flesh; if the shell does not break, the gull retrieves and drops it again, sometimes repeatedly. One study found that adult herring gulls average 1.6 drops for breaking open a clam, and that yearling birds require 2.3 drops. Sometimes the birds carry their prey far inland in executing this maneuver. Many of them, however, can't seem to distinguish a hard, shell-cracking surface (rocks) from softer ground (sand), so the stratagem often proves unsuccessful.

Herring gulls are common in the Northern Hemisphere throughout the world. In North America, they breed across the continent from the Arctic Circle south to the Great Lakes, New England, and coastal North Carolina. The herring gull provides a prime example of a ring species—that is, a species that varies over a circular range (in this case, circumpolar or Holarctic) to the extent that at each end of the circle, where the divergent subspecies rejoin (in northern Eurasia), they no longer interbreed. The *Larus* ring species complex probably evolved when parts of the ring distribution became fragmented and reproductively isolated during Pleistocene glaciation, then again became continuous.

Spring. A partial molt of body feathers occurs in March and April; fourth-year birds acquire full adult plumage at this time.

Adult herring gulls exhibit strong site fidelity *(philopatry)* to their natal and previous breeding colonies, often returning to the same territory they occupied the previous year, usually in April and May. Younger gulls, arriving later than the already paired adults, usually form territories at edges of the colony where competition from older gulls is less intense. But many subadult birds—gulls under age four or five—do not return to their home colony until they reach adulthood. These gulls wander widely in the intervening years and may show up almost anywhere in North America or Europe. Tinbergen believed that herring gulls usually pair for life but that mates probably do not remain together after breeding seasons. Yet, he wrote, "observations seem to show that both partners find and recognize each other in spring" weeks before they return to the previously occupied territory; "this shows an amazing faculty, not only of recognizing individuals, but also of memory."

Most herring gulls begin breeding in their fourth or fifth year. Females initiate pair formation within the social context of what Tinbergen termed the *club,* a dense association of unmated birds that gather in specific areas at the colony edge. Males attract flying females to land in the club by voicing the yelp or long call, an extended series of "ow ow" and "kyow" notes. Courtship behaviors include mutual displays—head tossing, pecking motions, foot scraping, feeding of the female with male regurgitant, and other actions. Herring gulls require larger territorial space than ring-bills—some thirty to fifty yards in diameter. Threat displays at territory borders consist of upright strutting and grass pulling, sometimes actual fighting. Pairs at this time spend only a part of each day on the territory, regularly flying from the colony to feeding areas, sometimes for distances of ten miles or more.

Both mates soon begin scraping slight ground depressions on the territory; eventu-ally they focus attention on one of them and construct the meager nest. Nesting usually begins in May.

EGGS AND YOUNG: typically three; female-female pairs sometimes lay superclutches of five to six (often sterile) eggs; eggs olive or bluish, blotched with brown and gray. INCUBATION: by both sexes, relieving each other every few hours; about twenty-six days; chicks hatch over a three-day period, are brooded in the nest for several days. FEEDING OF YOUNG: by both sexes (males more often before fledging, females more often after fledging); chicks initiate feeding by pecking at red spot on adult bill; mainly regurgitant of small prey items. FLEDGING: five or six weeks.

Summer. Herring gulls raise only one brood per year. Both fledglings and adults remain on the colony site through much of the summer. Fledglings continue to beg and be fed by parents for up to six months, a much longer period of feeding than in most bird species. Many fledglings, however, gather in groups, or *creches,* on the colony perimeters, where they forage by themselves and beg from any nearby adult.

Individual gull dispersal from the colony begins in late July, but most of the birds remain relatively near the breeding area, reassembling into large flocks only at abundant food sources. A wider general dispersal occurs in August, when the birds undergo their complete annual molt. The white adults' new plumage, marked with indistinct, brownish head and neck streaks, will be replaced with new white head and body feathers the following spring. Juveniles acquire a quite uniformly brownish plumage in August. As they age through three winters, successive spring and summer molts gradually lighten the head, bill, underparts, and rump. Experienced gull observers can usually identify an immature gull's year of age by these subtle though distinctive variations in plumage—particularly the wing pattern and amount of gray in the mantle.

Fall. Migrational movements in this species are age segregated. First- to third-year immatures are the foremost migrators. The youngest birds appear to move farthest south to milder climates, usually in October through mid-November, with second- and third-year birds traveling relatively less far. Most of the adult population remains throughout the year near the breeding area. Subadult gulls concentrate along the Gulf and southern Atlantic coasts, but many also winter inland in large lakes or reservoirs.

Winter. Adult herring gulls can be seen in the Great Lakes area throughout winter, foraging wherever open waters and other food sources permit. In the northern coastal states, many herring gulls move offshore during late fall and winter, finding richer food resources in the warm Gulf current than along shore. "A winter flock," observed Tinbergen, "seems to be made up of individuals, not of pairs." The birds defend winter feeding territories—usually areas of beach or intertidal flats—from other gulls. By March, the adult gulls begin to drift back to their continental breeding colonies.

Ecology. Secluded islands are the herring gull's foremost colonial breeding habitats. Major requirements are areas free of mammal predators and nest sites sheltered from prevailing winds. Feeding habitats include open sea, lake and ocean coastal areas, harbors, and inland landfills and garbage dumps. Roosting and loafing sites include beaches, landfills, parking lots, fields, and airport runways.

The nest, a scraped depression lined with grasses, mosses, and debris, measures a foot or two across. Occasionally, where remote island habitat is lacking, herring gulls nest solitarily in trees and on rocky ledges and rooftops. For nesting, herring gulls favor open, grassy sites near water, often in proximity to clumps of herb or shrub vegetation. Such nesting habitat is often shared with cormorants.

Omnivorous and opportunistic scavengers, herring gulls consume almost anything organic. Marine invertebrates (mollusks, worms, crustaceans, starfish, sea urchins), fish, insects, rodents, and carrion are common animal fare. Herring gulls follow plows on land for worms and grubs, trail ships and fishing boats for food and wastes thrown overboard. They also pirate food from other waterbirds. If opportunity offers, they attack undefended eggs and chicks of adjacent nesting gulls, terns, cormorants, puffins, and other birds; such predation appears uncommon, however, except where human intrusion into colonies disrupts normal behaviors, often causing the birds to vacate their nests temporarily. In company with other gull species, plus blackbirds, starlings, and others, herring gulls forage extensively at landfills and garbage scows. Several studies indicate that food from garbage dumps has much lower nutritive value for gulls than fish or fishery waste. Chicks fed by adults on garbage items show significantly lower growth and survival rates, thus belying the theory that the spread of landfills and garbage dumps significantly accounts for gull increases. At sea, herring gulls often associate with feeding groups that may include kittiwakes, cormorants, shearwaters, dolphins, and whales. Predatory fishes such as tuna may drive smaller fishes to the ocean surface, where the gulls capture many. Juvenile gulls in the Gulf of Maine often associate with surfacing humpback whales in fall and winter, feeding on fish driven to the surface by the whales. Herring gulls also consume algae and wild berries on occasion.

Mixed-species colonies are fairly common, with herring and other gull species and terns populating the site. Herring gulls defend their territories only from other gulls. This gull's foremost competitor in New England and Canada's Maritime Provinces is the great black-backed gull *(L. marinus)*, which sometimes hybridizes with it, often competes for nesting habitat and territorial space, and also robs its nests. Herring gulls have also hybridized with glaucous, glaucous-winged, lesser black-backed, and common black-headed gulls, indicating at least potential competitive interactions. Food competitors include all other gulls present plus predatory fishes and sea mammals.

Island breeding habitat restricts the number of mammal predators on gull colonies. At sites other than islands, red foxes, raccoons, minks, and rats consume gull eggs, and domestic dogs and cats kill chicks. Birds are more common predators: gull species, common ravens, and American crows on eggs; great black-backed and other gulls, great horned and short-eared owls, northern harriers, and herons on chicks. Adult gulls occasionally fall prey to bald eagles, peregrine falcons, gyrfalcons, and great horned owls,

plus sharks and harbor and gray seals. Some herring gulls become tangled in nets and fishing lines. Waste litter of plastic six-pack covers, in which birds strangle, has killed many gulls. Pesticides in lake ecosystems (especially DDT and DDE, as estrogen mimics) cause a skewed sex ratio (shortage of males) and consequent formation of female pairs that produce sterile egg clutches. Water pollution and contaminants, especially in the Great Lakes, resulted in much egg and chick mortality during the 1960s and 1970s, becoming somewhat alleviated in the 1980s. Yet herring gulls show remarkable physiological toleration of such toxins as PCBs, dioxins, and botulinus in amounts that are lethal to other waterbirds.

Focus. Shifts in herring gull abundance and distribution over the past century may have more numerous and complex causes than the human-created garbage sources so often cited as the simple explanation. No reliable figures exist for herring gull population size before European settlement in North America. During the nineteenth century, however, the birds were widely hunted for their plumage, used in millinery, and their eggs were widely sought as food, resulting in gull declines of massive proportions. Audubon considered the species rare; in 1900, only an estimated 8,000 pairs existed, all of them in Maine. Numbers recovered slowly after passage of the 1918 federal Migratory Bird Act prohibited hunting and egging (though gull egging remains legal in Canada).

From the 1930s through the 1960s, herring gull populations rapidly increased. In addition to the proliferation of garbage dumps during this period, equally or more important causes of increase included gull protection; the increase of commercial fishing activities, which generated large amounts of fish waste and reduced the abundance of large predatory fishes that compete with gulls for small fishes; and drastic decline of competitive whale and seal populations, again reducing competition for small fishes (especially capelin and sandlance) and invertebrates. Overfishing and new landfill techniques may account for the current leveling off of herring gull abundance in many areas. Also, based on figures from various studies from 1979 to 1984, the maximum fledging success of 3 chicks per pair lags below 25 percent in this species.

Today Massachusetts and Maine are the foremost herring gull states, but herring gull abundance has apparently peaked there, and may even be declining in the maritimes and New England. Causes are attributed to eggers in Canada and the southward expansion of great black-backed gull populations. Once the exclusive breeding gull of the Great Lakes (now ranking second after the ring-billed gull), herring gull populations continue slow growth there. In recent years, colonies have expanded southward along the Atlantic coast. Despite these relatively modest trends of increase, herring gulls have evoked considerable clamor besides their own in certain coastal New England areas. Recent government poisoning programs in Cape Cod—intended to eradicate thousands of herring gulls, thus making habitat available for terns and the endangered piping plover—met with storms of protest from local residents, whose motto became "save the seagulls." Studies show that such extermination programs usually don't work very well except in extremely localized situations; the gulls that are left simply expand their territories to fill available space, resulting in no appreciable gain of habitat for other species (bringing to mind ornithologist Pete Dunne's maxim: "That environment is maintained best which is juggled least").

Eider ducks and puffins benefit from gull vigilance and attacks on predators. Gull eggs have long been staple food items for human coastal dwellers. Gull expert Frank Graham, Jr., vouched for their pleasant taste, "which has a hint of the sea in it." Gull egging is still pursued on the birds' northern range outside the United States.

Typical adult herring gull longevity is 15 to 20 years, though ages over 30 have been recorded. As with most birds, chances for survival increase with age (up to a point), a fact reflected in the variously plumaged age classes seen in a gull flock (see Ring-billed Gull).

House and Purple Finches
(*Carpodacus mexicanus* and *C. purpureus*)

The two species resemble each other in size (five to six inches) and red male plumage. Purple finches are burgundy or plum red, more evenly colored over head and back; house finch color varies from pale yellow to bright red, with browner head and back markings and dark streaks (lacking in purples) on the lower breast and flanks. Females of both species are brown with heavy breast streaking. The purple's characteristic flight and perch call is a bluebirdlike "cheeyew"; males voice a rich, musical warble somewhat resembling that of the warbling vireo. House finch song is also fast and live-

ly, usually three-phrased and ending in a long, trilled "wheer."

Close relatives. Some twenty-one *Carpodacus* finches exist worldwide. Cassin's finch (*C. cassinii*) resides in the western United States. Eurasian *Carpodacus* finches are called rosefinches.

Behaviors. Purple finches are northern birds, breeding from the tree line in Canada to the northern states and south along the Pacific coast; house finches range throughout most of the continental United States. Not so long ago, house finch range was much more restricted, a fact that aided identification of these purple finch lookalikes. Now, however, the two species' ranges increasingly overlap, so observers may see both in many areas, especially at yard feeders in winter. Both species are gregarious for most of the year and feed in small flocks. Ground-foraging *Carpodacus* flocks tend to rise "impulsively" as they vacate one feeding site for another. When flying to cover, they usually favor higher branches rather than low shrubbery. Purple finches migrate, but house finch seasonal movements remain unclear.

Spring. Purple finches migrate to their northern breeding range in April and May, often in large, day-traveling flocks. House finches, of more southern distribution, are often incubating on their nests by this time. Males of both species sing lengthily at morning and evening, purple finches from high treetop perches, and house finches from prominent singing posts near the nest. Females sing only in brief bursts. House finch singing apparently bears no strong connection with territory, since several males may sing from the same tree. Hopping and strutting courtship displays are exuberant. House finch males often feed females at yard feeders; often two males follow and flutter around a single female.

House finch territory is considered as floating, centering mainly around the female. Territorial defense around the nest, mainly by females, is often weak and sporadic. Purples begin nesting in May. Both species may maintain pair bonds over more than one breeding season.

EGGS AND YOUNG: four or five; eggs pale bluish green, brown spotted. INCUBATION: by females; about two weeks. FEEDING OF YOUNG: by both sexes; mainly seeds. FLEDGING: two weeks for purple finches; eleven to nineteen days for house finches.

Summer. Parent birds continue to feed fledglings for at least several days. Whether purple finches typically raise second broods remains uncertain, as some are still nesting in July, but house finches usually raise two or more broods, continuing into August. By late summer, both species have abandoned their breeding territories and gather in gregarious flocks of twenty or more. Purple finches tend to form and migrate in unisexual flocks; house finches usually flock to fields en masse with no discernible age or sex segregation, paralleling the foraging behaviors of house sparrows at this season. Both adult species acquire new plumage from July through September. Males now appear duller, reduced to pinkish hues as buffy feather tips partially mask the underlying red plumage.

Fall. Purple finch southward migration proceeds through September and October, but movements vary in extent and abundance of birds from year to year. Banding studies indicate that west-to-east migration also occurs. At least some house finches shift southward in fall and winter.

Winter. Purple finch winter range extends from the northern Great Lakes and New England, where summer and winter ranges overlap, to the Gulf Coast and Texas. Flocks appear irruptively during some winters, invading in large numbers at irregular times and places, perhaps driven by low food resources in the northern range. House finches tend to remain on or near their breeding areas over winter, though extensive wandering may also occur. In northeastern areas recently colonized by these birds, yard feeders have probably aided or enabled their year-round survival. In the males of both species, the buffy feather tips erode, gradually revealing their red breeding plumage, and they sing with increasing frequency as winter advances.

Ecology. Purple finches favor northern coniferous and mixed forests and edges, as well as evergreen plantations and spruce bogs. House finches occupy generally the same habitats as house sparrows, though they increasingly appear in edge, dune, and semiopen countryside. Landscaped suburbs, nursery plantations, and building vicinities are typical habitats, as are weedy fields, for feeding sites.

Purple finches place their nests on horizontal conifer branches, often spruce, well out from the trunk at almost any height. Nests are camouflaged in needle clusters, making them almost invisible from beneath. The shallow cup built of twigs, grasses, and weed stems is lined with fine grasses, hair, and moss.

House finches build in a much greater variety of places, requiring only a stable base for the nest and at least minimal overhead shelter, such as an overhanging eave. Tree cavities, nest boxes, building ledges, ivy-covered walls, hanging planters, and ornamental conifers are all common nest sites. Open nests in trees usually abut the trunk. The open-cup nests consist of twigs, grass, debris, leaves, and other materials. House finches often appropriate vacated nests of Baltimore orioles, swallows, and other species. Sometimes they nest semicolonially within a few feet of each other.

Both finch species are primarily seed eaters, though purples depend less on weeds and ground foraging. In the spring, purple finches forage extensively in flowering trees and shrubs. They trim petals and consume the developing seeds and buds of many fruit trees, elms, maples, aspens, and others. Spring insect food consists mainly of aphids and cankerworms. In summer and fall, they feed extensively on the dry seeds of elms, ashes, sycamore, tulip tree, and ragweeds, as well as on the fruits of dogwoods, cherries, and many others. In winter, purples sometimes join feeding flocks of pine siskins and American goldfinches.

House finch diets consist almost exclusively of seeds and fruits. Seeds of dandelion, thistle, and other composites are highly favored, as are those of radish and field mustard in overgrown pastures or barnyards. House finches forage in almost any open, weedy area. In early spring, the birds relish dripping maple sap and tree buds. Sometimes they also pierce the bases of trumpet-shaped flowers, seeking nectar. Experiments suggest that they favor red-colored fruits, a diet that bears directly on the redness of male plumage (and thus, indirectly, on breeding success, as females of both species seem to prefer the redder males). In the western United States, house finches sometimes become orchard pests.

The foremost house finch competitors are probably house sparrows. Almost anyplace that a house sparrow nests, a house finch can do likewise, but house finches show a somewhat broader nest site tolerance and typically forage over larger areas. With the recent house finch explosion, many observers hoped that the newcomers would successfully compete with house sparrows. House sparrow declines have in fact occurred in some areas of house finch expansion, but countrywide data remain inconclusive.

The decline of purple finches in certain wooded suburban areas has been blamed on both house sparrows and house finches, but neither species' breeding habitats overlap widely with those of the purple finch. Food competition among the three probably becomes critical, if at all, in winter. At winter yard feeders, house finches often show dominance over purples, and house sparrows tend to dominate both.

Accipiter hawks likely capture some purple finches, and people once trapped them for cagebirds, but predation appears insignificant. Brown-headed cowbirds occasionally parasitize the nests of both species. House finches, more abundant than purples in urban areas, are exposed to frequent predation by domestic cats, as well as by American crows and blue jays. Mites frequently infest house finch nests, especially those that are repeatedly used. Disease epidemics, often prevalent in large populations of a species, include a widespread mycoplasma infection that affects the eyes of house finches, often encrusting them and swelling them shut.

Focus. The red pigment of both male finches is echinenone, metabolized from beta-carotene found in many plant sources, especially red fruits. Red coloring in males increases as they age.

Biologists continue to marvel at the house finch's explosive increase in the northeastern United States during the past fifty years. In Michigan, for example, none were seen before 1972. Populations grew exponentially through the 1980s until, in some urban areas

today, they outnumber house sparrows. Unlike European starlings and house sparrows, this is not an alien immigrant, though its rates of increase and dispersal resemble those of alien organisms. Thus its rapid spread offers unique opportunities for study. Biologists worry, however, that the hardy, adaptable house finches may displace other, less aggressive native birds, though current data show little sign of this.

All eastern U.S. house finches are ancestrally native to southern California. Trappers illegally shipped many Hollywood finches or red-headed linnets, as they were called, to New York City in 1940 for sale as cagebirds. Threatened with prosecution there, some pet dealers released their birds, which soon began to thrive in Long Island. By 1950, the species was pushing north, south, and west, spreading across the entire eastern continent over the next forty years. This expansion has occurred by two dispersal modes: diffusion, a gradual incremental process; and jump dispersal, in which a few birds establish satellite colonies in the vanguard of parent populations. The original California population at the same time expanded eastward. Today the two populations are bridging North America in the plains states, thus achieving continentwide distribution.

How to account for such vigor? Birds go where habitats invite them, and many researchers believe that the house finch explosion reflects urban and suburban growth, which provides numerous new habitats for the birds. Yet the likewise urban-loving house sparrow is declining, a trend that cannot entirely be attributed to house finch competition. The house finch's adaptiveness may relate to its opportunism in seeking nest sites and food and to its cohesive social structure. Unlike house sparrows, house finches show rigid dominance hierarchies in which each bird knows its place in the flock. They also show reversed sex dominance, rare in passerine birds: Winter females dominate males, and yearling males dominate older, redder males. These interactions are often visible at yard feeders.

You will find the scientific literature loaded with contradictory information about house finches. For example, they may wander as far as five hundred miles in winter, yet they are considered essentially sedentary; they are cold tolerant but adapt poorly to low temperatures; they often reuse previous nests but usually rebuild for each brood; they drive out house sparrows, but the latter are socially dominant over them; they compete with house sparrows for food but not nest sites, or vice versa; and so on. Probably all of these statements are correct for certain times and places; if so, we have only begun to measure the profile of the house finch. Clearly, this newcomer poses many questions that remain to be answered . . . or asked.

Purple finches have survived to ten years, but their life span probably averages three or four years.

The purple finch is New Hampshire's state bird.

House Sparrow
(Passer domesticus)

Old World sparrow family (Passeridae). This ubiquitous, six-inch-long sparrow thrives almost everywhere people live. Males have a gray cap, white cheeks, and black throat and bib. Male bills are blacker in spring and summer. Females and juveniles are dingy brown with no distinctive markings. The unmemorable song voiced by both sexes is a two- or three-part phrase of chirrups, background noise to a busy street; single-note chirps are also common.

Close relatives. The total of twenty-three *Passer* species are all native to Eurasia and Africa. In North America, the Eurasian tree sparrow (*P. montanus*), also an introduced species, resides in areas of Missouri and southern Illinois. Other family members include the pipits (*Anthus*), wagtails (*Motacilla*), and weavers (*Ploceus*).

Behaviors. Birders of a certain age grew up knowing this bird as the English sparrow. Although it was indeed introduced to America from England, it was also an immigrant there, having arrived from the European continent some two thousand years ago. Today, because of natural dispersion and deliberate introductions, it abundantly inhabits almost every temperate region of the globe. Superbly adapted to utilize habitats created by people, it has shadowed the spread of humankind through history and continues to rival rock pigeons, starlings, and dandelions as one of humanity's foremost biotic associates. Yet house sparrow distribution, though widespread, is patchy: These birds, once established, become relatively sedentary and seldom fly across areas of unsuitable habitat, such as wetlands or dense forests.

The hallmark of house sparrows is gregariousness. They feed, dust-bathe, water-bathe, roost (both day and night), and sometimes nest in communal flocks. Their sociability becomes most conspicuous—especially from summer through midwinter—at roost sites. Immense flocks often gather at these locales before sunset, noisily chirping and shifting positions. Birds may arrive from three or four miles away to settle communally for the night, often gathering at preroosting sites before approaching the primary roost in small groups. As relatively late sleepers, they seldom leave the night roost until after sunrise. Midday roosting of smaller congregations for an hour or so is also common. Unlike most gregarious birds, house sparrows show no rigid social structure or peck order; though aggressive interactions do occur, they seem largely circumstantial and inconsistent. A common habit is tail-flicking when perched, a sign of apprehension.

House sparrows reside year-round throughout most of their range, though northern populations often shift southward during periods of extreme cold. Nest building or repair occurs more or less continually except for a brief period in late summer.

Spring. Many house sparrows pair and use the same nest site for life. By early spring, light tips of the male's throat feathers have worn off to reveal the black bib breeding plumage, and courtship activities are well advanced. Small male flocks chase single female birds, performing hop-and-bow displays in front of them, and single males loudly chirp from perches near a nest site. These behaviors, though most prevalent in spring and fall, may be seen at any season. Pairs set about repairing previously used nests or rebuilding new ones. Territories average about two hundred feet or less surrounding the nest. Most actual nesting begins about April in the North, March in the South, but many February nesting dates are also on record. Human antipathy toward the house sparrow, especially earlier in this century, often extended to the birds' frequent copulations. Describing their "conspicuous venery," one sparrow hater fumed that "the male suffers from satyriasis, the female from nymphomania."

EGGS AND YOUNG: usually four or five; eggs white or greenish white, brown speckled. INCUBATION: by female; about thirteen days. FEEDING OF YOUNG: by both sexes; insects. FLEDGING: fifteen to seventeen days.

Summer. Fledglings continue to be fed, often by the male parent, for a week or so while the female begins renesting. Accounts differ as to whether females always reuse the same nest or sometimes move to a vacant one. Typically a pair raises two or three broods through September, occasionally more and later into fall. All-juvenile flocks feed and roost together through summer. After nesting ends, house sparrows molt into new plumage; males acquire light-tipped throat feathers, obscuring their new black bibs. Adult birds now join the juvenile flocks, deserting their nest sites to feed in grainfields and weedy, overgrown pastures.

Fall. In northern populations, a resurgence of territoriality occurs in late fall, with pairs and widowed mates returning to their spring and summer nest sites. Most juveniles disperse a mile or so from their birth sites, but some may return to the original colony to compete for available nesting space.

Winter. House sparrows use their nests through winter for roosting and shelter, defending them vigorously from neighboring sparrows. Juveniles continue to roost communally. As days begin to lengthen, nest site prospecting, courtship activities, mate replacement for widowed birds, and pairing of unmated birds begin to occur. A second dispersal of the previous fall's juveniles, as they seek nest sites and mates, may also occur. House sparrow females are dominant over males in winter, a behavior visible at yard feeders.

Ecology. Human and house sparrow habitats are virtually the same. Birds residing in urban areas usually look grayish and dingy, quite unlike rural house sparrows, which often appear neater and cleaner, with considerably lighter plumage. City air pollution presumably accounts for the difference.

For nesting, house sparrows favor outside crevices and crannies in houses, barns, and other buildings. Tree nesting usually occurs only when other sites are lacking. Nest sites are often located near a dependable food source, such as a barnyard or trash bin. Almost any sort of cavity can be used. Birdhouses, including colonial martin houses, are quickly claimed. Dense ivy growth on vertical walls and thick-foliaged ornamental plantings provide both nesting and roosting cover. Both sexes load the cavity with dried grasses and weeds, and sometimes cloth and string as well. Nest lining often consists of poultry feathers or fine grasses. Observers have reported that some house sparrows bruise and place pieces of tansy leaves, a possible parasite repellent, in the nest. Vine and tree nests are bulky, globular masses of vegetation with side openings. Occasionally house sparrows adopt swallow nests or build nests in the exterior walls of large, occupied hawk nests.

House sparrows are primarily ground-feeding seed eaters, despite the nineteenth-century propaganda extolling their virtues as a biological control on insects. A single house sparrow, it is estimated, consumes six to eight pounds of food—mostly grains—per year. Insects and spiders form only about 10 percent of the diet, mainly during the lengthy nesting season. Prey includes the Japanese beetle, a pervasive yard pest, caterpillars, and cankerworms. Grasshoppers, crickets, and ants are also frequently consumed.

In the spring, house sparrows often feed destructively on fruit tree buds. They also consume flower and grass fragments, shredding petals of apple blossoms, peas, beans, and others; in England, they seem to favor yellow flowers. In summer and fall, the diet becomes almost wholly granivorous, as the birds move into fields—seldom more than two miles from the breeding area. There they consume ripening wheat, oats, and sorghum and scavenge much waste grain, such as cracked corn. Field feeding occurs in tight flocks, usually within five yards of the field edge near hedgerows or other cover. In lawns and weedy fields, house sparrows also consume large quantities of ragweed, crabgrass, bristlegrass, and knotweed seeds, among others. Occasionally they raid orchards, pecking at fruits. Birdseed, elm seeds, organic garbage, and chicken-feed are common yard and barnyard foods.

House sparrows compete with almost all other cavity-nesting birds for tree holes, nest boxes, even using the ground holes of bank swallows. Their invasion and destruction of eggs and nestlings in already-occupied cavities are common occurrences; one observer compiled a list of seventy bird species that have been molested at times by house sparrows. Unless placed in suitable habitats, but sometimes even then, nest boxes erected for eastern bluebirds or purple martins may quickly attract house sparrows. House finches, recent invaders over most of the northeastern United States, have probably become the house sparrows' foremost competitors for food, though in most one-on-one competitive situations the more aggressive sparrows usually win. Summer and fall competitors in grainfields include blackbird and European starling flocks.

Raptors, American crows, and common grackles sometimes attack house sparrows. Nest predators, including black rat snakes and raccoons, take a toll as well. Many house sparrows are killed by heavy rain or sleet storms and collisions with automobiles. Because of their long occupancy, nests frequently become ridden with mites. The birds acquire and transmit other parasites in poultry yards and hog pens, where house sparrows often hang out. Persistent removal of nests and water spraying of roosts are probably the best human means of controlling house sparrow populations.

Focus. The record longevity for a wild house sparrow is thirteen years, but the average life span is probably two years or less. Nobody professes to like the little tramps—or can doubt that they are here to stay. Yet house sparrows have declined along with their food sources since their period of greatest abundance (1910–20) in North America. Animal feed and horse manure, a staple source of undigested grain, no longer litter city streets.

Multiple house sparrow introductions and establishment of house sparrow populations across North America occurred over a thirty-six-year period (1850–86). Many so-called experts initially hailed the bird as a biological weapon that would soon wipe out irruptive, foliage-eating inchworm caterpillars, especially the elm spanworm (*Ennomos subsignarius*). Once introduced, the sparrows quickly dispersed along highways and railroads, where waste grain and human garbage invited them to thrive. By 1890, the house sparrow's aggressive habits, omnivorous diet, competition with native birds, and increasing abundance had developed into a colossal ecological headache. Thus began the Great Sparrow War, a conflict marked by loud verbal fireworks. Die-hard sparrow defenders, led by Thomas Brewer, and the "I-told-you-so" camp of Elliott Coues, both prominent ornithologists, radically overstated their cases while science took a backseat. Brewer's arguments consisted mainly of denying the overwhelming data; Coues, a master of withering invective who labeled house sparrows "animated manure machines," and others blamed the birds for all sorts of hardly relevant environmental and social problems, including the scarcity of reliable household servants. Contrary to Coues's dire predictions, house sparrows never stripped the vast grainfields of the Great Plains; they remained most numerous in the cities, close to their human benefactors. And contrary to Brewer's optimism, the elm spanworm remains abundantly with us. In 1931, the prestigious American Ornithologists' Union finally allowed that this species had become a North American bird.

The Great Sparrow War amounted to a vastly entertaining show of sound and fury—but something else, too. Its surprising effect was a kind of national consciousness raising. Only rich people could afford to buy copies of Audubon's splendid bird folios, but two scholars with attitude enlivened the curiosity of the man in the street, where most house sparrows were. More people started looking at birds as creatures worthy of study and interest. Thus this dingy, disreputable immigrant helped democratize an eccentric specialty into the passion and pastime of increasingly numerous observers. The house sparrow, in some sense, trailed environmental awareness in its messy wake.

House sparrows also give us insights into the process of speciation, the way evolution works. Since its introduction to America, the bird has developed many geographical variations in size and plumage patterns, illustrating the operation of natural selection on sparrow gene pools.

House Wren
(Troglodytes aedon)

Creeper, wren, and gnatcatcher family (Certhiidae). All wrens have slender, slightly down-curved bills and often cock their tails upward. At five inches or less, the house wren, the most common North American wren, ranks midway in size among other wren species. It can be identified by its gray-brown color, lack of a pronounced white eye line, and stuttering, bubbling song. When alarmed or aggressive, it often voices a staccato chatter. Sexes look alike.

Close relatives. The only other northeastern wren of the same genus is the winter wren (*T. troglodytes*). Other eastern species include the Carolina wren (*Thryothorus ludovicianus*), Bewick's wren (*Thryomanes bewickii*), marsh wren (*Cistothorus palustris*), and sedge wren (*C. platensis*). Western U.S. species include the canyon wren (*Catherpes mexicanus*), rock wren (*Salpinctes obsoletus*), and cactus wren (*Campylorhynchus brunneicapillus*). More than sixty wren species range worldwide. Other northeastern family members include the brown creeper (*Certhia americana*) and the blue-gray gnatcatcher (*Polioptila caerulea*).

Behaviors. The male house wren's loud, gurgling song often sounds incessantly in spring and summer. Females sing occasionally, too. Native Chippewas, saddling this bird with even more syllables than its Latin name, gave it a name meaning "making big noise for its size." For its size, it also manifests extremely aggressive behaviors toward other birds; to a house wren, almost any other nesting bird in its territory threatens competition. It often claims all nest cavities anywhere near its own. If these cavities are occupied by any bird smaller than woodpeckers, punctured eggs or dead nestlings are the common result. House wrens may likewise attack open, noncavity nests. What one observer called this "Nazi trait" of house wrens may distress some bird lovers who discover wren mayhem in their bluebird boxes. Some studies suggest that unmated wrens are the main egg-destroying culprits.

House wrens are migratory birds with strong site fidelity to their previous breeding territories. Their breeding range spans the continent from southern Canada to the southeastern United States.

Spring. Older males arrive on the breeding range in April, preceding females (which precede yearling males) by a week or two. By song, a male establishes, or reestablishes, his territory of about half an acre or more. He explores every potential cavity site in his territory—in trees, fence posts, nest boxes—and clears them of old nesting material. Then he begins preliminary nest building in up to seven cavities. In nest boxes already occupied by such residents as tree swallows or eastern bluebirds, he may build atop the nest. Sometimes he lays only a base of dead twigs and other times almost fills the cavity with them, often leaving a single twig protruding from the entrance hole. Females, when they arrive, inspect all of these dummy nests. In mid-May, they select one for the actual nest, finishing it off with a deep cup of finer materials: grasses, plant fibers, feathers, insect cocoons, and bits of rubbish.

EGGS AND YOUNG: six to eight; eggs white, thickly speckled with reddish brown dots. INCUBATION: by female; about two weeks. FEEDING OF YOUNG: by both sexes; insects. FLEDGING: about seventeen days.

Summer. Most breeding house wrens raise two broods in a season. The male may exhibit polygyny, mating with two or more females that nest in his territory. Pair bonds also may shift to new partners between broods. After the first brood fledges in June, parent birds continue feeding the young for about two weeks. Then the female begins another nesting cycle. The male continues caring for the first brood while maintaining his territory and sometimes attracting new mates. Second broods usually fledge by early August, male singing declines, and the birds become much more secretive. The annual feather molt occurs in late summer; new plumage is darker and grayer than the breeding plumage.

Fall. Skulkers now in dense woodland underbrush, house wrens still voice an occasional, more subdued version of territorial song. Most depart their breeding range in September and early October.

Winter. House wren winter range extends from the Carolinas south along the coastal states into Mexico and northern Central America. The birds remain mostly silent and inconspicuous, foraging singly or in pairs,

The Carolina wren is becoming increasingly common in states where it used to be fairly rare. Like the house wren, it is a frequent backyard visitor. It's distinguished by its prominent white eye stripe and loud "tea-kettle, tea-kettle" song.

usually in dense thickets and undergrowth. As spring nears, the males begin to vocalize brief snatches of song. The lighter brown breeding plumage results from erosion of the darker feather tips acquired during the fall molt.

Ecology. House wrens favor edge habitats—thickets, open woodlots, orchards, and forest openings. Palmetto thickets, brushy tangles, and swampy undergrowth are typical winter habitats.

For nesting, the birds prefer open edge areas with extended visibility. It isn't Mister Loudmouth that persuades Jenny to linger but the aspect of his acre. The quality of a male's territory—that is, its insect resources and amount of properly spaced vegetation—

also may determine whether, and how often, polygyny occurs. House wrens are noted for the variety of nest sites they may improvise; tin cans, flowerpots, car radiators, boots, hats, and pockets in hanging clothes are only a few of the many places they may choose.

House wrens feed almost entirely on insects and spiders; grasshoppers, beetles, bugs (including negro bugs, stink bugs, and leafhoppers), and caterpillars rank high in their diet.

Nest-site competitors include woodpeckers, great crested flycatchers, eastern bluebirds, European starlings, black-capped chickadees, tree swallows, house sparrows, deer mice, and even paper wasps. Relatively few of these can withstand house wren persistence in claiming a cavity.

Foremost predators include cats and other house wrens, which occasionally raid nests outside their territories.

Focus. To wrens we owe the institution of the annual Christmas bird count, conducted by the National Audubon Society since 1900 to offset the then-widespread practice of Christmas bird shoots. Naturalist Charles L. Horn described these shoots as "the connecting link between the modern Christmas count and the medieval Hunting of the Wren," an annual rite in which a wren, sym-bolizing the king, was slain for good luck. Wrens remained untouchable at all other times of year. In Germany, the wren (*T. troglodytes,* our winter wren species) is still called *zaunkönig,* "hedge king." Why such a small bird—rather than a large raptor, for example—was chosen to represent royalty may have conveyed a message in itself.

House wrens are probably much more abundant today than in presettlement times because of the increase in edge habitats created by lumbering and farming. Where forests regrow, house wren populations usually decline.

Mallard
(Anas platyrhynchos)

This most common North American duck is also among the easiest to identify. Drakes show a glossy green head separated from the chestnut brown breast by a white neck ring; grayish back and sides; black, upcurled feathers centering the white tail tip; and yellow bills. Hens are straw brown streaked with darker brown, have orange bills splotched with black, and have whitish tails (a useful identity mark in separating this species from black duck hens). Both sexes show a violet-blue speculum (wing patch) bordered by white bars, visible in flight, and orange feet. The hen's loud, decrescendo quacking is virtually identical to that of American black duck hens. Drakes utter low "reeb-reeb" and "kwek" notes. Average length is two feet or slightly less.

Close relatives. American black ducks (*A. rubripes*) are so closely related to mallards that hybrids commonly occur. The mottled duck (*A. fulvigula*) is genetically similar. Less commonly, mallards also hybridize with almost all the other eight *Anas* species of North America.

Behaviors. Mallards are the most abundant ducks not only in North America but also globally in the Northern Hemisphere. In the eastern United States, along with mute swans, they are often the typical park waterfowl, associating comfortably with humans and easily becoming semidomesticated, sometimes to the point of being pigeonlike nuisances. Wild mallards, however, are a different story, seldom closely approachable by people. Though many mallards migrate, they may be seen year-round wherever open water exists except in their farthest-north breeding range. They often fly in large flocks of forty to sixty, sometimes many more, with relatively slow wingbeats in Vs or U-shaped formations.

Many of their social behaviors, especially courtship, closely resemble those of American black ducks, with which they often associate, but the two species also exhibit subtle differences. Sometimes, where they coexist (that is, almost everywhere in eastern North America except Atlantic coastal marshes), mallards seem to dominate interactions, but whether this is a simple reflection of larger mallard numbers or of innately greater mallard aggressiveness remains largely unknown (see Ecology on page 115). In other places, however, the two species seem behaviorally *conspecific* (as one species), and conflict is seldom observed. Solitary mallards are seldom seen; the birds are either paired, leading broods of young, or in flocks. Mallard range includes all of North America from the Arctic into central Mexico and almost the entire Northern Hemisphere worldwide. They have also been introduced into Hawaii, Australia, and New Zealand.

Spring. The mallard's North American breeding range encompasses the northern third of the United States to the arctic treeline, reaching the greatest density in the Canadian prairie provinces—the so-called "waterfowl factory" for the Central flyway. Most mallards that have wintered in the southern United States migrate north in February and March,

are already paired, and often begin to nest by late March. Travel to the northern range continues through April, most hens homing to their natal or previous nesting sites *(philopatry)*, their new mates accompanying them. Not all hens return to their previous breeding sites, however; food availability, habitat conditions, previous nesting success, and mate choice influence the rate of philopatry. Details of nesting chronology closely resemble those of black ducks.

April is the primary mallard nesting month throughout much of its range. The hen selects a nest site during evening reconnaissance flights, cruising low over marsh or field, followed closely by the drake. Paired drakes likewise establish one or more shoreline territories or waiting areas up to a quarter acre in size; these defended areas are separate from, but usually within one hundred yards of, the nest, which is not defended. The hen joins the drake in these areas during intervals off the nest. Size of the home range varies greatly, depending upon habitat and mallard density. As in other dabbling ducks, the drakes abandon nesting hens several days after incubation begins—or is it the other way round? One study suggests that hens may initiate drake desertion by abandoning the drake waiting areas. Despite the oft-repeated assertion that drakes invariably desert the hens during incubation, my own observations convince me that split-up of the mallard pair often occurs much later or less regularly than the experts tell us; I have witnessed too many instances of wild pairs swimming with broods to account it a rare occurrence. Yet many, probably most, drakes do fly to large marshes during hen incubation. There they gather in large flocks and, from May into summer, enter henlike eclipse plumage and become flightless for three to four weeks or longer.

Many broods hatch in May. The nest is often placed far from suitable brood-raising habitat, and hen and brood must swim or walk for a mile or more over a period of days, even after reaching the nearest water. Relatively high occurrences of extrapair copulations and multiple paternity are seen in mallards; in one study, at least 48 percent of broods revealed, by genetic testing, the involvement of more than 1 drake. When a paired drake mates with a hen other than his mate, it is often a quick, aggressive action *(forced copulation)* not preceded by courtship displays. Some biologists suggest that this behavior is a secondary reproductive strategy for both drakes and hens, helping assure the likelihood of fertilized eggs. This behavior is now seen to be fairly common among many so-called "monogamous" birds.

EGGS AND YOUNG: eight to ten; eggs greenish buff or whitish. INCUBATION: by hen; average of twenty-eight days. FLEDGING: fifty to sixty days.

Summer. The hen broods her ducklings for about twelve hours before leading them to the nearest water. Nest failure or predation usually results in a renesting attempt by hens; this could explain why some drakes remain paired beyond the initial incubation period. Also, unpaired drakes remain in breeding condition longer into the summer than paired drakes. As soon as the juveniles fledge (July or later), hens gather on marshes or remain in the rearing area during their own molt and flightless period. Summer is a time of movement off the breeding area as the birds assemble in traditional gathering places, usually large marshes. Most drakes have attained their new flight feathers and breeding plumage by mid-August. Toward late summer, flocks may build to thousands in size as hens and juveniles join the drakes. Mallard families have by this time ceased to exist as individual members disperse to various flocks and assembly locales. Pairing often begins in late summer as courtship behaviors recommence.

Fall. Mallards are generally late migrators, moving southward no sooner than weather forces them and no farther than they must to obtain food. Consequently, their migration is often irregular and prolonged, sometimes not peaking until November or December. The largest numbers of mallards travel from the Canadian prairies down the Mississippi flyway, sometimes called the mallard flyway for the millions of ducks that travel through and winter in this river corridor. Courtship flights and displays intensify through fall and winter; most adult mallards are paired by late October. Average fall populations consist almost equally of adult mallards and young of the year.

Winter. Mallards winter most abundantly between latitudes 34 and 36 degrees N in eastern Arkansas and western Mississippi. In smaller numbers, wintering populations extend to the Gulf and central Mexico, and northward to the Great Lakes and New England. Sudden spells of snow and cold will often send them south from the northernmost regions in dead of winter; then, as a warm spell sets in, they may wing back to the recently vacated area. Many, if not most, wintering mallards in New England join park mallard flocks, probably decoyed by the resident ducks. Hen mallards begin their pre-

basic molt in late fall or winter, replacing all body plumage in a period of six weeks or so. By early January, at least 80 percent of mallards are paired, though typically a few hens remain unpaired until their return to the breeding range. The paired ducks tend to segregate from the unpaired by moving to smaller, more secluded wetland spaces. Unpaired drakes remain gregarious in flocks in the larger marshes. By February, many mallards are beginning to leave their wintering areas. They "race spring itself," wrote one observer, "often forging ahead to be forced into temporary retreat by late winter blizzards."

Ecology. Optimal mallard habitat consists of a permanent marsh surrounded by small, shallow ponds, but mallards also inhabit other wetland complexes—swamps, lakes, and streams. Marsh habitat is especially important for brood rearing and for cover during

molting. In the Canadian prairie provinces, where mallard breeding density is greatest, spring ponds often dry up as the season advances to summer. Thus hens may find themselves far from water when broods hatch, necessitating long overland treks to water.

Most mallards nest on the ground within 100 yards of water, often in marsh growth. Not uncommonly, however, they also nest far from water in upland meadows and hayfields or on dikes, muskrat lodges, and small islands. One study found that nesting success in marsh sites was about 40 percent higher than in drier upland sites. Whatever cover type mallards choose, the nest is usually placed in dense plant growth about two feet high. The hen scrapes a nest bowl, rimming it with fragments of vegetation and adding down as incubation proceeds. Often the final structure is a bulky mass. Exceptions to the typical nest placement often occur, but as waterfowl biologist Joe Johnson states, "the ancestry of females choosing strange nesting sites [such as forested areas, tree hollows, flower boxes, landscape plantings] is worth questioning, as many semidomestic [mallards] have been released."

Primarily seedeaters, mallards consume a large variety of wetland food items. Seeds of wild rice, pondweeds, and smartweeds are favored in the Northeast, as are wild celery, barnyard grass, corn, and acorns. Fields of wheat and barley stubble are frequently invaded by feeding flocks; mallards, more than any other duck, have adapted to agricultural land use and in some areas consume large amounts of spring-planted wheat and barley. Given a choice, the birds seem to prefer their native wetland foods, but this option appears increasingly limited. Mallards also eat aquatic insect larvae and mussels—about 10 percent of the spring and summer diet.

Mallard-black duck interactions have been discussed in the previous account. Mallards have been known to hybridize with some forty other duck species, producing mostly sterile offspring. Many ducks, including mallards, occasionally lay eggs in nests of other birds of their own or other duck species. Mallards are often nest-parasitized by redhead ducks in areas where the two species overlap.

Mallard nest predators include American crows, skunks, foxes, coyotes, and ground squirrels. Hayfield mowing, trampling by cattle, and flooding also destroy many nests. Lead shot ingestion remains a toxic hazard for mallards. A blood parasite common to both mallards and black ducks, causing much duckling mortality, is the protozoan *Leucocytozoon simondi*, transmitted by black-flies. In some northeastern duck populations, 100 percent of the ducks may be infected.

Focus. Many mallard populations stem from propagation by game farms and pen-raised park flocks. Releases of these semi-domesticated fowl have no doubt helped swell mallard range expansion throughout the Northeast. Until the twentieth century, mallards were mainly prairie ducks, rarely seen from the Great Lakes eastward. Before 1900, only occasional wanderers had been spotted in New England. Thoreau makes no mention of the bird in his journals; he apparently never saw one. Land clearing evidently encouraged the eastward spread of the species, bringing it into frequent contact with its conspecific, the American black duck, which occupied eastern woodland habitats.

Like black ducks, most breeds of farmyard ducks, including the white Pekin (but not the Muscovy), are basically mallards in genetic makeup. Individual mallards have survived for three decades and longer in the wild, but average longevity is much less owing to high annual mortality rates. Some 50 percent or more of the mallard population dies each year; hunting pressure plus natural losses account for this figure. Because it is the most numerous game duck, the mallard is also the most widely hunted. In most years, however, more than one offspring per adult survives, thus maintaining or increasing population levels. In years when production falls below this ratio, as it did during the 1980s, the population declines.

The name *mallard* (from the French *maslard*, "wild duck") is actually a sexist label, with the Latin root *masculus*, "male." In Old World lexicons, evidently, the entire species thus became identified with the gender.

Mourning Dove
(Zenaida macroura)

Our most abundant native dove is a foot-long brown bird with a pointed, white-edged tail and a black spot behind each eye. Male birds show a rose-tinted breast and grayish cap, while females are duller brown on breast and head. The distinctive cooing notes are one of the most familiar bird sounds of spring.

Close relatives. The white-winged dove (*Z. asiatica*) has a southwestern U.S. range; the zenaida dove (*Z. aurita*), a West Indies species, occasionally appears in Florida. Other family members include the common ground dove (*Columbina passerina*), the Inca dove (*C. inca*), and the rock pigeon (*Columba livia*).

Behaviors. Be reminded when you observe mourning doves of their extinct North American relative, the passenger pigeon (*Ectopistes migratorius*), which they resemble in general form; passenger pigeons were larger, with reddish breasts. Mourning doves are tree nesters and ground feeders. Except when nesting, they are gregarious, often feeding and roosting in flocks. They walk and drink like rock pigeons. In flight, their wings make characteristic whistling sounds, especially when the birds are alarmed or displaying, though they can also fly silently. Overhead, a mourning dove can sometimes resemble a sharp-shinned hawk or American kestrel, but the dove's pointed tail is the giveaway.

Mourning doves are the only native North American birds to breed in every state—they have even been introduced to Hawaii. Most doves migrate south in the fall, but increasing numbers remain on their northern range over winter.

Spring. The plaintive cooing notes that give this bird its name are usually uttered by an unattached male advertising for a mate, though females and mated males occasionally voice this call, too. Males often use favorite perches for calling, but the perch-coo does not signify territoriality (beyond the perch itself), since the birds may range and call over a large area. Migrants arrive back at their birth or previous nesting locales in late winter or early spring; from then through summer, courtship and nesting activities are continual. Males bow and coo in front of females and perform a flap-glide flight, ending in a long, spiraling glide. The short coo, a briefer version of the perch-coo uttered by either sex, often signals selection of a nest site. Three-bird chases occur when an unmated male pursues the female of a mated pair. Perch-cooing ceases when a pair bond is formed.

Territoriality begins with nest building. The territory may radially extend fifty or more yards from the nest but often shrinks in size as incubation proceeds. Males select the nest site and collect sticks from the ground, bringing them to the female; sometimes he stands on her back as if supervising her arrangement of sticks. More than two eggs in a nest usually indicates *brood parasitism*, or dump nesting—an invading female dove has added one or two eggs to those already present. A parent bird, if frightened off the nest after the eggs hatch, may launch into a dis-traction display, fluttering on the ground. Mourning doves are monogamous throughout the nesting year; sometimes the pair bond lasts over several nesting seasons.

EGGS AND YOUNG: two; eggs white. INCUBATION: by female at night, male during the day; about two weeks. FEEDING OF YOUNG: by both sexes; pigeon's milk and regurgitated seeds, insects. FLEDGING: about two weeks.

Summer. Fledglings may roost in the nest tree and follow the parents about for ten or twelve days. Juvenile doves can be recognized by their shorter tails, the scaled appearance of wing and breast feathers, and lack of head spots. Adult females may begin renesting several days after their first offspring fledge, often while the male is still feeding them away from the nest. In their northern range, mourning doves average two or three matings per season, an average nesting cycle requiring about thirty-two days. A small percentage of doves are still nesting in September and October. Young doves often gather in all-juvenile flocks that feed, roost, and wander together. As nesting ceases, adult pairs also form flocks that often merge.

Fall. From September to November, mourning doves molt into a drabber winter plumage. Migration timing and sequence appear related to age and sex—a system called *differential migration*—though some mixing does occur. Juvenile flocks begin staging on electric wires and other perches and start moving south in late August and September; adult female flocks and finally male flocks follow. The young birds also move farthest south, some to Panama and Costa Rica. Most doves, however, winter in the southeastern

United States and Mexico. Doves migrate leisurely, both day and night at fairly low altitude in flocks of fifty birds or less. Banding records indicate that movements of nineteen to thirty-four miles per day are average and that the Wabash River valley in Indiana marks the boundary between southeast- and southwest-migrating doves.

Winter. Many if not most resident doves of the southern United States remain in place and do not migrate farther south. Mourning dove winter range lies south of the thirty-ninth parallel. But small population segments, consisting mainly of males, remain in their northern breeding range, probably held by a reliable food supply such as waste or stored grains and yard feeders. Harsh winter weather takes a lethal toll on them each year; not uncommonly one sees frozen toes and feet on north-wintering doves. Wintering flocks in the South tend to mingle sexes, and dominance hierarchies, or peck orders, govern social relations within the flocks. Whether another plumage molt occurs before spring migration or spring breeding plumage results from wear of the winter plumage, as in several passerine bird species, remains uncertain.

Ecology. Mourning doves range over a broad spectrum of habitats. The basic environs are woodland edges, but agricultural land practices and suburban yards have expanded mourning dove options. Landscaped areas, hedgerows, and parks with a mix of trees and open areas attract, these birds. Because of such habitat expansion, probably many more mourning doves exist today in eastern North America than in presettlement times. This trend of expansion in both breeding and winter ranges has continued over the past century.

The nest, hardly a construction marvel, is a loose, flat platform, mostly unlined. Often it is so flimsy that the eggs can be seen from beneath. It is placed in a tree fork or, more often, on a horizontal branch up to forty feet high, occasionally even on the ground. The birds favor conifers, especially spruce, as well as hawthorn thickets. Though surprisingly strong for their frail appearance, branch nests often blow down in storms. Mourning doves build about 40 percent of their nests atop their own previous nests or on vacated nests of other birds, especially those of blue jays, American robins, and common grackles. Occasionally doves nest semicolonially, with several pairs building in the same tree.

In most areas, mourning dove diet consists almost entirely of seeds foraged from the ground and plant stalks. Most preferred are cereal grains and other grass family seeds, such as canary grasses, corn, common oat, wheat, millets, foxtail grasses, and panicums. Seed sources also include buckwheats, common ragweed, poke-weed, knotweeds, sunflowers, and white pine, all highly nutritive. Animal food is insignificant, most frequently snails taken during the nesting season for their calcium content. Sand and gravel grit are essential for dove digestion, and the birds also ingest salt, often along winter-salted roads.

There is little evidence of any large-scale food competition. Blackbird and house sparrow flocks scavenge grainfields where mourning doves feed; one study, however, indicated that blackbirds favor cracked corn damaged or scattered by harvesting or livestock, whereas doves consume mainly whole-kernel corn. Food competition probably becomes severe at times for north-wintering doves.

High on the list of mourning dove predators are domestic cats and dogs (though their ranking compared with hawk and owl predation may reflect observer bias). American crows sometimes consume the eggs. If the mourning dove's most important habitat benefactors are humans, so also are we their major predators. Mourning doves are classed as gamebirds in thirty-seven states, and fall hunting seasons harvest about fifty million doves annually—more than all other migratory wildfowl combined. Southeastern states account for more than half of this harvest.

Focus. Prehistoric native peoples consumed mourning doves as food; the birds figured prominently in Native American folklore and mythology, and various tribes still have dove clans. It was probably a migrating mourning dove blown off-course that greeted Columbus before his West Indies landfall in 1492. Early American explorers and naturalists named the bird turtledove, identifying it with its Eurasian relative of that name (_Streptopelia turtur_). English naturalist Mark Catesby first distinguished the differences for science in 1731. Nineteenth-century market hunters largely ignored mourning doves, since the larger, more trusting passenger pigeons were far easier to kill in quantity. In a few states, such as Michigan, which officially classifies doves as songbirds, the issue of declaring them a legal gamebird is highly controversial. Hunters generally favor it; birders and naturalists generally fight it. From a purely biological view, little evidence exists that hunting seasons severely affect mourning dove populations. Why one would consider them worthwhile shooting is another matter.

Banding studies indicate that about 75 percent of mourning doves live less than a year, mainly because of predation and weather factors, though life spans of twelve years and longer have been recorded.

Northern Cardinal
(Cardinalis cardinalis)

Both sexes of this eight- to nine-inch-long finch have a prominent, pointed topknot and a heavy, reddish bill with a black patch at its base. Male plumage is otherwise all red; females are brownish, showing red tinges on wings, tail, and crest. The cardinal's loud, clear whistles, often "whoit whoit whoit," "cheedle cheedle cheedle," or "what's here, what's here, here, here," occur in several variations, some of which resemble tufted titmouse song; a loud "chip!" is also characteristic.

Close relatives. The cardinal's southwestern U.S. counterpart is the pyrrhuloxia (*C. sinuatus*). Vermilion cardinals (*C. phoeniceus*) inhabit South America. Most of the five other species called cardinals are South American and Hawaiian emberizine finches.

Behaviors. One of the most familiar and colorful of the birds that frequent suburban yards, the cardinal resides year-round in most of its continually expanding range. Its rich, pure voice makes it most conspicuous in late winter and spring, but this bird remains relatively unshy at all seasons and often becomes a reliable visitor at yard feeders. One observer described the chunky, restless cardinal as "rather a clumsy fellow" when moving on the ground with its stiff, hopping gait. Though it loosely associates with other cardinals for much of the year, males often show aggressive dominance behaviors toward those that try to share a feeder, including its erstwhile mate. Breeding season hormones work changes as the pair bond grows stronger, and the birds become extremely attentive mates and parents.

Cardinals breed throughout eastern and central North America from southern Canada to the Gulf, and westward through Mexico to Guatemala.

Spring. Many, if not most, cardinals remain monogamously paired year-round. Territorial behaviors are well advanced by early spring, with males singing loudly from high perches. Females also sing, most frequently after the territory is established but before nesting begins in March to May. Listen for *countersinging,* in which cardinals on adjacent territories, as well as paired males and females on their own territories, alternate matching songs as if in imitative "sez-you" bouts. Cardinals aggressively chase other cardinals of the same sex that venture onto their territories, which are generally three to ten acres, but they tolerate the presence of opposite-sex cardinals. Cardinals are also very well known for shadow boxing, battling their own images, sometimes for lengthy periods, in reflective surfaces such as windows and auto hubcaps. Both sexes perform a lopsided, swaying courtship display when perched; males will also perform song flights and often feed their mates, tilting their heads sideways to do so, on both perches and nests. Females build the nests, often accompanied by their mates as they gather materials. Nesting for the cardinal usually begins in late April.

EGGS AND YOUNG: usually three; eggs grayish or bluish white, brown spotted. INCUBATION: by female, which is fed by male; eggs are also occasionally incubated by male; about twelve days. FEEDING OF YOUNG: by both sexes; regurgitated insects at first, then whole insects. FLEDGING: about ten days.

Summer. Many cardinal pairs raise two or more broods, and nesting may extend into August. Females build a new nest on the same territory, leaving their mates to feed the first-brood fledglings. Fledglings achieve independence in three to four weeks, when renesting parents sometimes drive them off. The annual molt begins in late summer, extending into fall.

Fall, Winter. The new male plumage, showing feather tips edged with gray, is somewhat duller than the scarlet breeding plumage, which is acquired during winter by simple wear of the gray edging. If you examine individual feathers of a male's body plumage, you will see that most of the feather length is gray; only the upper third or so is pigmented red, giving the cardinal its brilliance.

The pair bond becomes relatively lax as the birds join other cardinals in fall and winter groupings (flocking is too social a term for most cardinal aggregations). These groups are usually small, with six to twenty birds, but occasionally many more. Some wandering groups probably consist entirely of first-winter juveniles. Many cardinals remain in the breeding locality year-round, ranging no more than a few miles during their entire lifetime. About February, males start to become more tolerant of close female presence and begin courtship behaviors and early-morning singing.

Ecology. Northern cardinals favor open-edge habitats, and originally they probably occupied forest openings. Today just about any thicket vegetation, wet or dry, in forest or suburban yard, may host cardinals. Isolated patches of dense shrubbery seem to be the vital habitat element, conditions ideally met in many human residential areas, as well as along roadsides and in overgrown fields and hedgerows.

Nests, seldom placed over six feet high, often occupy the densest part of a thicket or brier tangle. Multiflora rose and honeysuckle hedges are frequent sites, as are hawthorns, lilac and gray dogwood shrubs, and thick-foliaged conifers. Securely placed in a vertical fork or mat of vines, nests consist of four more or less distinct layers of plant materials: a foundation of stiff twigs or weed stalks,

often stalks and seed bases of yellow avens (*Geum aleppicum*); leaves or bits of paper and bark strips; weed and grass stems; and a fine grass lining. Cardinals differ extensively in their nest-building styles. Some nests are compact and thickly lined; others are loose, flimsy, and unkempt, with little lining. Gray catbird nests, found in similar habitats, may resemble cardinal nests but are usually bulkier, contain many more foundation leaves, and are lined with rootlets. White-footed mice frequently use vacated cardinal nests as feeding platforms and may also load the nest with plant down and move in themselves.

Omnivorous in diet, cardinals consume a huge variety of plant and insect foods, the latter mainly during the breeding season. Caterpillars, grasshoppers, true bugs, beetles, and other small invertebrates constitute some 60 percent of the spring diet. The birds eat almost any kind of fruit, with wild grapes, dogwood fruits, and mulberries ranking high. Smartweeds, corn, oats, and sedges provide much of the seed diet; in winter, seeds of sumacs, vervains, and tulip trees are favored, and anyone who maintains a yard feeder knows how much these birds relish sunflower seeds.

The cardinal's foremost food and nest site competitor in many areas is the gray catbird, which usually dominates any interaction, often driving cardinals to the less optimal fringes of their mutual habitats. As a relatively recent arrival in much of its present northern range, the cardinal appears still in the process of adjusting, in an ecological sense, to prior resident species. Yet its year-round presence, habitat and diet opportunism, early and lengthy nesting season, and promptness to renest after predation give it many competitive advantages.

Cardinal nests fall victim to many predators, including blue racers and black rat and milk snakes; American crows, blue jays, and house wrens; gray, fox, and red squirrels; eastern chipmunks; and domestic cats. Brown-headed cowbirds frequently parasitize the nests, and cardinals raise many cowbird nestlings.

Focus. Cardinals have expanded their original southern U.S. range northward during this century, a trend that continues. They began their northward expansion up the Mississippi valley late in the last century. Appearing first as casual visitors in the North, they rapidly increased from 1910–70, after which their range expansion slowed. Reasons for their successful northward invasion remain speculative; frequently suggested possibilities are the abundance and increase of edge habitats, a period of mild winters during the early 1900s, and a more recent climatic warming trend. Much of their range expansion has apparently occurred in winter, as the birds gravitated toward yard feeders and fruit-rich swamps, thus establishing nuclei for local populations. Despite their southern origins, cardinals apparently suffer few lethal effects from cold, though I have occasionally found a cardinal frozen on the ground beneath evergreens after an exceptionally cold night.

Often called the redbird, the cardinal, named for the red-robed princes of the church, was once commonly trapped in the southern states and sold as a cagebird.

The cardinal's spectacular color does not always make it conspicuous, as paradoxical as that sounds. "If a species evolves to become brightly colored, and if it lives in shady green places," wrote biologist Stephen Fretwell, "red or blue are good colors to be." This is because deciduous foliage absorbs most of the blue and red spectra, shedding green light that is not readily reflected by red plumage in the shade. Thus in its nesting habitat, at least, the cardinal may become relatively inconspicuous.

Average yearly adult survival rate is estimated at about 50 percent. This bird's longevity record surpasses fifteen years, but two or three years is probably a typical life span.

Seven states—Illinois, Indiana, and Ohio being the northernmost—have named the northern cardinal their state bird. The cardinal outnumbers any other bird species for this distinction.

Northern Flicker
(Colaptes auratus)

This conspicuous, jay-size woodpecker (twelve to fourteen inches) is brown backed and speckled on the breast. It has a narrow black bib, black tail, and red patch at the nape of the neck. Males display a black facial smear, or mustache. A prominent white rump patch is visible when the bird flies; this mark plus the bird's deeply undulating flight are distinctive field characters. Its "wicka-wicka" and "klee-yer!" calls also identify it. Three North American subspecies vary in plumage details; our common northeastern flicker, with golden yellow underwings and tail, is sometimes called the yellow-shafted flicker (*C. a. auratus*).

Close relatives. In the western United States, the gilded flicker (*C. chrysoides*), once considered a subspecies, is now classified as a species. Where their ranges overlap, the red-shafted and yellow-shafted subspecies hybridize, producing intermediate forms. Some five other *Colaptes* species range into South America.

Behaviors. Their size, abundance, and conspicuous behaviors make northern flickers the most easily observed woodpeckers. The way they soar *up* to a perch when landing plus their loud call notes and variety of squeals and other sounds also call them to our attention.

Flickers spend much more time on the ground than other woodpeckers. On the ground, however, they are awkward walkers and scarcely move, usually feeding, sunning, or preening from a stationary position. Flickers are migrants, though small numbers often remain over winter in the north. Their breeding range extends throughout east-central North America, from upper Canada to the Gulf.

Spring. Migrant flickers move north during March nights in large, loose flocks. Males usually precede females by a few days. If both birds of a pair have survived from the year before, they rejoin on their previous territory, which the male reestablishes by drumming, calling, and displays. Commonly heard now is his "wicka-wicka-wicka" call (which "really *quickens* what was dead," observed Thoreau), accompanied by much head bobbing. Resonant drumming, sometimes described as like a drumroll or miniature pneumatic drill, is done by both sexes, often alternated with loud "klee-yer!" calls around the nest tree. By the time egg laying begins in May, the defended territory has usually shrunk from a half acre or more to the nest site vicinity.

EGGS AND YOUNG: five to eight; eggs white. INCUBATION: by both sexes (males at night); two weeks or less. FEEDING OF YOUNG: by both sexes; insects (males feed regurgitant). FLEDGING: about four weeks.

Summer. After fledging, the juveniles, both sexes of which show black cheek marks like adult males, remain in family groups and continue to be fed for several weeks. As with many woodpeckers, the parent birds often revive courtship displays for a brief period following fledging. This is the period when flickers seem to be everywhere. A behavior known as *anting* (described under **Ecology**), seen in many birds, is especially conspicuous in flickers and often noticeable at this season. By late summer, the juveniles have dispersed, pairs have split, and adult birds are undergoing their annual molt.

Fall. Juveniles now acquire their first adult plumage. Small, pre-migratory flocks assemble, may briefly revive some courtship displays, then join other flicker flocks as migration begins. Flying at night, most of the northern population travels no farther south than the Gulf states, though some fly to Cuba.

Winter. Winter range coincides with the permanent range of southern resident flickers, from the middle tier of states southward. Little social interaction occurs among the birds until late winter, when flocks begin to gather for northward migration.

Ecology. The flicker's ability to reside in a variety of habitats helps explain its success as North America's most abundant woodpecker. Open woodlands, forest edges, orchards, roadsides, parks, and suburban areas are typical habitats, which the birds favor over dense, mature forests.

More than any other woodpecker, flickers tend to reuse their previous nest cavities, though they also excavate new ones, often in a previously used tree. Their slightly curved bills make flickers weak excavators; a pair may start and abandon several holes before selecting a final site, often below fifteen feet in a well-decayed tree or in the dead top of a broken-off trunk. A female will occasionally lay an egg in the nest of another cavity-nesting bird, including red-headed and pileated woodpeckers, tree swallows, eastern bluebirds, and house sparrows.

At least half of the flicker's diet consists of insects. No other North American bird consumes as many ants. Flickers spend much of their time at ant mounds, licking into the tunnels with their extremely long, sticky tongues. The sticky substance, strongly alkaline, probably counteracts the formic acid ants contain. The birds also consume ground beetles and grasshoppers. In fall and winter, wild fruits become the staple, including berries of poison-ivy and Virginia creeper, dogwood and sumac fruits, cherries, and various nuts and grains.

As with all woodpeckers, strong competition exists for nest sites. Dead trees are also sought by red-headed and other woodpeckers. Flicker nest holes, whether occupied or vacant, attract eastern screech-owls, American kestrels, great crested flycatchers, European starlings, and red, gray, and flying squirrels. Soft, decayed wood, which flickers prefer, makes their excavated cavities highly vulnerable to predation by raccoons, which often claw open weak-walled nest cavities and consume eggs or nestlings.

Researchers disagree about the functions of *anting* behavior, in which the bird picks up ants and rubs them vigorously on its plumage. The traditional view is that the ants' formic acid acts as an insecticide or fungicide against feather and skin parasites. Anting often occurs during periods of high humidity, lending weight to the fungicidal theory. But other investigators find no correlation between anting and parasite or fungus presence; they speculate that anting, like sunning, is simply a comfort activity, stimulating the skin, especially during the summer molt. A recent theory suggests that anting forces the insects to expel their formic acid, thus making them more palatable to consume. Observed in more than two hundred bird species (mostly passerine) worldwide, anting needs many more detailed observations.

Focus. Flickers bear numerous vernacular names, including yellowhammer, goldenwing, pigeon woodpecker, and hairy wicket. The word *flicker*, according to one source, is an old English term for "one who strikes."

About one-third of all northeastern flickers show some degree of past genetic mixing with the western subspecies, the red-shafted flicker. Traces of red or orange in wings or tail are believed to be common indicators of such lineage.

Northern Mockingbird
(*Mimus polyglottos*)

This conspicuous, long-tailed, robin-size bird is drab grayish with large white wing and tail patches, which are best seen when it flies. A frequent mimic of other bird species, it utters snatches and phrases of various songs in its own musical, repetitive phrasings. Sexes look alike.

Close relatives. Nine other *Mimus* species plus some seven mockingbirds of different genera reside in Mexico, the West Indies, and South America.

Behaviors. Ornithologist Frank M. Chapman called the Northern Mockingbird our "national songbird." One of the most accomplished vocal mimics in the bird world, the mockingbird advertises its presence loudly and incessantly, often from a conspicuous perch. Its song largely consists of multiple plagiarism, bits and pieces lifted from the repertoires of almost any other bird it has heard, plus frog croaks, dog barks, cat meows, gate squeaks, and tire squeals. One Indian tale, however, reverses the sequence: The mockingbird taught all the other birds to sing, so *they* are the plagiarists. In any case, no two mockingbirds ever sing exactly alike. A single song bout may last up to ten minutes, a medley that itself may differ from the bird's next or past performances. It may repeat particular notes up to a dozen times before switching to another arrangement. Some male mockingbirds, writes researcher Randall Breitwisch, "have repertoires in excess of two hundred songs, certainly the acoustic equivalent of the peacock's tail." Probably their repertoire has no upper limit, as the birds add new songs and sounds throughout their lives. For birders, mockingbird medleys of stolen song offer a postgraduate course in listening. Human ears are easily fooled by mimicry, but most bird species that mockingbirds imitate seem to ignore them (although this is a subject that may bear further investigation).

Note the mockingbird's wing action. In flight, the bird plows through the air like "oaring an old rowboat," as one observer wrote. As it drops to the ground, where it forages much of the time, it often holds its wings aloft for an instant after landing, much as some shorebirds do. While foraging, it slowly elevates and spreads its wings, displaying its white patches. Some researchers suggest that this wing-flashing behavior may startle insects into movement, making them easier to capture.

Highly aggressive toward territorial intruders, mockingbirds seem to relish diving upon dogs, cats, and snakes, with other mockers often joining in. They also attack blue jays and other birds, and occasionally even people, that venture too close to a nest.

Mockingbirds reside most abundantly in the southern United States. Since about 1920, however, their breeding range has expanded northward to southern Canada, but northern populations remain sporadic and local. Many of these northern birds migrate in fall to the South. Most mockingbirds, however, remain on or near their breeding territories year-round.

Spring. Seasonal timing of mockingbird breeding varies with latitude; northern populations may not begin nesting until early summer. Males precede females on the breeding territory—usually one or two acres—in late April and May, or earlier southward. Loud song uttered from conspicuous perches plus aerial loop flights mark the male's initial territorial behaviors. Singing peaks as females arrive and nesting begins, then rapidly declines during incubation and the nestling period. Male mockingbirds that fail to find mates continue singing on their territories into midsummer, often into the night. Mockingbirds usually form long-term pair bonds, though pairs occasionally split between successive nestings. Polygyny, in which one male mates with two or more females, also may occur.

EGGS AND YOUNG: usually four; eggs blue-green, heavily brown spotted. INCUBATION: by female; about twelve days. FEEDING OF YOUNG: by both sexes; insects, fruits. FLEDGING: about twelve days.

Summer. Males continue to feed fledglings for up to a month on the territory as the pair builds a new nest and females begin a second brood. Should a nesting fail through predation, the male immediately begins singing again, signaling his mate to start over—but sometimes, in that event, she deserts to another male's territory. "Females may be programmed to try a new [perhaps more protective?] mate when no young are fledged," suggests Breitwisch. The annual molt, as juveniles finally disperse and territories are abandoned, occurs in late summer.

Fall. Individuals of both sexes plus mated pairs again become territorial in the fall, and now both sexes sing. These territories are centered around a food source, usually a fruit-bearing tree or shrub, and are vigorously defended. They tend to fluctuate in size, depending on the durability of the food source and on the weather; often they roughly coincide with the breeding territory. Wandering flocks of mockingbirds, mostly unpaired juveniles, often intrude on these territories and are aggressively chased. After fall territory formation, often in November, you may see the border dance, which might be described as an exercise in bird diplomacy: Two mockingbirds of adjacent territories meet on the ground, strutting, darting, generally aping each other's behavior. Sometimes this action provokes a brief scrap, but usually the birds simply fly off to their own territories, their borderlines apparently reaffirmed. In many areas, pair bonding of previously unmated birds probably occurs in fall and winter. Mockingbird migration consists mainly of females and juveniles; many males tend to remain in their northern range.

Winter. Mockingbirds sing infrequently now; their only defensive behavior consists of chasing other fruit-eating birds from their food territories.

Ecology. Mockingbirds occupy open and semiopen edge habitats, mosaics of plant cover and open space, including pasture thickets, orchards, and hedgerows. They have adapted especially well to urban and suburban gardens, parks, and yard shrubbery, seeming to favor sites near houses. A tall sentry tree or perch from which to sing and survey the territory seems essential.

Mockingbirds typically place their nests up to ten feet high in a shrub, small tree, or vine. In the Northeast, they favor red cedar, spruces, hawthorns, privet hedges, and osage orange and multiflora rose thickets for nest sites. The male usually builds the nest foundation of thorny sticks, forming a bulky mass; then the female lines the nest with grasses, plant stems, and brown rootlets. Mockingbird nests are virtually identical in site, size, and appearance to gray catbird nests.

The mockingbird's diet, like the catbird's, closely balances between animal and vegetable, with fruits holding a slight edge. Spiders and insects—mainly beetles, ants, and grasshoppers—are consumed most abundantly during the breeding season. Nestlings are fed animal matter for about a week, until they have developed *endothermy*, or body temperature control; then they consume increasing amounts of fruit. Summer, fall, and winter diets include fruits of hollies, greenbriers, sumacs, and pokeweed, as well as blackberries, common elderberries, and grapes. Where sufficient wild fruits exist, mockingbirds seldom invade orchards or berry farms. Mockingbird range expansion in northern states since the 1950s has closely paralleled the spread of multiflora rose (*Rosa multiflora*). This thorny alien shrub, once widely touted for wildlife plantings, has become an aggressive nuisance in many areas. Its high-nutrient fruits remain on the plant through winter, however, and in the North it now ranks as the mockingbird's chief winter food source. In some areas, the birds nest in multiflora rose thickets, so this plant-bird association extends year-round.

Mockingbird territorial behaviors reveal strong competitiveness with other mockingbirds for nest sites and food sources. Though precise data are lacking, potential nest site competitors in areas where breeding ranges coincide include gray catbirds, some of the forest thrushes, and northern cardinals. Food competitors include all other frugivorous, or fruit-eating, birds—blue jays, American robins, European starlings, and common grackles, among others. A food tree claimed by a mockingbird, however, often becomes strictly off-limits to other frugivores.

The mockingbird's innate pugnacity drives off many would-be predators, yet most mockingbird nesting failures apparently result from predation. Snakes (kingsnakes, racers, and rat snakes), accipiter hawks, blue jays, American crows, opossums, raccoons, and domestic cats are the foremost threats. Brown-headed cowbirds rarely parasitize mockingbird nests.

Focus. Mockingbirds in the wild have been known to live for twelve years. Many Native American legends treated the mockingbird with awe, often associating it with the divine gift of language. English naturalist Mark Catesby, exploring in the Carolinas, first named it the mock-bird in 1731. Audubon associated the bird mainly with Louisiana, where he first saw it. Today, five other southern states—Arkansas, Florida, Mississippi, Tennessee, and Texas—honor it as their state bird. Some regional writers have proclaimed its music the ultimate "song of the South" or the "voice of the realm." The mockingbird's symbolism extends to such works of American literature as Walt Whitman's poetry and Harper Lee's 1960 novel, *To Kill a Mockingbird.*

Bird-song analyst Charles Hartshorne expressed the interesting idea that each mockingbird's song is, in a sense, an autobiography—a record of the bird's exposure to the sounds, and thus the environs, of its lifetime.

Red-bellied and Red-headed Woodpeckers
(*Melanerpes carolinus* and *M. erythrocephalus*)

Both sexes of adult red-headed woodpeckers have all-red heads, jet black backs, white bellies, and conspicuous white wing patches; juveniles have brownish heads, backs, and white wing patches. In red-bellied males, red crowns extend over the nape; in females, the red covers only the nape; juveniles of both sexes are brown headed, devoid of red. The zebra-striped back of red-bellies is distinctive in all sexes and age groups. Orange hues of male red-belly underparts, whence the bird derives its inaccurate name, may represent display coloration, since these birds spend much of their foraging time upside down. Red-bellies measure about an inch longer (to ten and one-half inches) than red-heads. The churring calls of both species sound somewhat alike, though red-heads usually sound louder, shriller, and more emphatic.

Close relatives. Nearest North American relatives include the gila woodpecker (*M. uropygialis*), golden-fronted woodpecker (*M. aurifrons*), acorn woodpecker (*M. formicivorus*), and Lewis' woodpecker (*M. lewis*), all western species.

Behaviors. Distinctive red-head traits include fly catching, sallying briefly from a perch to capture winged insects. Red-bellies frequently forage upward on tree trunks, and both species also feed occasionally on the ground. Northern red-head populations often migrate southward depending on food availability. Both woodpeckers reside in the eastern United States from Canada to the Gulf, but red-heads range farther north and west (to the Rockies) than red-bellies. The latter's range continues to expand northward from southern states.

Spring. Both species exhibit conspicuous territorial behaviors as they begin breeding activities in May and June—chasing, calling, reciprocal tapping, and drumming. Red-heads drum in well-spaced bursts; red-bellies drum in short bursts often preceded by a few slower taps. But both species drum less frequently than other woodpeckers. Both also excavate their own nest cavities in dead trees. Red-heads, however, often use natural cavities or their own previous cavities and tend to nest somewhat later than red-bellies.

EGGS AND YOUNG: four or five; eggs white. INCUBATION: by both sexes (males at night); about two weeks. FEEDING OF YOUNG: by both sexes; insects. FLEDGING: about one month.

Summer. In most areas, these woodpeckers nest only once a year. Young birds fledge and feed in family groups beginning in early summer; the groups split in September concurrently with the annual molt of adult birds.

Fall, Winter. Juveniles molt into their first adult plumage throughout fall and winter. Individuals of both species establish and defend fall and winter territories, which enclose roost and feeding locales. One researcher suggests that the same coloration of both sexes in red-heads relates to fall territories. Such similarity permits red-head females to hold their own with males, which might otherwise force the females into inferior feeding areas. Sexually distinct male red-bellies are dominant over females, but this species exhibits less territorial defensiveness in the fall than the more aggressive red-heads.

Ecology. Both species reside in woodlands, but red-heads are said to favor drier country—open stands, old burns, or edges containing solitary dead trees and snags. My own observations run counter to this, however; the largest red-head population near my home occupies a flooded creekbottom. For nesting, red-bellies usually prefer denser forest, often in river lowlands; after breeding, they tend to inhabit parks and suburbs with large trees. The two species often occupy closely adjacent territories, especially in fall and winter.

For nest cavities, red-heads favor isolated, long-dead, barkless trees and snags. They also use utility poles and fence posts. Often they begin excavating at a preexisting crack. Red-bellies usually select dead limbs of living trees or recently dead trees that retain the bark. Red-head nest cavities average forty feet in height; red-belly cavities are usually low. The unlined cavities average about a foot deep.

Both species are vegetarians to a larger extent than all other eastern woodpeckers. Acorns and beechnuts (mast) become staples during fall and winter, and mast abundance probably governs whether the birds remain in a locale over winter or shift elsewhere. Both birds also relish corn and wild fruits; red-bellies occasionally raid Florida orange

groves. Mulberries and Virginia creeper and poison-ivy berries are particular favorites. Both species store acorns, berries, insects, and other foods in the fall, hammering them into bark furrows, tree crevices, and various other apertures; red-heads often seal up their caches with plugs of moist splintered wood. After a period of hasty collection and storage, the birds often remove some of their caches, distributing their contents over wider areas. Such caches provide the main winter food supply, and the birds jealously guard them from intruders. Red-heads also feed at sapsucker wells during winter and spring and create their own sap wells by scaling off bark and consuming fragments of the cambium layer beneath. Insect foods become important in spring and summer diets. The birds consume ants, wood-boring beetle larvae,

grasshoppers, wood roaches, and caterpillars in abundance, and red-heads frequently capture large flying insects, seeming to prefer bright-colored ones.

Food competitors, especially for acorn and beech mast, include other woodpeckers, blue jays, European starlings, squirrels, and many other birds and mammals. Competition between the two woodpecker species for nest cavities is minimal because of the birds' differing site preferences, but squirrels, smaller woodpecker species, American kestrels, great crested flycatchers, and European starlings may usurp old or freshly excavated holes. Starling competition for nest cavities probably accounts for some degree of red-head declines over the past fifty years. One study, however, showed that red-heads often instigate nest cavity conflicts with starlings, which usually nest earlier than red-heads, and that the less aggressive red-bellies are much more frequent victims of starling aggression.

The northern black racer, a tree-climbing snake, sometimes invades woodpecker nest cavities and consumes eggs and young. Cache robbers include other woodpeckers, blue jays, European starlings, and squirrels. But human cleanup of standing dead timber from woodlots is probably the foremost antiwoodpecker act, guaranteed to deplete their local populations. Dutch elm disease, which virtually wiped out American elm trees in many localities during the 1950s and '60s, indirectly benefited red-head populations by providing dead timber for nesting cavities. Subsequent uses of DDT and other pesticides for elm disease control, however, erased many of the benefits along with many birds.

Focus. Alexander Wilson, the Scottish cofounder of American ornithology, shot a red-headed woodpecker in Delaware the first day he stepped off the boat in 1794. The sight of the gorgeous bird inspired him to begin compiling his classic *American Ornithology* (1808–14), the first comprehensive attempt to describe New World species. Naturalist John Burroughs reported red-heads as more numerous than American robins in Washington, D.C., during the late 1800s, an abundance long since vanished. Red-head populations have fluctuated widely, but the trend over the past century has been downward. Habitat depletion, woodland sanitation, and starling abundance are the reasons usually suggested for their decline. Red-bellies, though, are on the increase; like so many southern native birds in the past fifty years, they continue to push northward.

Red-tailed Hawk
(Buteo jamaicensis)

In flight, this large hawk with a four-foot wingspread displays the typical *Buteo* shape: chunky body, broad wings, and broad, rounded tail. Typical redtail adults have brown backs and copper red tails; viewed from beneath, their white chests and brown-streaked bellies are distinctive. Plumage variations are common, however, ranging from almost all black to nearly white. Viewed overhead, the most reliable field mark is the dark *patagial bar* on the fore edge of the wing. Immatures have gray, banded tails. Females are slightly larger than males. Listen for the redtail's raspy squeal, which some have likened to the sound of steam escaping from a valve.

Close relatives. Other *Buteo* hawks of eastern North America are the red-shouldered hawk (*B. lineatus*), broad-winged hawk (*B. platypterus*), and rough-legged hawk (*B. lagopus*). Western U.S. species include the Swainson's hawk (*B. swainsoni*) and ferruginous hawk (*B. regalis*). The buzzard (*B. buteo*) is a Eurasian resident. Some twenty other species exist worldwide.

Behaviors. This is our most common and widespread *Buteo*, or buzzard hawk, a soaring predator whose distribution spans the continent. Redtails are mainly still-hunters, often perching for long periods on telephone poles or electric towers as they scan the countryside. A large hawk perched in a roadside tree is usually a redtail. But it also hover-hunts; in a strong wind, sometimes it hangs motionless in place (kiting). Often it quarters back and forth over a field in low flight. It also hunts while soaring; when it spots prey, it may plunge, or stoop, into a steep, fast dive.

Redtails are only partially migratory, withdrawing south in the fall from the northernmost parts of their range. Their breeding range spans the continent south to Panama.

Spring. The redtail's spectacular courtship flights, begun in winter, continue through early spring and at intervals thereafter. Pairs usually mate for life. Breeding territories average more than a square mile in size but are often larger. Yearling birds occasionally nest, but most first-time breeders are at least three years old. Often a pair reoccupies one of several previous nests in March or April, adding fresh material, or builds a new nest nearby. Until their eggs hatch, redtails are extremely sensitive to disturbance and may quickly abandon the nest at slight provocation. Incubation begins with the laying of the first egg, and thus eggs hatch at successive intervals. An older nestling sometimes kills a younger sibling. By late spring, the surviving young become conspicuous by their noisy calling and rambunctious movements in the nest vicinity.

EGGS AND YOUNG: two or three; eggs white, brown spotted. INCUBATION: by both sexes; four or five weeks. FEEDING OF YOUNG: by both sexes; meat fragments. FLEDGING: six or seven weeks.

Summer. Juveniles often continue to roost in the nest vicinity, even returning at times to use the nest as a feeding platform. They soon begin to develop strong flight, learning to hunt by trial and error; those that can't consistently find and kill prey soon starve to death. By midsummer, they may still linger near their parents or disperse in any direction. The adult annual molt begins after fledglings depart the nest, proceeding gradually and with great variation in timing, sequence, and duration. Older birds sometimes show evidence of molting throughout the year.

Fall. Immatures attain their full adult plumage (including their red tails) by autumn of their second year. Northern populations may remain on their breeding range or migrate slightly southward, depending on the amount of snow cover. Southern redtails usually remain on their summer territories. Young redtails tend to move earlier and farther than adult birds, sometimes as far south as Panama. The birds migrate singly or in small groups, soaring on thermals.

Winter. Redtail nests in deciduous trees become most visible in winter, when both hawks and foliage are gone. Spotting the nests provides advance notice of where the birds are likely to nest again, either on the same nest or nearby. Since many old nests are taken over by other raptors in winter or early spring, they're always worth checking out.

Influxes of fall-migrating redtails on the winter range sometimes result in territorial conflicts with year-round redtail residents. The newcomers may be forced into marginal

feeding territories, which they seem less inclined to defend than resident birds on permanent territories.

Migrants begin moving northward in late winter and early spring. Courtship behaviors may become conspicuous in late February through March. The pair soars together, circling, spiraling, recrossing each other's flight paths. The male sometimes dives toward the female, and the two briefly interlock feet. Many of these aerial maneuvers resemble the birds' territorial displays. The pair also perches closely together, preening and feeding each other.

Ecology. Redtails favor forest edges or woodlots surrounded by open fields and pastures.

Nests are usually placed high in tall trees that give the hawks an outlook on the coun-

tryside. Frequent nesting sites include crotches of oaks, American beech, American elm, and (especially in the hawks' northern range) white pine. Redtail nests are large—repeatedly used ones may measure three or more feet high and four feet across. Like many hawks, redtails often add green sprigs of white pine, northern white cedar, hemlock, or other leafy twigs to their nests. Presence of fresh greenery reveals an active nest. Theories suggest that this habit helps camouflage the nest, aids nest sanitation, or helps inhibit the growth of insect parasites. Nest lining includes long grasses, bark strips from red cedar and wild grape, pine needles, and corn husks. Redtails may recycle old squirrel or crow nests as foundations for their own.

"To list the feeding menu of redtails in summer," writes one hawk researcher, "would be to name almost every living creature within their domain, from the larger insects to half-grown wood-chucks." The preferred prey of the redtail—some 90 percent of the diet where abundant—is rodents, especially meadow voles and ground squirrels. Red squirrels, cottontail rabbits, moles, bats, and shrews are also commonly taken, as are crayfish, toads, garter snakes, and carrion. Among bird prey, red-winged blackbirds and ring-necked pheasants are frequent victims.

Although the breeding ranges of other *Buteo* hawks concur with the redtail's, habitat preferences reduce competition between these species. A raptor associate in some areas is the great horned owl, sometimes called the redtail's nighttime counterpart. This large owl favors similar food and habitats and often nests close to redtails, probably because it often adopts old redtail nests.

Redtails have no significant predators except humans, but blue jays and American crows often mob and harass perched hawks.

Eastern kingbirds fearlessly chase and strike hawks, as they do most large birds. Insect parasites are often numerous in redtail nests. Most redtail nestlings suffer from myiasis, a nonfatal disease caused by bloodsucking fly larvae. Bird lice (Mallophaga) may damage flight feathers to an extent that flying ability is affected.

Focus. The oldest leg-banded red-tailed hawk on record lived twenty-three years, probably far longer than the average. Redtails make easy targets for gunners and are still illegally shot by dimwits who believe in overpopulating the countryside with mice and rabbits. Formerly legal bounty hunting all but wiped out redtails in many northeastern states. Now protected, their populations are thriving and increasing throughout their range. Redtails seem more tolerant of human activities than most other hawks. Their habitat preferences coincide with agricultural land use, and public enlightenment about predator ecology is on their side.

Red-winged Blackbird
(Agelaius phoeniceus)

One of our most common and familiar wetland birds, the redwing (seven to ten inches long) is easily identified. Males are glossy black except for a red shoulder patch (epaulet) bordered by a lower yellow strip. Females and juveniles are brown and heavily streaked with a light line over each eye. Redwing sounds are also distinctive: the male's gurgling "konk-kee-ree" song and shrilly whistled "cheee-er" alarm call, and the harsh "chack" note of both sexes. Female song is a chattering "spit-a-chew-chew."

Close relatives. Still listed as a separate family (Icteridae) in some classifications, the blackbirds are included as a subordinate tribe (Icterini) of finches in the Monroe-Sibley DNA classification scheme. Almost 100 species exist, all in the Western Hemisphere and most in South America. Twenty-one species reside in North America—orioles, meadowlarks, and grackles, among others—and eleven breed in the Northeast. Other *Agelaius* species include the tricolored blackbird *(A. tricolor)* of the western United States and nine residents of tropical South America and the Caribbean.

Behaviors. Many ornithologists believe that the red-winged blackbird is the most abundant bird in North America. It is probably also the most widely studied; every aspect of its biology and behavior has been inspected and analyzed repeatedly, and more research accumulates each year. This attention owes not only to its abundance but also to its easy accessibility, observability, and conspicuous actions. It is, in biologist Robert W. Nero's words, "an ornithological white rat." Yet many facets of its life history still pose interesting problems.

Vital to behavioral interactions of the red-winged blackbird is its most distinctive feature, the red epaulets (lesser wing coverts) of the male. Males fully expose and display them during their so-called "song-spread," in which the perched bird leans forward, partially spreads his wings, flaunting the red shoulder patches, spreads his tail, and utters his liquid "konk-kee-ree" song. Song-spread is mainly a threat and advertising action, aimed at other males and at arriving females. Aggressiveness in redwings, the ability to establish and hold a territory or successfully challenge a territory holder, is also a function of badge display and apparently is proportional to epaulet size and conspicuousness— the bigger and gaudier the epaulets, the more belligerent and successful the bird. Yet actual combat and fighting are rare; most boundary disputes are settled by threat displays alone.

Redwing males often stray when seeking food or vacant territories, frequently trespassing onto occupied territories. When they do, they cover their red badges with black scapular feathers of the wing so that only the lower yellow margins of the epaulet show, thus reducing chances of being attacked by the territory holder. Casual observation might indicate large amounts of variation in size of red patches among male redwings. The fact is that all males have epaulets of about the same size but, unless displaying, the birds often cover them to greater or lesser degrees. The epaulets form only a single component of the threat display complex; others are the bird's vocal sounds and movement patterns.

Redwings, like several other blackbirds, are polygamous breeders; indeed, this is one of the most highly *polygynous* of all bird species. Males may mate with one to six females (average of three, but up to fifteen have been recorded), and male competition is intense. "Polygyny," as Robert W. Nero wrote, "is related to the fact that first-year [that is, second-summer] males do not usually breed, whereas first-year females do, thus providing . . . a surplus of females." Many males, called "floaters," never gain territories or mates.

Redwings forage frequently, though not exclusively, on the ground. Like many blackbirds, they walk and can double-scratch in a quick hop-skip backward like juncos and towhees. A flock of redwings foraging in a field often appears to "roll" across it, as birds in the rear continuously leapfrog over their flock mates to the front of the flock. "The advantage of the system," wrote redwing researcher Gordon H. Orians, "is that each bird has exclusive use of foraging sites that have not yet been visited by other flock members, and yet has to make only short flights between feeding locations." A feeding adaptation common to many blackbirds including redwings is *gaping*—inserting the closed bill into crevices or vegetation or beneath rocks, then forcibly opening it (the jaw muscles work in reverse fashion, snapping open rather than shut), exposing insect larvae or other prey unavailable to most other birds.

Redwing flight is strong, with bursts of wingbeats followed by slight pauses, producing a slightly undulating course. Large winter flocks tend to fly in long, strung-out columns; during migrations, however, the birds usually fly side by side.

Redwings are highly gregarious for most of the year, not only with other redwings but also with other blackbird species (common grackles, brown-headed cowbirds, rusty blackbirds), European starlings, and sometimes American robins as well. An important element of redwing social dynamics is the roost, or sleeping area, where thousands of birds gather in the evening after foraging all day. Some roosts are used almost year-round; others are seasonal. Males and females tend to roost apart, and most roosts are also age segregated. Spring roosts are mainly occupied by subadult, nonbreeding males. Age and gender components of roosts, however, may change seasonally. Roost numbers and occupancy dramatically increase in late summer, often reaching peak size in winter. The birds establish dominance hierarchies in roosts and maintain them by the same sorts of song-spread displays and aggressive behaviors they exhibit during the breeding season. Adult males, for example, are dominant to younger males, which remain at the roost periphery.

Red-winged blackbirds breed across most of North America, from the arctic tundra to Costa Rica, the Bahamas, and Cuba. Breeding redwings in Alaska, Canada, and the northern United States are migratory, but most lower-latitude breeding populations remain resident year-round. Fourteen races or subspecies are currently recognized; these vary in size and, to some extent, plumage and behaviors.

The redwing subspecies occupying almost the entire eastern continent (thus the main focus of this account) is *A. p. phoeniceus.*

Spring. In southwestern Michigan, I can usually count on seeing the first returning redwings about mid-February. All-male flocks continue to pass, arriving throughout the northern breeding range through March. Arthur A. Allen, in his classic 1914 study of the redwing, divided spring migrants into seven classes, beginning with "vagrant" birds and ending with resident immature females. Probably the movements are not this distinct or easily seen in many cases; many noisy male flocks that settle temporarily in the marshes are en route to distant breeding areas. Site fidelity to previous territories *(philopatry)* is strong in both sexes, though some dispersal of previous territory holders to nearby marshes occurs each spring. Almost all redwings breed within thirty miles of where they hatched, most at much shorter distances than that. Subadult males (yearlings) do not often breed, though many do establish territories and *can* breed if replacement males are needed.

Arriving adult males immediately establish territories (rarely *exactly* the same in size and locale as in the previous year) by means of song and display behaviors. In addition to song-spread displays, they also engage in territorial song-flight, a slow, stalling flight between perches as they flare their epaulets and sometimes sing. Sex chases—rapid, acrobatic flights over the marsh—occur between males and females. Two birds at their territorial borders often exhibit the bill-tilt display: Both birds elevate their bills and flare their epaulets but remain silent.

Male territory size varies greatly. Territories are usually fairly small, averaging to ¼ acre in size. Intense competition for territories in good habitat often results in *territory compression*—that is, the squeezing of many small, adjacent territories into optimal sites. Most food foraging, however, is done off territory. Usually a male territory holder retains a territory from the time he first establishes it until his death (about 2.6 years, on average). Territorial boundaries may shift within a breeding season and from year to year, but the site generally remains stable. Each year a small proportion of males change territory locations or are evicted by competing males. Most males do not begin breeding until their second year (that is, their third summer), though they incessantly try to invade and establish territories. They wander nomadically for most of the summer. Redwing floaters often include many former territory holders that have been displaced.

Females, which arrive several weeks later than males, also exhibit song-spread and bill-tilt displays. Researchers disagree on whether females also establish and defend subterritories within male territories. Female display perches overlap considerably in male territories. Evidence indicates that females choose a desirable male territory rather than a specific male. Thus a female occasionally ends up with the same polygynous mate two years in a row but not because of any durable pair bonding beyond a single breeding season.

The *harem*, which consists of all females nesting within a male territory, exhibits both cooperative and competitive aspects. Dominance hierarchies apparently do not exist as such in harems. Harem members seldom operate at the same stage of breeding; one may be building a nest, another incubating eggs, another feeding young. Harem females may help defend each other's nests; they also compete for male paternal care of nestlings. Complicating the parental situation is evidence that female residence on a male territory does not necessarily indicate exclusive mating with the territory holder; thus *polyandry*—the mating of two or more males with a female—may also occur. Most nesting occurs from mid-May through mid-June.

EGGS AND YOUNG: three to five; eggs bluish green, streaked and blotched with brown. INCUBATION: by female; about eleven days; hatching asynchronous, within twelve hours to two days; nestlings altricial. FEEDING OF YOUNG: mostly by female; variable feeding also by male (little in some populations, up to 90 percent frequency in others; male tends to feed fledglings with greater frequency than nestlings); insects (mainly dragonflies and damselflies in marsh habitat, caterpillars in upland habitat). FLEDGING: eleven to fourteen days.

Summer. Most northern redwings nest only once per year, though double brooding does occur. Anybody who walks the marshes in late spring and early summer knows the protocol of redwing defense. One's distance from a nest becomes obvious from the male's behavior. As one approaches a territory, he voices his piercing "cheee-er" calls from a perch and utters harsh "check" notes. Then, as one nears the hidden nest, the bird's excitement increases; he dives or circles and hovers just above one's head. The female often joins in, both hovering just behind or at the sides of one's head ("like earmuffs," reported a researcher). The commotion often attracts other redwings, eliciting mobbing behavior. Intensity of redwing attack is unpredictable. In many years of checking redwing nests, I have seldom been actually struck, but many other observers have been, usually from behind by the diving male; typically he twists in the air, striking one's head with his feet, not his bill. A broom or jacket on a stick held above one's head often deflects the focus of attack. Perched fledglings just out of the nest also elicit strong defense behavior by adults.

Parents continue to feed fledglings for up to two weeks on the territory, up to another two weeks off territory. The independent juveniles then join flocks of adult, postbreeding females, which they strongly resemble. Flocks often feed in upland fields during the day, roost in cattail marshes at night. From late July through early September, however, redwing flocks seem to vanish quite mysteriously. This is the annual molting period; the birds secrete themselves deeply in secluded marshes, becoming relatively quiet and inconspicuous. Juvenile males emerge with variable plumages; some have brown streaking like females, others look quite black, and most show orange-red shoulder patches. Yearling males (that is, in their second summer) develop their first full adult plumage. Adult males wear new black plumage, much of it edged with brown and buff (this edging wears off before the next spring), and red shoulder patches.

Fall. Redwings on the northern range congregate in dense premigration flocks in the marshes. Sources differ on whether adult males depart before or after the females and young. Migration begins in force by mid-October, continuing through November. The day-flying flocks are often joined by flocks of common grackles and brown-headed cowbirds. Migrant flocks vary in size but tend to number less than one hundred birds. They stop en route to feed in grain-fields and often do not arrive at wintering areas for several weeks. A few migrants from farther north may remain on the northern breeding range through winter but seldom linger where snow cover prevents ground feeding. Most northern interior redwing populations use the Mississippi flyway, fanning out to join year-round resident redwings in the central areas of Kentucky, Tennessee, and Alabama. Atlantic and Gulf coastal marshes also hold many migrants and permanent residents.

Winter. The lower Mississippi valley holds the largest concentrations of wintering redwings on the continent—upward of 200 million redwings and starlings, often roosting together. At least 150 major blackbird roosts exist in the southeastern United States, each containing a million or more birds—some as high as 20 or 30 million. Individual birds may be site-faithful to certain roosts during a winter but not often to the same one over succeeding winters. Redwings sometimes travel up to 50 miles between roosting and foraging areas. Most northern-range redwings are migrating by mid-February.

Ecology. Red-winged blackbirds are highly adaptable to both wetland and upland habitats, accounting in large part for their abundance. Common wetland habitats include swamps, freshwater and salt marshes, and wet meadows. Cattail marshes are probably the places most associated with redwings. Within such habitats, however, a few song perches are necessary, sometimes on trees outside the marsh. "It's important to be able to perch above the tops of the cattails," wrote Robert W. Nero. Hayfields (especially alfalfa) are also frequent nesting habitats, and the birds forage extensively in grainfields. Redwings in presettlement America (and until the

1940s) apparently dwelt almost exclusively in wetland habitats; forest clearing, agricultural development, and wetland shrinkage resulted in habitat shifts so that today the birds thrive in both environments.

The redwing nest is a four-inch-deep, sturdy cup usually attached to and suspended from surrounding stems. Inside nest diameter is about four inches. In marsh vegetation, nests typically hang some two to four feet above the ground or water surface. Cattails, bulrushes, sedges, *Phragmites* reeds, and bur-reeds are typical nest-cover plants in wetlands, as are willow, alder, and buttonbush shrubs. Nests in fields are commonly on the ground or a few inches above it. Tree or swamp-shrub nests may sometimes be placed fourteen to twenty feet high. Tall grasses provide domi-nant cover for upland nests. Nest materials consist of dried cattail leaves and other marsh vegetation, grasses, willow bark, rootlets, and mud or soft, decayed wood fragments molded for the inner cup and lined with fine grasses. The birds often use the silvery inner bark of swamp milkweed, if available, for the suspended hammock of fibers upon Which the nest is built. Female redwings often immerse cattail and other leaves before weav-ing them into the nest structure. "Often," wrote Nero, "a peculiar sound heard on the marsh in spring is the tearing sound made by female Redwings as they pull off a strip from a wet cattail blade."

Redwing diet largely consists of insects in spring and summer, seeds in fall and winter. It captures many insects by gaping (see **Behaviors**), by gleaning from vegetation, occasionally by fly-catching on the wing.

"Arguably the most critical attribute of marshes for redwings is their role as insect reservoirs," wrote researcher Les Beletsky; "redwing breeding in many regions is tied to marsh insect emergence." These insects—primarily mayflies, caddisflies, dragonflies, damselflies, midges, gnats, and mosquitoes—are sequentially abundant for limited periods, which coincide with redwing nesting. This high insect productivity ensures that a single parent (usually the female) can capture sufficient prey to feed nestlings, in effect freeing males to court additional mates ("Monogamy almost certainly would prevail if redwing young could not survive without feeding assistance from males," wrote Beletsky). The birds seem to take whatever insect offers in greatest abundance. Early-spring arrivals often feed on cattail moth larvae within cattail heads; redwing feeding activities "serve, in part, to bring about the characteristic puffing out of portions of cattail heads as spring advances," wrote Nero. As calorie needs decrease after nesting, redwing diet turns to seeds of weeds and farm crops: corn, rice, wheat, oats, millet, foxtail-grass, smartweed, and sunflower seeds, among others. Corn provides some 75 percent of the August–September diet in agricultural areas. Ragweed and cocklebur seeds are common winter foods, as are seeds of crotons (doveweeds) and docks.

Male redwings compete intensively for territories. Size of the floater population—itinerant, unmated, often second-summer males that constantly challenge older, territorial males through the breeding season—determines competition levels. Actual fights between competing males are rare; intimidation by song or display is the rule. Another foremost competitor, where its range overlaps with those of redwings, is the yellow-headed blackbird, also a marsh dweller. Each species defends its territories from the other where both are present. Larger than redwings, yellow-heads arrive after redwings are on their territories; yellow-heads compete directly for the redwing-occupied areas, often displacing them to the landward marsh periphery. They do not always evict redwings, however. Yellow-heads favor bulrush over cattail habitat, deeper water over shallow areas, more productive over less productive lakes and marshes. Thus both species can and do coexist, not only on the same range but often in the same wetland area. Even though yellow-heads dominate redwings, redwings seem more adaptable to habitat variability, thus far surpassing yellow-heads in abundance and distribution. Redwings and tricolored blackbirds are also mutually territorial in the latter's narrow western range. Common grackles compete with redwings for territorial space in some marshes; the redwings usually succeed in restricting grackle movement near or across redwing territories. Redwings, however, will mob or attack just about any bird or mammal that ventures too close to a nest.

Foremost redwing nest predators include black-billed magpies, American crows, marsh wrens, raccoons, and minks. Redwings are especially hostile to marsh wrens, which puncture eggs and kill nestlings, and they chase them vigorously. The two species seldom nest in proximity. Brown-headed cowbirds may parasitize almost 75 percent of redwing nests in some areas, usually in peripheral sites. Hawks and owls capture adults and fledglings. Mobbing behavior, in which several redwings from adjacent territories may jointly harass or assault a large predator, is a typical defensive action.

Focus. "Unfortunately," as Nero wrote, redwings "are one of the major agricultural pests and nuisance birds over much of the eastern and central United States, California, and southern Canada." Flocks of redwings may strip husk and kernel from entire fields of standing corn. Late-summer crop damage may also extend to oats, barley, flax, sunflowers, rice, and others. Migrating flocks consume much unharvested as well as waste grain, but local flocks probably account for most crop damage. Although redwings and common grackles inflicted considerable losses on even colonial farmers, losses for farmers swelled with agricultural development and increases in cropland acreage, consequent increases of redwing populations, and the addition of grain-feeding European starlings to our avifauna. Commercial rice crops in Louisiana and Texas are often hard hit, though less so today, with mechanized harvesting and drying, than formerly. In cornfields, it is male redwings that apparently do most damage; females, with slightly smaller bills, favor smaller grains and seeds. Even in colonial days, redwings showed adaptability for nesting in hayfields when marsh habitat was unavailable, and this versatility in habitat use further increased their abundance (the dearth of tribal lore about redwings makes one wonder how abundant they really were in America before European settlement). Today in the Midwest, most redwings now nest in upland habitats owing to the decline and loss of so many wetlands.

Redwings provide ample demonstration that introduced species from abroad do not bear exclusive blame for achieving pest status in our environments; native organisms such as redwings, brown-headed cowbirds, some gull species, and many irruptive insect species can also burgeon when habitats are changed. Their numbers not only cause economic losses to humans but, in many cases, compete with and threaten less adaptable native species. Yet agricultural authorities recognize that redwings also consume large amounts of crop-foraging insects at the time of year when these services are most vital to farmers. The redwing's heavy consumption of periodical cicadas and corn rootworm beetles, for example, has been well documented.

Efforts to control blackbird and starling populations—especially mass destruction at winter roosts, where the birds gather in greatest numbers—have met with unspectacular success. An amendment to the 1918 Federal Migratory Bird Treaty Act, which protects all nongame migratory species, allows American farmers to kill redwings that threaten crops. They remain wholly unprotected in Canada. Cost-benefit analyses, however, indicate that control of redwings may be cost effective only where crop damage is heaviest.

Annual survival of adult redwings probably averages about 60 percent. About 6 percent of eggs fail to hatch, and losses to nest predators can range from 30 to 50 percent. The longest wild redwing lifespan is fifteen years, but mean life expectancy ranges from about two to four years. Highest mortality probably occurs during migrations and in winter cold. Like many if not most American birds, redwings were once market-hunted— "few could distinguish them from bobolinks," wrote ornithologist Arthur C. Bent—and sold as "reedbirds." The "four-and-twenty blackbirds baked in a pie," however, referred to the Eurasian blackbird *(Turdus merula)*, which is actually an all-black thrush.

Rock Pigeon
(Columba livia)

Also known as the rock dove, this is the common or domestic pigeon, noted for its ubiquitous presence in urban and rural areas alike. Plumage colors vary, as any glance at a flock reveals; the birds may be gray, brownish, mostly black or white, or any combination thereof. Typical coloration is gray or slate blue with a whitish patch above the tail and reddish feet. Iridescent feathers often color the neck and upper breast. The birds utter various cooing and gurgling sounds, all of them given in social, usually sexual, contexts. The only visible differences between sexes are behavioral. Rock pigeons reside on every continent except Antarctica.

Close relatives. Nearest North American relatives include the band-tailed pigeon (*C. fasciata*) and red-billed pigeon (*C. flavirostris*), both southwestern U.S. residents, and the white-crowned pigeon (*C. leucocephala*), which inhabits the Florida Keys. The stock dove (*C. oenas*) and wood pigeon (*C. palumbus*) are common European species.

Behaviors. Anybody who has sat for five minutes in a park where pigeons converge for handouts or to scavenge food already knows something about their behaviors. These birds *walk* in a rather stately manner (often pigeon-toed) rather than hop or run. Their thrusting head movements when they walk are also characteristic. These movements may be an innate balancing act to compensate for the bird's small head and consequently skewed center of gravity. Another common behavior is wing clapping in flight, most often done by male birds, perhaps signaling a readiness to mate.

Rock pigeons feed mainly on the ground. Gregarious in every aspect of their life history, they feed, fly, roost, and nest together. Individual birds may shift between flocks, but the flock itself remains the dominant social structure. In a flock, the birds fly close together; this flock pull instinct is probably a protective adaptation that distracts a hawk predator from focusing on a single bird. In a turning or wheeling flock, each bird is geometrically repositioned.

Rock pigeons are generally nonmigratory, though some far-northern populations apparently shift southward in winter.

Spring, Summer, Fall. In contrast to most North American birds, rock pigeon breeding activities are not seasonally based, although northernmost populations seldom nest during winter months. Nesting in many areas is continual; a female may nest up to nine times per year. Stylized courtship behaviors are easily observable; in any large flock, one may see various phases of the breeding cycle occurring simultaneously. A male inflates his neck feathers, bows, and turns in front of a female or chases her on the ground and in the air. Courtship has reached the ultimate stage when a pair *bills*—the female places her bill inside the male's, and the birds bob their heads rhythmically in this posture. Rock pigeons are monogamous; the pair bond is apparently lifelong. Five months after hatching, the young are sexually mature and ready to mate.

Even though pairs often nest in close proximity, they vigorously defend their nests. The nesting territory, writes one researcher, "is remarkably compressible or expandable according to circumstances." Where more than one pair occupy a single ledge or beam, the birds defend only the immediate area around their nests. Renesting pigeons usually build new nests near the previous site.

In late summer, rock pigeons undergo their molt, an annual "change of clothes" signified in the city by pigeon feathers everywhere.

EGGS AND YOUNG: two; eggs white. INCUBATION: by both sexes; about seventeen days. FEEDING OF YOUNG: by both sexes; pigeon's milk for first few days, then seeds. FLEDGING: about three weeks.

Winter. Even in areas where rock pigeons reproduce year-round, the frequency and success of winter nesting lag because of harsh weather and decreased access to food. Sheltering and feeding are the main pigeon activities during this season.

Ecology. The rock pigeon's foremost associate is humankind, a coexistence dating from the Neolithic period. The farmer is its friend, the city dweller its closer friend. Pigeons seldom exist apart from people.

Safe nesting shelter is a foremost necessity for pigeons. The nest locale is usually a partially enclosed or semisheltered flat surface on a building or bridge. Window ledges, cornices, bridge beams, and barn rafters are common sites. The male collects short sticks or pieces of straw, selecting them for their stiffness, and brings them to the female, which arranges them beneath her. The final structure is a shallow, flimsy platform.

The abundance of city pigeons directly reflects the feeding attention lavished upon them. For many people, bird feeding consists entirely of feeding pigeons in the park. Without such handouts, huge city flocks could not exist, for these birds invariably breed to the limit of their food supply. Rock pigeons are mainly seed eaters, preferring vetches and cultivated grains, but they have learned to consume popcorn, peanuts, french fries, bread, meats—just about any fast food item—and they scavenge sidewalks, streets, and parks for garbage debris. Rural flocks are mainly grain scavengers. Insects, snails, and other invertebrates are sometimes taken, especially for nestlings graduating from a pigeon's milk diet. Rock pigeons rarely eat green vegetation.

Scavenger competitors include American crows, house sparrows, and squirrels, among others. In some places, pigeons may compete with barn swallows, eastern phoebes, and American robins for ledge nesting sites.

The rock pigeon's foremost natural predator is the peregrine falcon, which shares similar habitats to ancestral rock pigeons. A few American cities have released pairs of these cliff-dwelling raptors in the canyons of tall city buildings, hoping to control rock pigeon populations. The results so far remain unspectacular. American crows sometimes raid pigeon nests and devour the eggs. In most cities with pigeon problems, however, people's ample provision of food items swamps all efforts to curb rock pigeon populations by biological controls.

Rock pigeons carry numerous parasites. The birds' gregarious habits permit rapid transmission throughout a flock, sometimes leading to disease epidemics. Probably 80 percent of all pigeons are infected with trichomoniasis, caused by the internal protozoan *Trichomonas columbae*. Ornithosis, also called psittacosis or parrot fever, results from primary infection by *Chlamydomonas*, a green alga that resembles bacteria. Although it is seldom fatal to mature rock pigeons, this disease is highly contagious to humans, who may experience flulike symptoms. Pigeons also transmit the fungus *Cryptococcus neoformans*, which in humans may cause the often fatal cryptococcal meningitis. Many human cases of these diseases are air-transmitted during cleanups of pigeon droppings from roost sites; wearing of face masks is advised while performing such tasks.

Focus. Native populations of rock pigeons exist today in only a few scattered locales, mainly in remote coastal mountains of northern Europe and the Balkans. In such places, the birds nest on cliff ledges and in caves. Several European dove species, including the rock pigeon, figured in the early flood myths of various civilizations. The dove's early symbolic connection with love, sex, procreation, and the goddess Venus probably resulted from observations of the birds' conspicuous courtship and nesting behaviors. Doves later came to represent various aspects of divine love in Christianity. As a popular icon of peace, the bird regularly appears in editorial cartoons.

Opinion is divided on whether most of today's rock pigeon populations are feral (that is, descended and escaped from domestic flocks) or, like house sparrows, simply opportunistic, having successfully adapted to human-created environments. Both possibilities exist, and for U.S. populations, at least, the distinction between them remains unclear. The spread of some fourteen worldwide subspecies plus numerous strains developed by pigeon husbandry and dovecote cultures have thoroughly mixed the genes of this species. Variations in plumage color alone indicate the genetic mixtures present in any flock. Researchers point out genetic behavioral differences between wild rock pigeons and our common city pigeons; many even fear that the native populations of Europe have become endangered by genetic leakage from feral pigeons.

Our North American rock pigeon populations stem from dovecote pigeons domesticated by artificial selection. These were introduced into Britain by the Romans (c. A.D. 100) and brought to this continent by French and British colonists in the early 1600s. They became so common that nobody bothered to study them, an appalling neglect of scientific opportunity. We would know far more than we do about the pigeon's history in North America if naturalists and ornithologists had not, until the 1970s, regarded them as a trash species. Today, even if pigeons remain uncharismatic to birders, numerous cadres of experts who raise, train, study, and value them feel otherwise.

Throughout human history, pigeons have provided blessing and curse, both in abundance. They are important food (squab) and pernicious pests. They are readily bred and trained for fancy show racing and homing activities. For science, they provide easy subjects for experimental and behavioral research. As pests, their overpopulations befoul public structures. Cleanup involves much labor, cost, and potential health hazards.

Medieval monasteries throughout Europe raised pigeons for meat. Dovecote architecture became a specialty, and pigeon fancy, the term used for the breeding and care of flocks, grew into an avocation of the very rich. Today the aviculture of some two hundred breeds and many varieties of rock pigeons—bred for color, plumage patterns, flight, speed, and meat—parallels the development of rose and iris culture. Numerous organizations and journals explore nuances of pigeon fancy.

The homing ability of rock pigeons—actually their nest-site tenacity, which drives them to return to their dovecotes, sometimes from hundreds of miles—was put to extensive use during World War I. Trained carrier pigeons delivered messages, often from the front lines at night, back to support units. Pigeon use continued during World War II and the Korean War, usually in situations where telecommunications became impractical or dangerous. Some thirty-two pigeons have received medals citing them for "brave service."

How pigeons are able to home on their dovecotes from long distances has puzzled researchers for many decades. Visual cues are apparently of minor importance. The birds seem to orient themselves by innate sun and magnetic compasses, but compass direction is only part of the complex. One discovery is that rock pigeons are sensitive to infrasound ranges far below the capacity of human ears, down to .05 hertz, twelve octaves below middle C. But the whole story of how pigeons navigate remains elusive. The secrets still held by this lowly draper of our statues may give even "The Thinker" pause.

Ruby-throated Hummingbird
(Archilochus colubris)

Hummingbird family (Trochilidae), order Trochiliformes. Measuring only slightly more than three inches and weighing only one-tenth of an ounce—less than a penny—the ruby-throated hummingbird, the smallest bird of northeastern North America, can hardly be mistaken, except, perhaps, for a large moth. Its buzzing flight and needlelike bill are obvious identity marks. The male has a bright red throat, iridescent green back, and forked tail; the female, slightly larger, has a green back but lacks the red throat and has a blunt, white-spotted tail. Juveniles of both sexes resemble the female in coloration. Ruby-throats voice no song, only a variety of squeaks, twitters, and grating notes.

Close relatives. Some sixteen other hummingbird species reside mainly in the western United States. The black-chinned hummingbird (*A. alexandri*) and rufous hummingbird (*Selasphorus rufus*) are the most common of these. All of the more than three hundred hummingbird species reside in the Western Hemisphere, most in the Neotropics. Most are vividly colored.

Behaviors. Ruby-throats are most often seen hovering, their wings beating fifty-five times per second, or darting in quick zigzag patterns. They can fly in any direction—

forward, back, or straight up and down. Forward wingbeats number seventy-five or more per second, producing a wing roar similar to that of a hawk moth or bumblebee. Measured in ratio to body weight, however, hummingbird wingbeats are slower than those of most birds. Hummingbirds require vast amounts of energy to keep those wings buzzing. The hummingbird's metabolic rate is extremely high, more than six hundred heartbeats per minute, and it must feed almost constantly during the day. Most feeding occurs as it hovers and probes in front of a nectar source, but it also perches at frequent intervals. Hummingbirds feed not by sucking but by licking three times per second. The grooved, forked tongue fills with nectar, which is pumped by capillary action along the tongue, then swallowed. At night, hummingbird temperature drops, metabolism slows, and the bird enters a state of torpor; without this adaptation, it would starve overnight. Highly aggressive, especially toward other hummingbirds but also toward other birds and even large insects, hummingbirds are extremely territorial and spend much of their nonfeeding time chasing, threatening, and displaying.

Ruby-throats are migratory. Their breeding range spans the eastern United States from lower Canada to the Gulf.

Spring. The sexes migrate north separately, beginning in late March and early April. Hummingbirds usually migrate singly during daytime hours. Males arrive on the breeding range in early May, a week or so before females. Males and females, in fact, do just about everything separately except mate—and researchers still haven't discovered how hummingbirds subdue their innate hostilities long enough to do that. Spring migration precedes the flowering of most hummingbird food plants, necessitating the use of other food sources. Each male establishes a small territory of about a quarter acre, which usually contains a nectar food source and a perch overlook or two. As the season advances, these territories may shift boundaries to coincide with the flowering of new nectar sources.

There is a fine line, if any, between threat and courtship displays. Most spectacular, perhaps, is the male's pendulum flight, in which he swings back and forth in a buzzing, U-shaped arc that rises from three to forty feet on either side. I have sometimes elicited this display in front of my face by wearing red, a color that always attracts these birds. Two other displays are a horizontal back-and-forth motion and a straight up-and-down flight performed by two hummingbirds facing each other. Most mating occurs in June. A female entering a male's territory is threatened and chased, probably leading the male off his territory, where copulation (some observers suggest rape) occurs on the ground. The mates then go their own ways—the male to continue defending his feeding territory and mating promiscuously with other wandering females, the female to establish her own nesting territory and build a nest or reuse a previous one. After fledging, young birds remain in the nest vicinity for several days, gradually learning to feed themselves.

EGGS AND YOUNG: two; eggs white, pea-size, oval. INCUBATION: by female; about two weeks. FEEDING OF YOUNG: by female; regurgitated nectar, small insects. FLEDGING: two to three weeks.

Summer. Nesting continues in July and sometimes into August with second broods. Occasionally a female may tend two successive, closely spaced nests at the same time, feeding young in the first and incubating the second. But feeding is the main summer activity. The females, though defensive of feeding territories, seem generally less so than males and often bring the fledglings to food sources. Fall migration begins in late summer, males departing two weeks or more before females and juveniles.

Fall. Flying singly and in daytime, often quite low over land and water, ruby-throats migrate to southern Florida, Louisiana, and Texas. Most move on to Mexico and as far south as western Panama, crossing the Gulf of Mexico nonstop.

Winter. Ruby-throats continue to feed territorially on nectar in their winter habitats. Now occurs their annual molt, when juvenile males acquire their red throats.

Ecology. In their breeding range, male and female ruby-throats often select different habitats. Males favor woodland edges, hedgerows, orchards, and flower gardens. Mated females seek out dense woodland cover, often near a stream, for nesting. Open woodlands and edge thickets are the main habitats in hummingbird winter range.

The nest site, often a downward-slanting twig or small branch some ten to twenty feet high, is frequently leaf-sheltered from above. The female collects bud scales and saddles them to the branch's upper side with spider silk, then adds lichen fragments on the exterior and lines the interior with plant down, which may include fuzz from the underside of sycamore leaves or down from willow flowers. The result is a soft, flexible cup resembling a lichened knot on the branch.

Nesting trees vary, but rough-barked species coated with the foliose lichen *Parmelia* seem to be favored.

Researchers once thought that hummingbird spring migration was timed to coincide with the opening of favored nectar flowers. This may be true for their southern breeding range but is not so in the North, where the birds may arrive weeks before most flowering occurs. Then observers discovered that a *commensal* feeding relationship—one in which one species benefits and neither suffers—exists between ruby-throats and yellow-bellied sapsuckers, whose northern range encompasses ruby-throat breeding range. Some researchers speculate that the limits of ruby-throat northern range may actually have more to do with sapsucker range than with nectar flower distribution. The sapsuckers drill rows of small holes, or sap wells, mainly in birches but also in other trees. The exuding sap feeds not only the sapsuckers but also the hummingbirds. Sap wells, oozing sucrose and amino acids chemically similar to floral nectar, provide a reliable food source for hummingbirds until seasonal flowering occurs. The birds also feed on the numerous small insects attracted to the sap wells.

Some remarkable relationships have coevolved between hummingbirds and their food flowers, which are usually tubular, odorless, nodding down, and brightly colored. Ruby-throats forage upon more than thirty nectar-producing species, plus numerous garden flowers; at least nineteen of these are *ornithophilous*—adapted for pollination by birds. Pollen is deposited on the base of the bill and carried to another flower as the bird forages. Since hummingbirds are attracted to bright red, orange, and yellow colors, hummingbird pollination has probably

influenced the evolution of colors and structure in these flowers. Examples include cardinal-flower, wild columbine, Oswego-tea or beebalm, and Indian paintbrush. Wild or mountain honeysuckle, red buckeye, fire pink, and trumpet creeper are also foraged. The white, heavy nectar-producing flowers of black locust and horse-chestnut feed many hummingbirds, as do jewelweeds, the last especially during fall migration.

Some western hummingbird species, and probably others, transport not only pollen but tiny flower mites (*Rhinoseius epoecus*) to and from Indian paintbrush flowers. The mites ride in the bird's nostrils, moving down its bill into the flower as it hovers to feed.

The ruby-throat's chief food competitors are probably other ruby-throats. Not uncommonly, while one hummingbird is aggressively chasing another, a third hummingbird will sneak in on the food source. Large nectar-feeding insects, such as bumblebees and wasps, may discourage hummingbird feeding at times, but insect competition is probably insignificant.

Hummingbirds occasionally fall victim to bizarre circumstances. They become enmeshed in spiderwebs and are sometimes captured by leaping leopard frogs and bass, even by insects such as mantids and large dragonflies. American kestrels, merlins, and great crested flycatchers occasionally seize a hummingbird. Natural predation, however, is probably negligible. A recent hazard on farms is red insulators on electric fences; if the attracted hummingbird perches near one and its tail brushes a tall weed, the resulting ground circuit electrocutes the bird. Far more hazardous than these occurrences, however, are the bird's semiannual thousand-mile migration flights.

Focus. Wildlife folklore has long held that hummingbirds hitch rides on migrating geese in spring and fall. Aside from the fact that northern geese arrive earlier and depart later than hummingbirds, there is no evidence that this occurs. The tale probably stemmed mainly from incredulity that this tiny bird can wing so far on its own power.

But genuine superlatives abound. The hummingbird family is the largest family of nonpasserine, or nonperching, birds, has the relatively largest breast muscles of all birds, carries the fewest feathers (less than a thousand in ruby-throats), and has one of the proportionately largest bird brains, at 4 percent of body weight. Mobile shoulder joints enable hummingbird wings to twist in flight, generating lift in both forward and backward strokes.

In recent years, a minor industry has grown from public interest in attracting hummingbirds to suburban yards and gardens; advertisers display many styles of hummingbird feeders plus colorful plantings for hummingbird gardens. Probably such activities have helped compensate for natural habitat loss through urbanization and wetland food-plant depletion. Present ruby-throat populations seem relatively stable.

Sharp-shinned Hawk
(*Accipiter striatus*)

Short rounded wings, a long square-cornered tail, and several quick wingbeats alternating with short glides characterize the sharp-shinned hawk in flight. The sharpie is about pigeon size, ten to fourteen inches long, and females are larger than males. Adult birds have a dark bluish gray back and rust-colored, horizontal barring on the underparts. Immatures are brown backed and brown streaked. Not vocal at most times, the birds often utter a series of shrill cackling notes when alarmed near the nest.

Close relatives. Other North American bird hawks, so called because their prey is chiefly birds, are the Cooper's hawk (*A. cooperii*) and northern goshawk (*A. gentilis*). Some thirty-eight other accipiters range worldwide.

Behaviors. The sharp-shinned is our smallest accipiter, but female sharpies and male Cooper's hawks often appear to overlap in size, making positive field identification difficult—in fact, one of birding's toughest challenges.

The sharp-shinned hunts mainly by ambush from inconspicuous woodland perches or by low, gliding

The Cooper's hawk also preys on birds, including those that visit backyard feeders. Similar in appearance to the sharp-shinned hawk, the Cooper's hawk is larger and presents a different flight silhouette. Their ranges overlap considerably.

flights amid trees and thickets. Unlike the larger *Buteo* hawks, it can quickly maneuver, abruptly turning or dropping when it spots prey. It may suddenly snatch a warbler from its perch or chase a bird into dense brush at top speed. During bird-banding operations, I have watched sharpies dive into mist nets after captured blue jays, often tearing through the net with the force of their attacks. Their deft reflexes "seem not just to mirror the escape tactics of prey," wrote hawk biologist Pete Dunne, "but to anticipate them." Observers also cite instances of play attack, when a sharpie suddenly scatters a group of finches for the apparent sport of it. Even toward birds larger than itself, it some-

times feints an attack. Sharpies also soar high, usually in the morning and extensively during migrations.

Spring. In April, most sharp-shinneds move north from their winter range as far as the tree line in Canada, traveling singly and in small or large flocks. They sometimes accompany other accipiters or *Buteos*, such as broad-winged hawks. On the breeding range, which spans most of the continent, aerial courtship displays occur near the future nest site, which is often located in a previous nesting vicinity. Within a home range of two or three miles, a pair occupies a territory of several acres. Usually the birds build a new nest each spring.

EGGS AND YOUNG: four or five; eggs white, splotched with brown. INCUBATION: by female, which is fed by male; about a month. FEEDING OF YOUNG: by both sexes; bits of meat. FLEDGING: almost a month.

Summer. Family groups remain together, often in the nest vicinity, for most of the summer as the juveniles gradually learn hunting skills. By late summer, most have dispersed from their family groups. The prolonged annual feather molt extends into fall. Yearling birds gain full adult plumage during their third summer. Juveniles and yearlings often begin migrating in mid-August.

Fall. Migration numbers peak in mid-September. This movement usually coincides with warbler and sparrow migrations, and sharpies capture many of these smaller migrants. The hawks often travel in large numbers, both by active flight and by riding thermal updrafts.

Winter. Some sharp-shinneds travel as far south as Central America, males and juveniles apparently migrating farthest south. Many winter in the southern and central midwestern United States, however, and some wintering sharpies typically remain in the lower Great Lakes and New England areas. These and Cooper's hawks are the predators that frequently haunt suburban yard feeders, sometimes crashing into picture windows while chasing a junco or sparrow.

Ecology. Open woods, edges, and openings in dense forests are the sharpie's favored habitats.

For nesting, the sharpie often selects a tree near the outer edge of a small, dense conifer grove, building a twig nest close to the trunk. Nest height averages about thirty

feet. Occasionally sharpies adopt and refurbish old crow or squirrel nests.

About 96 percent of the sharpie's diet consists of birds, almost any species smaller than itself. Probably it captures more adult passerines—finches, warblers, and other perching birds—than anything else, but it also takes nestlings, rock pigeons, and young chickens in poultry yards (so-called chicken hawks, however, are usually Cooper's hawks). The sharpie's diet also includes mice, young rabbits, frogs, and large insects. A common feature of this hawk's near-nest vicinity is a butcher's block or plucking post—a stump, fence post, or other perch where the bird habitually brings its prey, tears it apart, and feeds. Feathers or other remnants on the ground may indicate a butcher's block perch and nearby nest. Often, however, the birds leave little refuse at such sites. Probably sharpies find their easiest, most abundant prey during migration seasons as they trail or accompany passerine flocks.

The foremost food competitors are probably other bird hawks, depending upon habitat and weather conditions. Accipiters seldom share the same woodland acreage with other accipiters, however, so sharpies largely avoid competitive encounters. In areas where sharp-shinned and Cooper's hawks do coexist, the latter apparently forage lower in the tree canopy.

Sharp-shinned predators are mainly larger raptors, including Cooper's hawks, northern harriers, red-tailed hawks, and peregrine falcons.

Focus. This bird's common name results from its pencil-thin legs, or *tarsi*, a helpful field mark when the bird is perched in good light. But even veteran observers find it difficult to distinguish sharpies from Cooper's hawks in the field; the sharp-shinned's squarish tail, contrasted to the Cooper's less squarish tail, is often an unreliable mark. In flight, the sharpie's head barely extends in front of the wings, while the Cooper's head extends quite visibly. The key visible difference between the two is size, plain to see and measure in the hand but hard to judge through binoculars; any birder who says otherwise is leading you astray. As one raptor expert states, "One should not be too proud to list a bird as an 'unidentified *Accipiter*' or even 'unidentified hawk or falcon.'"

Along with Cooper's hawks, sharp-shinneds sometimes evoke the wrath of poultry farmers, gamebird hunters, and even some bird lovers who still believe that hawk attacks on yard feeders are heinous crimes of nature. It's true that any bird hawk can get into the habit of raiding a chicken yard or yard feeder. Hawks are opportunistic predators, and as such they cull the weak and unwary. Yet they usually avoid human environs unless hunger drives them to bold actions.

Gunners once shot sharpies by the hundreds during fall migrations. Widespread use of DDT caused a dramatic decline of sharp-shinneds in the early 1970s, but populations are now recovering in many areas. Eastern seaboard censuses, however, show massive declines of this species in recent years, which some observers attribute to concurrent declines in passerine bird prey. Sharpie eggs, once regarded as the handsomest of all hawk eggs, were prized by egg collectors for their rich brown markings. Egg collecting has been legally banned since 1918.

Song Sparrow
(Melospiza melodia)

O ur most common native brown sparrow is five or six inches long and shows heavy breast streaking that converges into a large central spot. Song sparrows characteristically pump their rounded tails as they fly. Male song begins with a series of three or four introductory "sweet sweet sweet" notes followed by a variable musical trill. Sexes look alike.

Close relatives. The Lincoln's sparrow (*M. lincolnii*) and swamp sparrow (*M. georgiana*) are both North American species. Vesper sparrows (*Pooecetes gramineus*) somewhat resemble song sparrows in plumage and song but usually occupy more open habitats.

Behaviors. One bright day in the dead of every winter, the song sparrow, joined by the tufted titmouse, launches into loud, insistent song, marking for me the true if invisible turning point of the seasons.

Song sparrows breed across most of the continental United States and Canada. The large number of subspecies—thirty-four geographic forms, more than for any other North American bird—reveals song sparrow populations as highly adaptive; the species is extremely sensitive to localized environmental influences and is undergoing rapid evolutionary transition. This variability extends to migration patterns: Most song sparrows migrate, arriving early and staying late, but many remain on their breeding range all year. One can observe them almost year-round in the right habitats, often as they move in short, bounding flights between patches of cover. Thoreau remarked that "they generally bring some object, as a rail or branch, between themselves and the face of the walker." When foraging on the ground, they scratch simultaneously with both feet. Unlike many sparrow species, song sparrows rarely flock together habitually, usually appearing solitarily or in pairs.

Spring. Most male song sparrows are on their breeding range by early spring, and territorial song is loud and frequent. Both nesting and feeding occur within the territory, the size of which depends on song sparrow abundance; it may range half an acre in crowded habitats, but it can range up to more than an acre in less populated sites. Territorial males sing, chase, and display, habitually using several song perches, but they often tolerate song sparrow intruders who don't sing or act territorial. Females arrive one or two weeks later than males, returning to the previous year's territory and thus frequently returning to the same mate. *Pouncing* behavior, in which the loudly singing male dives on the female, often marks pair formation at this time. Male singing decreases when females arrive; then, as nest building begins in late April and early May, song again becomes frequent. The female constructs the nest—often repeatedly, for nest predation is frequent in this species. If disturbed with young in the nest or vicinity, parent birds exhibit a showy distraction display, where they begin running about with stiffly erect wings and dragging tail.

EGGS AND YOUNG: typically three or four; eggs greenish white, heavily brown spotted. INCUBATION: by female; about twelve days. FEEDING OF YOUNG: by both sexes; insects. FLEDGING: about ten days.

Summer. Fledglings typically leave the nest before they can fly, hiding in ground cover. They begin to fly in about a week but remain in the nest vicinity, following and being fed by a parent, usually the male, for three or four weeks before dispersing. The female often renests only days after the first brood fledges, sometimes using the same nest, sometimes building a new one. She may produce two or even three more broods, nesting well into August. Most song sparrows probably remain monogamous only through a single breeding season. Polygyny, in which one male mates with two or more females, may occur when a male dies and his mate pairs with another already mated male or when females of a population outnumber males. As nesting declines toward late summer, territorial behaviors and song also cease, a signal that the annual plumage molt has begun. Molting may extend through September.

Fall. Males often become briefly territorial again after molting, but song is seldom heard after November. Song sparrow migrations are *partial*; portions of a population—most juveniles and adult females and about half the adult males—usually migrate, but individual males may migrate one year and remain on their breeding range the next. Some juvenile males establish territories in the fall, then migrate and return to them the following spring. Fall migration usually lasts into November, as individual birds drift away.

Winter. A broad overlap of breeding and winter ranges extends across the northern United States south to the central tier of states. Winter residents on the breeding range consist of birds remaining on or near their summer territories plus arrivals from farther north. South of this range overlap, song sparrow winter range spans the southern United States, extending into central Mexico. Song sparrows never become actually gregarious, but they often form small foraging flocks during migrations and in winter, especially during severe weather. They frequently mix with dark-eyed juncos, American tree sparrows, and northern cardinals at this season. At yard feeders, they are among the most belligerent of birds. In January and February, song commences, increasing in frequency as migrants head north in late winter. A large percentage of first-year birds, it is reported, return to areas near their birth sites.

Ecology. Song sparrows favor dense, brushy thickets, often near water, in both summer and winter ranges. Any shrubby area near a pond or stream may host one or more pairs. Hedgerows and overgrown fields are also typical habitats.

Song sparrows usually build their first nests of the season on the ground, half hidden by a tuft of grass, low shrub, or brush pile. Later nests are often placed two or three feet high in a shrub or young tree, frequently a conifer. The cup, formed almost entirely of dried grasses and lined with finer grasses, looks pocketed in the ground but bulkier when placed above ground.

Song sparrows usually feed on or close to the ground. Insect prey makes up 34 percent of the diet, chiefly beetles, plus grasshoppers, caterpillars, ants, and others, consumed mainly during the breeding season. The year-round seed diet includes smartweeds, bristle-grass and other grasses, ragweeds, oats, pigweed, and sedges, plus berries and cherries in season.

Competition with other species is probably negligible. Birds of its size that often nest in similar habitats include American goldfinches, yellow warblers, and common yellowthroats. Song sparrows often defend their territories from these species, but most competition is probably between the sparrows themselves as they conflict with unmated floaters that seek territories.

Song sparrow predators are many, but the amount of predation that occurs seems strongly correlated to density of cover. "A well-situated population is practically immune to predation," wrote ornithologist Margaret Morse Nice, "while a badly situated one suffers heavy losses." Accipiter hawks, falcons, and owls prey upon the birds; nest predators include snakes, box turtles, common grackles, opossums, raccoons, skunks, and domestic cats. One recent study found that song sparrow nesting success increased with the abundance of local coyote populations, suggesting that these canine predators may control other predators that prey on the nests. The sparrows may mob potential predators on occasion. This species is one of the most frequent hosts of brown-headed cowbird parasitism. A high percentage of the song sparrow nests I find contain one or more cowbird eggs; some studies estimate cowbird parasitism at about 40 percent. But in optimal habitat, according to Nice, the sparrows easily tolerate this parasitism, and loss of sparrow nestlings is minimal. In marginal habitat, cowbird nestlings often survive while the sparrow young die of starvation.

Focus. The song sparrow has probably been the most intensively studied of all passerine birds, mainly because of Ohio researcher Margaret Morse Nice. Working on her own time and with minimal resources, she spent years observing this species, ultimately providing a classic model for life history studies. Nice's work, conducted during the 1930s, also added vastly to our knowledge of passerine birds in general. In the roster of great American ornithologists, Margaret Nice ranks near the top.

Eleven years is the maximum recorded life span for wild song sparrows; probably two or three years is average. Nice estimated that only about 12 percent of hatched young survive long enough to breed. Adult yearly survival is an estimated 60 percent, however, and song sparrows remain one of our most abundant native birds, second only to American robins in many areas.

Tree Swallow
(Tachycineta bicolor)

Identify this five- to six-inch-long swallow by its metallic greenish blue upper parts; clear white chin, breast, and belly; and notched tail. Sexes look alike, except that yearling females show mixed brown and greenish blue plumage on the back. Juvenile tree swallows are brown above and white below, with a dusky, incomplete breastband. Calls include various twittering notes associated with courtship and a liquid "chee-leep," mainly voiced in flight.

Close relatives. Eight other *Tachycineta* species reside mainly in South America. These include the violet-green swallow *(T. thalassi-* *na)*, mangrove swallow *(T. albilinea)*, white-winged swallow *(T. albiventer)*, white-rumped swallow *(T. leucorrhoa)*, and Chilean swallow *(T. leucopyga)*. Bank swallows *(Riparia)* and a group of South American hole-nesting swallows also appear closely related.

Behaviors. Seldom seen on the ground, tree swallows usually perch on bare branches, power lines, nest boxes, or other above-ground sites in the open. Tree swallows tend to circle and glide more than most swallows, readily diving at the head of a person in the nest vicinity, swerving aside with a raspy note. Mobbing and diving potential predators are common behaviors in nesting areas. Yet these birds do not fly especially fast, typically less than 20 mph.

Mainly aerial feeders, tree swallows sometimes fly long distances from nests to prime feeding areas such as over-water sites or open acres sheltered from wind. They are social birds for most of the year, sometimes semi-colonial nesters, yet are fiercely territorial and protective of individual nest sites. Although most pairs remain seasonally monogamous, *polygyny* (a single male pairing with two females, each with her own nest) occurs at about 5 percent frequency.

Tree swallow breeding range extends across North America, from the arctic treeline south to the middle tier of states. The birds are migrators.

Spring. As the earliest swallow migrants, tree swallows typically arrive at their breeding sites from mid-March to early April. I thus noted their arrival in my notes of a recent April 14: "Tree swallows returned, exuberantly, about mid-AM, circling, dipping, vocalizing as if greeting the area anew, checking it all out. As they course around and over the cabin, their note might be described as a chewed or chewy chirp." Older birds precede yearlings. Females, especially, exhibit highly variable rates of *philopatry* (fidelity to previous nesting areas), though the birds usually return to sites where breeding has been successful. "Occasionally," one research team wrote, "a pair breeds together for several consecutive years in the same or a nearby nest site . . . most likely a result of each individual having strong site fidelity rather than long-term pair bond."

Migrating by daytime in small, loose flocks, males usually arrive a few days before females. The birds pair soon after female arrival, exhibiting several courtship behaviors, though many females seem to "play the field" for several days after initial pairing. The pair may examine several potential nest cavity sites, and soon the male establishes a territory, which extends to distances of up to twenty-five feet or so from the nest site. Some twelve different call notes have been identified, plus a male dawn song and day song, repetitive phrasings of one- and two-note series, usually given while perched at the nest site. The male hovers and flutters near the female, and the pair bows toward each other and touches bills. Courtship displays continue until incubation begins. A social display of apparent exuberance, if nothing else, is *towering,* in which a bird circles high over its home range; other tree swallows join, calling softly as they wheel high in the air before dropping to their nest sites.

Tree swallows are slow to begin nesting, usually in May. Nest building, done by the female, can encompass several days to two weeks, and egg laying may not begin for a week or more after nest completion. In contrast to the frenetic nesting activities of many birds, tree swallows seem deliberate, almost casual, in their timing and sequence of nesting events. Nest building usually occurs only during the morning. Both sexes fiercely compete for and defend nest sites, grappling in midair, on the ground, even over water with intruding tree swallows. Territorial disputes, attacks, and chases commonly occur before incubation begins. The birds' fierceness extends to other occupied nests; a male tree swallow moving in to replace a dead or missing male will often kill nestlings of the widowed mate before breeding with her and claiming the same nest site. Before and sometimes even during incubation, tree swallows may completely abandon the nesting area for up to several days. Eggs already laid do not seem to lose viability. This behavior may be related to a temporary lack of aerial insect food during cold or wet weather; the birds may fly twenty miles or more to forage elsewhere. This volitional abandonment of territory for such lengthy durations—thus far seen in no other North American bird—is a remarkable adaptation for a bird dependent on aerial insect prey.

Tree swallows have been subject to much field research. The more they are studied, the more complex their social relations appear. For example, the yearling female, so distinctive in plumage (the only North American female passerine bird that does not gain full breeding plumage in a year), has been found to assume an important backup role in breeding. She arrives two to three weeks later than adults, just after pairs have settled on their territories. Although she is sexually mature, her migration timing has placed her at a competitive disadvantage with older females. She thus becomes part of a population of "floaters," wandering, unpaired birds (about 25 percent of female tree swallows in a given area) that constantly revisit already occupied nest cavities throughout the nesting season. She approaches these nests with a distinctive flutter-flight, hovering with shallow wingbeats; if she finds the nest resident absent, she may immediately claim the site and proceed to defend it as her own. The male partner of the displaced female generally does not respond aggressively to such a takeover, apparently accepting any female present on the nest as belonging there. The juvenilelike plumage of the invading female, as well as its submissive flutter-flight display, may permit it to approach active nests without challenge.

In checking my own tree swallow nest boxes, I occasionally find other evidence of puzzling domestic events. One of the strangest situations I encountered occurred in the spring of 1996, when I found a tree swallow sitting on three of its own eggs in the lined portion of a nest box crammed with house wren sticks; several hundred feet adjacent, a nest box contained six house wren eggs lying in the feathered nest of a tree swallow. The root cause of such anomalies probably lies in the birds' intense competition for nest cavities, which are often in short supply. Occasionally, nesting groups—a male and two or more females—may tend or occupy the same nest cavity. Being dived upon by a trio of tree swallows when checking my nest boxes became a fairly common occurrence.

EGGS AND YOUNG: four to six; eggs white. INCUBATION: by female; fourteen or fifteen days; hatching asynchronous, over one to two days. FEEDING OF YOUNG: by both sexes; insects. FLEDGING: average of three weeks.

Summer. Tree swallows raise only one brood per year. After fledging, juveniles continue to be fed by parents for several days. Sometimes juvenile tree swallows attempt to pirate food at still-functional nests of other tree swallows (*kleptoparasitism*). Researcher Michael R. Lombardo's 1987 "exploratory-dispersal" hypothesis suggested that such visitors are exploring potential nest sites for the next year. (The relatively low frequency of yearling philopatry in this species would seem to argue against this thesis.)

Annual molt of flight and body feathers begins in July, sometimes before nesting is completed, continuing through October. After fledglings become independent, young and adults alike usually abandon the breeding area, often flocking and roosting together in open marshy habitats where aerial insects are abundant. To persons who have witnessed them, the evening preroosting aerial displays—"tornadoes of tree swallows," Roger Tory Peterson described them—are spectacular events. Hundreds or thousands of tree swallows gather over a marsh roosting area, swirling down from the sky in a funnel cloud of birds similar to the evening flights of chimney swifts into smokestack roosts. Such roosting flights can occur during any season except spring.

Premigratory flocking begins in August, sometimes earlier. Large flocks—up to millions along the Atlantic coast—may gather with much noise and confusion in marshes or on power lines. Some researchers have described "mass examinations" of nest boxes by tree swallows during this period—an extension of Lombardo's hypothesis? Flocks may remain on the northern range into October, however, making this species the latest of fall migrant swallows.

Fall, Winter. Tree swallows migrate in daytime, moving in much larger flocks than in spring (many more birds now exist). Again, they sometimes investigate potential nest sites during fall migration. Migration peaks during September. Two main migration channels exist: Most tree swallows east of the Great Lakes travel along the eastern seaboard, wintering from New Jersey south to Florida and the Caribbean. Midwestern and Great Plains populations move down the Mississippi flyway, wintering on the Gulf coast and south to Venezuela. Local populations also winter south of San Francisco on the Pacific coast. A certain field near Chiapas, Mexico,

hosts up to a million tree swallows that roost there from December through March. Tree swallows may occasionally linger over winter in parts of New England and Long Island owing to their dietary versatility. Often in fall and winter, tree swallows roost communally with other swallows, including bank, barn, cliff, and northern rough-winged swallows and purple martins.

Tree swallows are about half molted when migration begins in late summer, and they complete their annual molt by October or November. Most tree swallows are en route northward by late February or early March.

Ecology. Tree swallows require open areas, but they may frequent several habitat types within that designation: fields, marshes, open bogs, shorelines and dunes, savannas, pastures, roadsides, and hedgerows. Often they favor open country near lakes or ponds, but not invariably; my own heavily used tree swallow nest boxes stand on a dry upland savanna miles from open water. The most important components of tree swallow breeding habitat are nest cavities—standing dead trees in ponds or wetland margins, or nest boxes within or adjacent to open areas for foraging. Beavers indirectly benefit tree swallows by creating ponds, flooding out trees that die, become excavated by woodpeckers, and ultimately serve tree swallows. The birds frequent the same types of habitat in winter, except that cavities are unneeded.

Tree swallows never excavate their own tree cavities but "recycle" the work of woodpeckers. The tree swallow's semicolonial nesting habits probably owe as much to the spacing of cavity sites within a habitat as to social preference of the birds. Most tree swallows favor a spacing of at least thirty to fifty feet from their nearest neighbor, though occasionally they nest much closer together; they also prefer substantial open space around the nest site. Eastern bluebird nest box programs, which have widely benefited that species, have probably also resulted in tree swallow population increases (see Eastern Bluebird). Tree swallows seem to prefer south-facing cavities for nest sites. Most nests within cavities consist mainly of dried grasses, sometimes other plant materials as well. Some tree swallows, however, collect very little nesting material. In my own nest boxes, a scant-covered, practically bare floor during tree swallow occupancy is not uncommon. A characteristic of many tree swallow nests is a lining of feathers—often quite large ones—in and around the nest cup. These are not the swallows' own feathers but those of other species, usually added after egg laying and incubation begin. The male collects them, and the female places them so that the quill ends stick into the nest and the feather tips curl over the eggs, covering them when the bird leaves the nest. Collected feathers are mostly white contour feathers, sometimes from waterfowl (probably collected from water), gull rookeries, and poultry yards. Almost any size and color of bird feathers may be used; I have seen ruffed grouse tail feathers in nests, and the birds will even collect from torn feather pillows. Researchers speculate that feathers in the nest may provide added insulation and a barrier to moisture and skin parasites. Occasionally tree swallows occupy rural mailboxes, wall crevices, and even holes in the ground as nest cavities.

Tree swallow diet mainly consists of flying insects captured over land or water, rarely from water or ground surfaces. Some 40 percent of the insect diet consists of flies, with lesser amounts of beetles, ants, grasshoppers, dragonflies, stoneflies, mayflies, and caddisflies. During winter and early-spring migration, at least in northeastern coastal areas, tree swallows become almost exclusively frugivorous (fruit eating), with especially heavy consumption of *Myrica* fruits (wax-myrtle and bayberry species). While many birds consume *Myrica* nutlets, tree swallows probably depend upon them to a larger extent than most; the birds readily digest the waxy coating of these fruits, which in these areas may form the entire diet for long periods in winter. Tree swallows also occasionally eat fruits of red cedar, Virginia-creeper, and dogwoods plus seeds of sedges and bulrushes. This ability to turn vegetarian in the absence of insects enables tree swallows to adapt more efficiently than most other swallows to cold spells and the vagaries of weather.

Competitive interactions abound for most hole nesters, and tree swallows are no exception. They contend for nest cavities not only with each other but also with purple martins, great crested flycatchers, northern flickers, eastern and mountain bluebirds, house wrens, European starlings, and house sparrows. The wrens, flickers, and sparrows are known to destroy tree swallow eggs and nestlings on occasion; bluebirds usually successfully defend their nests against tree swallows, which may occasionally kill bluebird nestlings. Food competition appears insignificant, but competition with other tree swallows for nest-lining feathers may become intense at times. Aggressive "feather chasing" among tree swallows often seems to show elements of play behavior: A bird may repeatedly drop its feather, then retrieve it, attracting other swallows to the chase. Feather chases may also occur after the breeding season, leading one researcher to speculate that "chases for feathers may possibly serve some social function in addition to acquiring feathers for the nest."

Bird predators on tree swallow eggs and nestlings include northern flickers, American kestrels, American crows, and common grackles. House wren and house sparrow predation is probably a secondary result of nest cavity competition. Rat snakes, chipmunks, weasels, raccoons, deer mice, and feral cats also raid tree swallow nests. Flying or perched tree swallows are vulnerable to sharp-shinned hawks, American kestrels, merlins, peregrine falcons, great horned owls, and black-billed magpies. Nest parasitism by brown-headed cowbirds, as for most cavity-nesting species, seldom occurs. Nestlings, however, are frequently parasitized by blowfly *(Protocalliphora sialia)* larvae, which rarely kill them but may reduce vigor and growth rates. The larvae attach to the nestlings at night, sucking their blood, then hide in the nesting material during the day. Hypothermia or starvation from a lack of flying insects may result from abnormally cold weather during the nestling stage. "Weather, pesticides, draining of wetlands, elimination of fruits, and local shortage of nest sites aggravated by competition with introduced species [starlings and house sparrows]," according to one researcher, covers the gamut of threats to tree swallow populations.

Focus. Availability of cavity nesting sites is probably the chief limiting factor on tree swallow breeding populations. Over the past few decades, regional eastern and central populations appear relatively stable or increasing, and the birds have also extended their breeding range southward. How much of this abundance owes significantly to human placement of nest boxes remains un-

clear. Opinions differ; some researchers believe that, although nest boxes may tend to increase local populations of tree swallows, the number of tree swallows annually fledged from nest boxes probably does not exceed 2 or 3 percent of the total; others consider the percentage much higher. Birders erect relatively few nest boxes specifically for tree swallows; usually the swallows occupy boxes intended for wood ducks or eastern bluebirds. Nest-box interiors should be roughened or grooved to facilitate the bird's exit; tree swallows often die when they become trapped in smooth-walled boxes.

When I check my nest boxes in spring, I find that tree swallows claim their sites soon after their arrival; they often vigorously defend them weeks before actual nesting begins, which invariably occurs only after bluebird nesting has begun in some of the adjacent boxes. A defending swallow often remains perched atop its nest box as I approach, not flying up until I stand at arm's length, then circles overhead and dives at me. Later in the season, when nestlings are present, the birds seem much more tolerant of intrusion. It remains unclear whether they have become somewhat habituated to it by then or have eased defense because of diminished territorial impulses—maybe both.

Thoreau, who called this species the "white-bellied swallow," noted its tendency to perch on wires; he identified the birds as "among the phenomena that cluster about the telegraph."

Average life span of tree swallows is about 2.7 years, with maximums of 8 to 11 years. Only about 20 percent of fledglings survive their first year, after which annual survival ranges from 40 to 60 percent.

Tufted Titmouse
(Parus bicolor)

At about six inches long, the tufted titmouse is the largest parid and the smallest crested bird of the eastern United States. It can be identified by its gray upper parts, black forehead patch, tufted crest, and rusty flanks. Its whistled songs and buzzy call notes are also distinctive. Sexes look alike, but juveniles lack the dark forehead patch.

Close relatives. Plain and bridled titmice (*P. inornatus, P. wollweberi*) are southwestern species. Other North American parids of the same genus include the chickadees.

Behaviors. Tufted titmice, which much resemble chickadees in their agility and foraging behaviors, are likewise familiar visitors to yard feeders. The clarion sounds that emanate from this plain little bird in spring—most typically a clear "peter peter peter"—are altogether disproportionate to its size. Its less musical notes resemble those of chickadees but sound more nasal and grating. Like chickadees, titmice are cavity nesters and gregarious for most of the year, but unlike chickadees, their flocks consist mainly of family groups. Few birds display such abruptly contrasting styles of behavior in a breeding season, from loudly conspicuous exhibitionism to utter stealth and silence. Titmice are also more sedentary and range less widely than chickadees and are not so adaptive to various habitats.

Titmouse range spans most of the continental United States east of the Great Plains. During the past fifty years, observers have traced this bird's remarkable northward range expansion, a movement that somewhat parallels that of the northern cardinal but is slower paced. Since about 1965, however, this expansion has slowed and halted in many areas. Tufted titmice are year-round dwellers and do not migrate.

Spring. By early spring, titmouse flocks have largely dispersed into pairs and solitary birds. Breeding territories typically comprise about two to five acres, depending on habitat. Territorial skirmishes and incessant singing of males, with males often chasing females and feeding their mates, mark this period. As nesting commences in April and May, titmice fall silent and become difficult to detect.

EGGS AND YOUNG: five or six; eggs white with fine speckles. INCUBATION: by female, which is fed by male; about two weeks. FEEDING OF YOUNG: by both sexes; insects. FLEDGING: about eighteen days.

Summer, Fall. Where second nestings occur (mainly in the birds' southern range), juveniles of the first brood may help feed second-brood nestlings. The noisy fledglings continue to be fed by the parents for a month or more after leaving the nest. In contrast to the young of most passerine species, which disperse from their birth areas in late summer or fall, titmouse juveniles remain in family groups for several months, often on a home range of fifteen to twenty acres. The annual feather molt occurs in August.

Winter. Titmice become most visible in winter as they forage in plain sight and visit yard feeders. Small family flocks remain together through much of the winter, sometimes joining temporary mixed flocks of black-capped chickadees, downy woodpeckers, nuthatches, and kinglets. The pair bond apparently lasts all year, as in chickadees, but details of titmouse flock behaviors, dispersion, and pairing are not well understood. As territorial impulses quicken in late winter, the yearling birds finally disperse widely, many to form their own pair bonds. Listen in February for the ringing songs of male titmice as they begin to establish or reestablish their breeding territories. In many places, titmice are the first vocal songbirds of the year, providing the first loud, sure forecast of spring.

Ecology. Primarily a woodland bird, the tufted titmouse favors deciduous and mixed forests, moist bottomlands, and swamps. Dead trees with suitable cavities for nesting are important habitat needs. For feeding, titmice range outside these habitats to edges, thickets, suburban yards, and parks.

Unlike chickadees, titmice do not excavate their own nest cavities but use natural cavities or vacant woodpecker holes. The female brings huge billfuls of mosses, grasses, and often wet dead leaves, as well as bits of fur, string, cloth, and cast snakeskins, packing them into the cavity and lining the cup with finer materials. Occasionally a pair uses the same cavity for succeeding years.

Spring and summer foods consist mainly of caterpillars, plus wasps, scale insects, ants, beetles, and spiders. Like chickadees, titmice also forage on twigs and bark for insect and spider eggs and insect pupae. In fall and winter, the diet turns mostly vegetarian. Apple fragments, blackberries, elderberries, blueberries, and wild grapes are favored fruits; acorns, beechnuts, and corn become staple winter items. Observers believe that this bird's heavy use of yard feeders in the North accounts at least in part for its range expansion. Like chickadees, titmice often cache food items for short periods in such places as bark crevices, among foliage, or under moss or soil.

Small cavity-nesting species such as downy woodpeckers, chickadees, nuthatches, and house wrens may contend with titmice for nest sites. In areas where dead or dying trees are few, titmice may use nest boxes. Food competition probably becomes significant only in winter. The many bird and mammal consumers of acorns and beechnuts often strip these trees in the fall; competition becomes even tighter in years when nut production is poor. In areas where titmouse and chickadee ranges overlap, the potential for competition between these close relatives seems likely, but field observations thus far are inconclusive.

Raccoons are probably the foremost nest predators on titmice. Around yard feeders, sharp-shinned hawks and domestic cats often menace the birds. Brown-headed cowbirds rarely parasitize cavity-nesting birds.

Focus. The tufted titmouse longevity record is thirteen years, but most titmice probably survive only two or three years. If only half the amount of research lavished on chickadees had focused on titmice, we would know much more than we do about these

birds. Many of their flock patterns and behaviors may be found to parallel those of chickadees; other parid species vary extensively in certain social and behavioral features, however, so maybe this common bird holds some distinctive surprises for us.

The name *tit* originated in England (where the name *titmouse* is unknown), apparently from the Icelandic word *tittr*, which meant anything small; the Anglo-Saxon *mase* signified "a small bird." Another explanation is that the bird's large black eyes, supposedly mouselike, account for its mammalian moniker. Tomtit is a common local name.

Turkey Vulture
(*Cathartes aura*)

New World vulture family (Ciconiidae), order Ciconiiformes. Both sexes of these large birds are brownish black with small, red, featherless heads and silvery under wings. The shallow-V (*dihedral*) posture of their five- to six-foot wingspread and their rocking, tilting flight as they soar are also characteristic.

Close relatives. Other North American species include the black vulture (*Coragyps atratus*) and the California condor (*Gymnogyps californianus*). Three other species reside in South America.

Behaviors. Vulture flight requires daytime updrafts of warm air, known as *thermals,* on which the birds, seldom flapping their wings,

ride. As they circle and coast from one updraft to another, they sink at a rate slower than the warm air rises. Thermals usually begin rising at midmorning, and that's when vultures go aloft. You'll see few vultures in the air on a cold, cloudy day without strong thermals.

The ratio of low body weight to area of their broad, planklike wings gives turkey vultures their tippy flight; primary feathers at the wing tips extend like fingers, providing deeply slotted air flow that reduces turbulence and lowers stalling speed.

Except when nesting, turkey vultures are social birds, often soaring at different levels in groups of three, four, or many more. These spiraling formations are called *kettles*. Turkey vultures also feed together on large animal carcasses. They are most gregarious at night, when hundreds may roost together, often in tall electric towers or large trees. These communal roosts occur year-round, and the birds' fidelity to the same roosting sites may last for years. Before leaving roosts in the morning, vultures often stand with wings outspread in the sun, raising their lowered nighttime temperatures. On the ground, turkey vultures are awkward and graceless. They hop, shuffle, and sidle as if crippled, sometimes uttering hisses and raucous grunts. They often defecate on their legs, which gives the legs a whitened appearance and may help regulate their temperature on hot days.

Turkey vultures are migratory in North America. Their breeding range spans the Western Hemisphere from southern Canada to Cape Horn.

Spring. Turkey vultures move into their northern breeding areas from early March through May. From Panama they travel by day, covering more than three thousand miles to the upper Midwest in about ten days without feeding. Often while traveling, they ride up over advancing storm fronts, sometimes up to four miles high. Courtship behaviors include follow flight, in which a female leads a male in a series of soaring maneuvers. Breeding territory probably extends only around the nest vicinity. Turkey vulture home range, however—the aerial distance it covers in hunting for carcasses—probably extends many miles. One study arrived at a figure of about eleven thousand acres.

Regurgitation of carrion makes the nest a putrid-smelling site. When threatened near the nest, turkey vultures often vomit; the stench may have the same defensive function as a skunk's spray. If that doesn't work, the birds may collapse and play dead. Vulture pairs, which probably mate for life, often return to the same nest sites year after year.

EGGS AND YOUNG: two; eggs white with brown spots and blotches. INCUBATION: by both sexes; five or six weeks. FEEDING OF YOUNG: by both sexes; regurgitated carrion. FLEDGING: about six weeks.

Summer. Juvenile vultures have brownish, smooth heads instead of red, wrinkled ones, and their beaks are dark tipped in contrast to the adult's uniformly ivory-colored one. The juveniles join adult birds at communal roosts, which may serve as information centers; that is, birds may follow roost mates to known carcass sites. Often the birds settle into roosts about an hour before sunset. The annual feather molt of adult birds proceeds gradually through summer into fall.

Fall. Turkey vultures begin their withdrawal from northern areas in September and October, often grouping into large, soaring kettles that circle steadily southward. Probably even southern U.S. turkey vultures shift southward as northern vultures supplant them. Wintering turkey vultures reside north to the Ohio River; isolated vultures may remain farther north, especially during mild winters. But much of the North American population passes south through Mexico and Central America. Peak flights in early November over Panama City have numbered almost two hundred thousand birds per day.

Winter. Winter activities consist solely of hunting carrion and feeding. In the Neotropical rain forest, turkey vultures cruise low above the dense tree canopy. Their northward movements begin in late winter. During this migration, they appear at certain locations with great regularity, seldom varying by more than a day or so each year.

Ecology. Nesting and feeding habitats differ. The birds favor isolated nest sites—dark recesses in caves, rocky cliffs, hollow logs, tree snags, or brush piles; on the ground in dense thickets; or in abandoned barns or other buildings. Foraging habitats, except in the rain forest, are open lands and fields where carrion may be easily located.

Turkey vultures use no nesting materials. The nest itself is merely a bare surface of gravel, rotted wood debris, or old flooring.

Debate raged for years among scientists over whether vultures locate carrion primarily by sight or by smell. Probably they use both senses. Vultures cannot detect a carcass by smell until it is about twelve hours old, and they prefer fresher carcasses over badly rotted ones. Above a certain height, it seems unlikely that their smell apparatus, good as it is, can detect food. In the rain forest, where they must cruise low, they apparently locate carcasses exclusively by smell. Their keen vision, equaling that of hawks, enables vultures to spot carcasses from high altitudes and also to watch the movements of other soaring vultures or ground scavengers that may find food.

A favorite food is dead snakes. Often a vulture's first item of choice is the eyes of a carcass. When feeding on dead skunks, they leave only bones and scent glands (great horned owls are not so fastidious). Occasionally they also feed on vegetable matter such as rotting pumpkins. One study found that turkey vultures fed on carcasses mainly during midday hours; during later afternoon, when thermal updrafts were strongest, they soared at high altitudes, possibly searching for the next day's meal. A few records exist of turkey vultures' attacking small or weak living prey, but these cases are rare. After feeding, the birds regurgitate pellets containing fur, bones, and other indigestible materials.

Especially in the rain forest, vultures must compete with mammal and insect scavengers in finding carcasses quickly. In North America, American crows, common ravens, and many mammals, including foxes, coyotes, and raccoons, vigorously compete with turkey vultures, especially at large carcasses.

No regular predators exist, though eggs and young may sometimes be taken by ground mammals such as skunks or raccoons that may brave the foul "barf barrier."

Focus. Turkey buzzard is a popular name for this vulture, though the true buzzard (*Buteo buteo*) is not a vulture at all but a European hawk. The turkey designation refers to the bird's red, turkeylike head (a few American colonial hunters, thinking they had shot turkeys, reported a "most disagreeable flavor"). The word *vulture* derives from a Latin word meaning to pluck or tear.

New World vultures were long classified as raptors closely related to hawks, ospreys, and falcons. Recently, however, bird taxonomists officially certified what vulture researchers had long known—that the birds are "nothing but short-legged storks," as one eminent ornithologist stated. Vulture feet, unlike those of raptors, are not adapted for grasping; the talons are weakly hooked, and the foot cannot fist.

The vulture's image in our culture is one of grim death, symbolizing the charnel house; it is the sinister, patient awaiter of a victim's certain demise. Even many famous bird lovers have found it difficult to accept this "winged ghoul" in the same class of creatures as robins and bluebirds.

Today, however, we know that vultures perform vital environmental services. Not only do they scavenge dead animals, helping recycle their bodily constituents, but they also are sanitarians in another sense: Their corrosive digestive system kills several deadly disease organisms, including *Salmonella* and bacteria that produce hog cholera, anthrax, and botulinum toxins. Other vulture adaptations include their bald heads, which shed gore, allowing them to probe deeply into carcasses; their razor-sharp, hooked beaks, efficient as butchers' shears; and their rough, raspy tongues.

Turkey vulture populations have shifted remarkably at various times and places. Since about 1920, the birds have expanded their range considerably, and they continue to do so. Probably the abundance of road-killed carcasses and increasing white-tailed deer populations account for much of this expansion. In some areas they have become aircraft hazards. The U.S. Air Force blamed them for the loss of ten military planes from 1989 to 1994 and began mapping their seasonal densities. Highest concentrations—up to forty vultures per ten square miles—were found in skies over Florida and Texas.

The northward movement of turkey vultures in March has put one small town on the tourist map. Hinckley, Ohio, located south of Cleveland, celebrates a Buzzard Sunday festival every year on the first Sunday after March 15, the date when townsfolk claim the vultures show up. The vultures usually are there by that date, but most years they probably first appear days or weeks earlier, when the chamber of commerce isn't looking.

White-throated Sparrow
(Zonotrichia albicollis)

This seven-inch-long northern sparrow can be recognized by its white throat patch and the yellow mark between eye and bill, in the area known as the *lore*. Its clear, plaintive song begins with two or three long, whistled notes followed by a series of three-note phrases: "Oh-h-h swee-e-et Canada Canada Canada Canada." A cardinal-like "chink" note is also characteristic. Except for morphic differences in pairs, sexes look alike.

Close relatives. The white-crowned sparrow (*Z. leucophrys*) is the white-throat's nearest northeastern kin. Harris' sparrow (*Z. querula*) resides in the west-central United States; the golden-crowned sparrow (*Z. atricapilla*) is a Pacific coastal species.

Behaviors. Its ringing, melancholy song heard from afar voices the northern wilderness as hauntingly as loon, raven, and wolf but is more commonly heard than all three. White-throats breed from the upper Great Lakes and New England throughout much of forested Canada. Like ruffed grouse and screech-owls, they are *polymorphic*, showing two distinct color forms: birds with black and white head stripes, and birds with brown and tan head stripes. Unlike grouse and screech-owls, however, white-throats tend to pair with their opposite-colored morphs. Research by James K. Lowther in 1962 indicated that behavioral differences may account for this tendency: White-striped males are more aggressive than tan-striped males toward singers of both morphs, driving them off; since white-striped females sing and tan-striped females do not, the upshot of this tendency is that white-striped males monopolize tan-striped females, leaving white-striped females to mate with the less aggressive tan-striped males. This system, called *negative assortative mating,* sounds more complex than it is.

Most white-throats migrate, though some, especially adult males, remain in the breeding range year-round. These birds are most commonly seen as they forage in flocks during spring and fall migrations.

Spring. A prenesting molt occurs in early spring as the birds arrive on their breeding range. Only head and body feathers are replaced; the white-striped morph acquires its black and white coloration at this time. Males arrive one or two weeks ahead of females in April and May, often returning to their previous breeding territories. Females return less often to the same sites, so most pairs remain monogamous only for the season. The male's territorial song seldom interrupts the song of a neighboring male, as if by mutual agreement to grant each other solos, thereby enabling each to vocalize its claim to the fullest. Not uncommonly, males also sing at night. Song decreases when the female arrives but usually recommences if predation or other failure causes renesting. She builds the nest, and the pair becomes silent and secretive. White-throats are excitable, easily aroused by a birder's pishing sounds, especially near the nest. Even then, however, they usually remain hidden in the underbrush. An incubating female may not flush from her nest until almost stepped on.

EGGS AND YOUNG: four to six; eggs glossy, whitish, heavily brown spotted. INCUBATION: by female; eleven to fourteen days. FEEDING OF YOUNG: by both sexes; insects. FLEDGING: eight or nine days.

Summer. I have found white-throat nests containing nestlings in July, and nesting may even continue into August. Since pairs seldom attempt to raise two broods, however, these later nestings probably result from one or more previous nest failures. Renesting white-throats usually rebuild more than one hundred feet away from the previous site. The relatively short duration from hatching to fledging may relate to the low placement of nests and their consequent vulnerability to predators. Parents continue to feed fledglings for about a month. Then females and juveniles often depart the territory, while males may remain there until fall. White-throats molt their entire plumage in late July and August; both morphs acquire tan-striped head plumage that lasts until the following spring.

Fall. White-throats migrate, usually in small flocks and at night, through September and October. During the day, they settle in brushy areas to feed. Occasionally they sing during these layover periods in both fall and spring. White-throats exhibit differential migration, with the females and the heavily streaked juveniles traveling farthest south, while many adult males remain on or nearer the southern breeding range.

Winter. Most white-throats winter from the lower Great Lakes south to the Gulf Coast and northern Mexico. Individuals often return to the previous winter's site, which, in optimal habitats, may encompass less than an acre. Rigid dominance hierarchies govern white-throat flocks in winter. The flock, averaging five to fifteen birds, often forages in association with other ground-feeding sparrows and dark-eyed juncos. "The [eastern] towhee is the white-throated sparrow's best friend," wrote one old-time birder; although breeding ranges of the two species coincide only in a relatively narrow band, they often occupy similar winter habitats. North-wintering white-throats often appear at yard feeders.

Ecology. The white-throat's primary habitats are natural openings in northern coniferous or mixed forests, often in or near wetlands. Such areas include bogs, swampy alder and shoreline thickets, edges of burnt-over clearings, shrubby ravines, and windfall gaps. These favored edge habitats often border stands of large coniferous trees. The birds also frequent dense lowland and upland thickets and brush piles in both summer and winter. During migrations, however, they may appear in almost any habitat, including marshes, suburban lawns, and deciduous forests.

White-throats usually nest on the ground, occasionally two or three feet high in shrubs or small trees. Extremely well concealed in the low vegetation, the small, cuplike nests are usually sited at edges of clearings, though I have also found their nests in sphagnum bogs. Often the nest lies within several feet of a lookout perch such as a stump or small tree. Coarse grasses, bark fibers, pine needles, and rootlets form the nest, which the female lines with finer grasses and sometimes hair.

White-throats forage from the ground to treetops, seldom far from cover. Foraging methods likewise vary. On the ground, the birds scratch with both feet; in trees, they hop systematically along one branch after another. At times they also hawk insects in flight. In early spring, the birds devour several kinds of tree buds and blossoms (staminate flowers of beech are favorites), plus elm and maple seeds. The breeding-season diet consists mainly of insects, many gleaned from leaves and branches. Ants, small wasps, beetles, caterpillars, and spiders are the foremost items. In late summer and fall, the diet shifts to seeds—ragweeds and smartweeds alone may provide some 25 percent of the annual food intake—and pulpy fruits, minus skins and large seeds, including wild grapes, blueberries, bunchberries, and dogwood and poison-ivy fruits. White-throats are probably the foremost fruit-eating sparrows.

Its feeding adaptability probably gains the white-throat a degree of competitive advantage in its habitats. In many areas, it shares similar ground-nesting habitats with song sparrows and dark-eyed juncos. One study indicated that it favors a density of nesting cover midway between the sparser preferences of the song sparrow and the denser preferences of the junco.

Hawks and owls sometimes capture white-throats, but most predation probably occurs at the nest. As with all ground-nesting birds, white-throat eggs and nestlings are vulnerable to many mammal predators, such as raccoons, skunks, squirrels, and red foxes. Brown-headed cowbirds occasionally parasitize the nests, but white-throats are not common cowbird hosts, probably because most nest in remote areas outside typical cowbird habitats.

Focus. Vernacular names include Canada bird and Peabody bird, both referring to its characteristic song. The oldest white-throat on record survived almost ten years, but average longevity is probably less than half that.

White-throats seem to be declining throughout much of their breeding range. As edge dwellers, they probably benefited from lumbering, increasing their abundance from presettlement times. As north-country breeders, however, they seem caught in a habitat squeeze of sorts: Both extensive clear-cutting and the aging of mature forests deprive them of optimal habitat (though early-stage regrowth of clear-cut areas attracts them), and both continue to occur in numerous areas of the breeding range.

Yellow-bellied Sapsucker
(Sphyrapicus varius)

A white wing patch, bright red forehead patch, and dull yellowish belly mark adult sapsuckers. Sexes differ only in the throat patch, which is red in males and white in females. Juveniles lack the head coloring. Sapsucker drumming is a rapid series of thumps slowing to several slower, arrhythmic knocks. These birds emit a whining, catbirdlike, mewing note and a squealing "cheerrr."

Close relatives. Western North American sapsuckers include Williamson's sapsucker (*S. thyroideus*), red-breasted sapsucker (*S. ruber*), and red-naped sapsucker (*S. nuchalis*).

Behaviors. Sapsuckers don't really suck sap—they lap it from parallel rows of small pits they drill on living tree trunks. Such pitted areas always indicate sapsucker presence. Sapsuckers are also skillful fly catchers, sailing out briefly to snatch an insect. The sapsucker's long tongue is brushlike and blots up sap by capillary action. This bird, the red-headed woodpecker, and the northern flicker are the only true migrants among northeastern woodpeckers.

Spring. Sapsucker breeding range is the relatively narrow strip of northern hardwood forest that spans the continent. Males usually arrive in early April, several days before females. The monogamous pair bond is a function of territory, since both members return to their previous nesting area. Courtship activities—loud drumming, ritual tapping, bobbing motions, and snipelike wing-winnowing sounds—precede mating, which occurs in May and June. The territory, extending one hundred feet or less around the nest tree, is centered in the home range, which may include several acres enclosing sap well trees. Nestlings squeal and chatter almost constantly in the tree cavities; such "talking trees" make sapsucker nests relatively easy for a sharp-eared listener to find.

EGGS AND YOUNG: five or six. INCUBATION: by both sexes; twelve or thirteen days. FEEDING OF YOUNG: by both sexes; sap, fruits, insects, sometimes regurgitated. FLEDGING: about four weeks.

Summer. Young birds fledge by mid-July. About a week before they do, parent birds begin a brief period of renewed courtship drumming and displays but do not renest. Sapsucker families, bound to their territories by one or two sap trees where they regularly feed, remain together through summer. The annual molt begins soon after the nestlings fledge, continuing into early fall. Juvenile birds have acquired most of their adult plumage by the time they migrate. Many sapsuckers begin moving southward by late summer.

Fall. Sapsuckers migrate through the fall. Banding studies have shown that females travel farther south than males, an example of *differential migration.*

Winter. Sapsucker winter range extends from the central tier of states southward to Panama and the Bahamas. Although this sapsucker is sometimes called the most migratory of woodpeckers, small numbers often remain in southern locales of the breeding range through winter.

Ecology. Sapsuckers inhabit forests and woodlots, preferring hardwood or mixed stands often near water and forest openings. Mature aspen groves are frequent habitats.

Sapsuckers almost always excavate new nest cavities each year, frequently in trees showing their previous cavities. Cavities average about twenty-five feet high, often on the south side of large aspen trees infested with the hoof-shaped brackets of false tinder fungus (*Phellinus tremulae*). This fungus softens and decays the heartwood, making it easy to excavate; the surrounding hard shell of sapwood protects the nest cavity. Other fungus-infected trees often used by these birds include birches, American beech, and maples. Vacated sapsucker cavities near a functional nest hole are often reoccupied by gray, red, or flying squirrels, whose presence many sapsuckers seem to tolerate.

Except during the breeding season, sapsuckers feed mainly from the sap wells they excavate. They first feed on the soft inner bark exposed by drilling, then return at intervals to feed from the flowing pits. The birds defend their sap trees from other birds and mammals.

Sap well excavation follows a progressive pattern: First a bird drills a horizontal *primary band* of squarish holes, sometimes encircling the trunk. If sap flows, the bird then drills more holes above the primary band, eventually creating vertical columns of pits. *Bast bands* are series of ragged holes where the birds drill for inner bark, mainly in winter and spring. *Spiral sap bands* wind around the uppermost twigs. More than two hundred native tree species may be drilled for sap. Preferred above all are white birches, which have a sap sugar content of 20 percent. Other favored trees include Scotch pine, basswood, apple, and hickories. The birds often select scarred or injured trees, which often accumulate abundant nutrients near the point of injury as tissue healing begins. Except in early spring, the sap consumed is *phloem* sap, the nutrient-rich liquid being transported *down* the tree from the leaves. Although the sap in winter-dormant northern trees remains stationary, thawing days and freezing nights cause some sap movement, and the birds tend to drill on the sunny side of trunks. Conifers have sap storage cells and are favored in freezing weather.

Sapsuckers never entirely abandon their sap wells in either summer or winter ranges. But during the breeding season, when protein is needed, their main diet shifts to insects—carpenter ants, crane flies, mayflies, beetles, moths (including destructive spruce budworms and forest tent caterpillars), yellowjackets, and hornets. Many of these are probably captured at the flowing sap wells. In the fall, sapsuckers also consume berries and other fruits.

Since most woodpeckers do not excavate nest cavities in trees that contain previously used holes, the sapsucker's tolerance for such sites, shared mostly with squirrels, gives them a competitive edge over other cavity nesters.

European starlings are probably their foremost competitors for cavities.

Sap well users, however, include a host of opportunists that exploit a food resource made accessible by the birds. In most cases, such feeders are *commensals*—that is, they benefit from, but do not hinder, sapsucker activity. Among the thirty-five bird species that feed on sap or insects at sap wells, ruby-throated hummingbirds are the most frequent and may almost totally depend on fresh sap wells in early spring; sap well trees, especially near water, are good places to look for hummingbird nests.

Probably the sapsucker's foremost nest predators are raccoons. Trees containing many excavations may weaken with repeated use and heartrot. Unless the trunk walls of the nest cavity remain solid, a raccoon can chew through them to reach the nest. Squirrels are potential predators, but sapsuckers closely monitor their movements, readily attacking if the animal approaches a nest cavity.

Focus. Much controversy existed in past years about the amount of tree mortality caused by sapsuckers. Foresters once declared them outright enemies, but subsequent research has revealed that the birds kill relatively few trees by their girdling sap wells, often preferring fungus-infected or defective trees. Certainly they kill *some* trees; these are often extensively drilled birches. One researcher estimated that a sapsucker pair may account for the death of one or two trees per year. But weighed against the abundance of destructive insects they consume, especially during caterpillar irruptions, sapsuckers more than pay their dues.

Index

Page numbers in italics indicate illustrations.

hummingbirds
 black-chinned (*Archilochus alexandri*), 152
 ruby-throated (*Archilochus colubris*), 152, 152–56, *155*
 rufous (*Selasphorus rufus*), 152

jays
 blue (*Cyanocitta cristata*), 28, 28–32, *31*
 gray (*Perisoreus canadensis*), 28
 Steller's (*Cyanocitta stelleri*), 28
juncos
 dark-eyed (*Junco hyemalis*), 60, 60–62
 yellow-eyed (*Junco phaeonotus*), 60

kestrels
 American (*Falco sparverius*), *10*, 10–13
 common (*Falco tinnunculus*), 10–11
kingbirds, eastern, 139

Lee, Harper, 131
Leopold, Aldo, 24, 44, 45, 46, 47
Lowther, James K., 178

mallard (*Anas platyrhynchos*), *112*, 112–16, *115*
Miner, Jack, 48
mockingbirds, northern (*Mimus polyglottos*), *128*, 128–31
mourning dove (*Zenaida macroura*), *117*, 117–20
mynahs
 crested (*Acridotheres cristatellus*), 80
 hill (*Gracula religiosa*), 80

National Audubon Society, 111
Nero, Robert W., 141, 144, 146
nest box programs, eastern bluebird, 73, 169
Nice, Margaret Morse, 164
North American Bluebird Society, 73
northern cardinal (*Cardinalis cardinalis*), *121*, 121–24, *123*
northern flicker (*Colaptes auratus*), *125*, 125–27

northern mockingbird (*Mimus polyglottos*), *128*, 128–31

Ogilvie, M. A., 46
orioles
 Altamira (*Icterus gularis*), 18
 Audubon's (*Icterus graduacauda*), 18
 Baltimore (*Icterus galbula*), 18, 18–21
 Bullock's (*Icterus bullockii*), 18, 20–21
 hooded (*Icterus cucullatus*), 18
 orchard (*Icterus spurius*), 18
 Scott's (*Icterus parisorum*), 18
owls
 eagle (*Bubo bubo*), 89
 eastern screech (*Otus asio*), 74, 74–76
 flammulated (*Otus flammeolus*), 74
 great gray (*Strix nebulosa*), 89
 great horned (*Bubo virginianus*), *88*, 88–91, *91*
 scops (*Otus scops*), 74
 snowy (*Nyctea scandiaca*), 89
 western screech (*Otus kennicottii*), 74
 whiskered screech (*Otus trichopsis*), 74

pesticides, 17
pigeons
 band-tailed (*Columba fasciata*), 148
 passenger (*Ectopistes migratorius*), 117
 red-billed (*Columba flavirostris*), 148
 rock (*Columba livia*), 117, *148*, 148–51
 white-crowned (*Columba leucocephala*), 148
 wood (*Columba palumbus*), 148
pine siskin (*Carduelis pinus*), 6
Pinkowski, Ben, 73
polygamous breeding, 141
polymorphic birds, 178
purple finch (*Carpodacus purpureus*), 98–102
pyrrhuloxia (*Cardinalis sinuatus*), 121

ravens
 Chihauhuan (*Corvus cryptoleucus*), 1
 common (*Corvus corax*), 1
red-bellied woodpecker (*Melanerpes carolinus*), *132*, 132–35
red-headed woodpecker (*Melanerpes erythrocephalus*), 132–35
redpolls
 common (*Carduelis flammea*), 6
 hoary (*Carduelis hornemanni*), 6
red-tailed hawk (*Buteo jamaicensis*), 90, *136*, 136–39, *138*
red-winged blackbird (*Agelaius phoeniceus*), 57, *140*, 140–47, *145*
robins
 American (*Turdus migratorius*), *14*, 14–17, *16*, 67
 European (*Erithacus rubecula*), 14
rock pigeon (*Columba livia*), 117, *148*, 148–51
Root, Terry, 13
ruby-throated hummingbird (*Archilochus colubris*), 152, 152–56, *155*

sapsuckers
 red-breasted (*Sphyrapicus ruber*), 182
 red-naped (*Sphyrapicus nuchalis*), 182
 Williamson's (*Sphyrapicus thyroideus*), 182
 yellow-bellied (*Sphyrapicus varius*), *182*, 182–84
Scheifflin, Eugene, 84
seagulls, *see* gulls
shadow boxing behavior, 122
sharp-shinned hawk (*Accipiter striatus*), *157*, 157–60, *159*
Silent Spring (Carson), 17
Smith, Susan M., 24
song sparrow (*Melospiza melodia*), *161*, 161–64, *163*
sparrows
 American tree (*Spizella arborea*), 53
 black-chinned (*Spizella atrogularis*), 53
 Brewer's (*Spizella breweri*), 53
 chipping (*Spizella passerina*), *53*, 53–55